The author: James D. Crichton was born in 1907, educated in England and ordained in 1932. He has worked in various parishes in the Archdiocese of Birmingham since then. Since 1955, he has been parish priest at Pershore in Worcestershire.

His main interests have been liturgy and catechetics. For some years he was assistant inspector of schools. He has written many articles which have been published in various journals; he contributed an essay to *Shaping the Christian Message,* ed. G. Sloyan, 1959; a chapter, " An Historical Sketch of the Roman Liturgy," to the Downside symposium, *Worship,* 1963. He has lectured in liturgy at the Luman Vitae Centre in Brussels, and in 1963 at the Catholic University of America. Since 1951, he has been editor of the quarterly, *Liturgy.*

THE CHURCH'S WORSHIP

J. D. CRICHTON

THE CHURCH'S WORSHIP

Considerations on the Liturgical Constitution
of the
Second Vatican Council

SHEED & WARD — NEW YORK

THE PUBLISHERS WISH TO ACKNOWLEDGE THEIR INDEBTEDNESS TO REV. CLIFFORD HOWELL, S.J., AND WHITEGATE PUBLICATIONS FOR PERMISSION TO REPRODUCE THE TEXT OF THEIR TRANSLATION OF THE 'CONSTITUTION ON THE SACRED LITURGY.'

Library of Congress Catalog Card Number:— 64-22998

NIHIL OBSTAT: JOANNES M. T. BARTON, S.T.D., L.S.S., CENSOR DEPUTATUS.
IMPRIMATUR: P. J. CASEY, VIC. GEN.
WESTMONASTERII, DIE 23 APRILIS 1964
    THE NIHIL OBSTAT AND IMPRIMATUR ARE A DECLARATION THAT A BOOK OR PAMPHLET IS CONSIDERED TO BE FREE FROM DOCTRINAL OR MORAL ERROR. IT IS NOT IMPLIED THAT THOSE WHO HAVE GRANTED THE NIHIL OBSTAT AND IMPRIMATUR AGREE WITH THE CONTENTS, OPINIONS OR STATEMENTS EXPRESSED.

Manufactured in the United States of America

CONTENTS

v

PREFACE

It was somewhere in the middle of January of this year that
Mr Geoffrey Chapman inveigled me into writing a commentary on the liturgical Constitution of the Second Vatican
Council. It was not until the beginning of Lent that I was
able to begin writing and it will be seen that this book has
been written very quickly, too quickly. There was no time
to look anything up beyond the most simple references.
One had to go on writing. The results, for good and for ill,
are to be seen in the pages that follow.

The work would have been made considerably more
laborious if Father Clifford Howell, S.J., had not, at light-
ning speed, produced the translation of the Constitution
which he has very kindly allowed me to use here. The
leaders of the Centre de Pastorale Liturgique in Paris produced, in *La Maison-Dieu*, a Latin-French edition of the
Constitution with the references as given in the official
text as well as very valuable ones of their own. Later, in
March, they issued in the same periodical a full commentary
on the Constitution. This is done with all the learning and
thoroughness so characteristic of the French liturgical
scholars, although unfortunately it came a little too late to
be of much help to me. But anyone wishing for a fuller
commentary than will be found here will go to that.

Needless to say the commentary I have written is a purely
private venture and has no authority at all. If it appears to
be a rather personal commentary, it is the only sort I could
write. All I can say is that I have spent some thirty years in
the liturgical apostolate, and in reading the Constitution I
have recognized with delight much that I have been trying
to propagate in that time. It is a comfort to me at any rate to

think that I have not had to retract anything I have ever
said or written on the liturgy.

I have ventured to add a Reading List (see pp. 239–42).
The Constitution contains so much condensed liturgical
theology that it is quite impossible to do justice to it in a
commentary of this kind. I hope the list will supply sufficient
reading for those who wish to take their study of the Constitution a little further.

The writing of this commentary has meant that I have
had to give close attention to the Constitution for several
weeks on end, and after this prolonged study, I am filled
with admiration for it. It is a magnificent document,
whether from the viewpoint of its underlying theology or on
account of its urgent pastoral concern for the people or for
the sanity of its views on reform. But what strikes one more
forcibly than anything else is its determination that a
renewed liturgy shall become the means by which the
people may worship God in sincerity and truth. For years
in England and many parts of America there has been a
great reluctance to set in motion a liturgical movement of
the kind that we know has been vigorous in many other
countries of the Church. There has been a fear of the movement that is difficult to understand and sometimes a hostility
that was very saddening. Opposition to the liturgy has been
far from rational. Now at any rate the Church through the
Council has spoken so plainly that no one can plead in the
future that he does not know what the Church wants. What
the Church wants is set out in the Constitution in no un-
certain terms and one hopes that the near future will see
the initiation of a really active liturgical movement and
give to the people a liturgy that is rightfully theirs.

J. D. C.

Pershore,
   Wednesday in Easter Week, 1964.

1.   This sacred Council has several aims in view: it desires
to impart an ever-increasing vigour to the Christian life of the
faithful; to adapt more suitably to the needs of our own times
those institutions which are subject to change; to foster whatever can promote union among all who believe in Christ; to
strengthen whatever can help to call the whole of mankind into
the household of the Church. The Council therefore sees particularly cogent reasons for undertaking the reform and promotion of the liturgy.

2.   For the liturgy, 'through which the work of our redemption is accomplished', most of all in the divine sacrifice of the
eucharist, is the outstanding means whereby the faithful may
express in their lives, and manifest to others, the mystery of
Christ and the real nature of the true Church. It is of the
essence of the Church that she be both human and divine,
visible and yet invisibly equipped, eager to act and yet intent
on contemplation, present in this world and yet not at home in
it; and she is all these things in such wise that in her the human
is directed and subordinated to the divine, the visible likewise
to the invisible, action to contemplation, and this present world
to that city yet to come, which we seek. While the liturgy daily
builds up those who are within into a holy temple of the Lord,
into a dwelling place for God in the Spirit, to the mature

measure of the fulness of Christ, at the same time it marvellously strengthens their power to preach Christ, and thus shows forth the Church, to those who are outside, as a sign lifted up among the nations under which the scattered children of God may be gathered together until there is one sheepfold and one shepherd.

3. Wherefore the sacred Council judges that the following principles concerning the promotion and reform of the liturgy should be called to mind, and that practical norms should be established.

Among these principles and norms there are some which both can and should be applied to the Roman rite and also to all the other rites. The practical norms which follow, however, should be taken as applying only to the Roman rite, except for those which, in the very nature of things, affect other rites as well.

4. Lastly, in faithful obedience to tradition, the sacred Council declares that holy Mother Church holds all lawfully acknowledged rites to be of equal right and dignity; that she wishes to preserve them in the future and to foster them in every way. The Council also desires that, where necessary, the rites be revised carefully in the light of sound tradition, and that they be given new vigour to meet the circumstances and needs of modern times.

Introduction

(1–4)

The Constitution on the Sacred Liturgy which was debated
and voted upon by the Council Fathers in the first and
second sessions of the Second Vatican Council and solemnly
promulgated by Pope Paul VI on 4 December 1963 has
already been widely recognized to be a document of the
greatest importance for the life of the Church. The findings
and experiences of the liturgical movement of the last
sixty years form the underlying basis of the document and
a window is opened on to a future the end of which no man
can see. While remaining ever the same, the body of Christ,
the Church, in the years that lie ahead, will put on a new
face through the renewal of worship which has now been
inaugurated in so impressive a manner.

As one looks through the Constitution, it is possible to
discern one or two dominant themes. The Church looks
back constantly to her immensely rich past and scrutinizes
the tradition, not so much to copy it but to find there the
creative principles of a reformed liturgy. Then the Church
looks out on to a new world into which she has so rapidly
moved and shows her concern for the millions of people of
many languages and cultures, some of whom have but recently come to Christ and many more of whom have still to
learn about him. The Church is conscious of their needs

3

and by this document seeks to adapt herself to them in all the ways that lie open to her. Above all, the Church looks at the people, the laity, and in this document expresses her wish again and again that they should have a living worship which they can grasp, take part in and make the centre of their lives. Finally, the Church shows her awareness of her essential duty to give glory to God and to procure the salvation of men. It is for these two purposes which cannot be separated (for it is only those who have been made holy who can give glory to God) that she exists and she achieves them principally through the liturgy Christ committed to her in the beginning.

These few remarks are sufficient to emphasize the importance of the Constitution and one would like to insist that it should not be regarded as a Chamber of Liturgical Horrors in which are to be found all the reforms that have worried some people. On the contrary, it is a magisterial statement of profoundly important doctrines that concern the Church, the liturgy and the members who make up the Church. It is only if it is accepted as such that it will be seen for what it is, that the reforms it suggests will be understood and that it will be able to enter into the life of the Church. That this, broadly speaking, is the view of the Council may be gathered from its opening statement. The Council has three aims: the renewal of the Christian life of the people within the Church; to promote union 'among all who believe in Christ'; and 'to strengthen whatever can help to call the whole of mankind into the household of the Church'. *For this reason*, the Council sees the necessity 'for undertaking the reform and promotion of the liturgy' and states the willingness of the Church 'to adapt more suitably to the needs of our times those institutions which are subject to change'. Among these the Council includes the liturgy.

It is clear from statements in the next article that the Church has realized that she has moved into an entirely new pastoral situation. There is not only running strongly in the world the current of ecumenism, there is not only the ardent desire among Christians of all communions for the restoration of Christian unity, but there are the vast numbers of men and women in so-called Christian countries who are out of contact with the Roman Catholic Church and indeed with any church, and millions more who are daily increasing in number to whom it is the Church's task to bring the Good News of Christ. In spite of the fact that the liturgy has no directly missionary function—and the Council is aware of this—yet it regards the renewal of the liturgy as central to the whole pastoral situation in which the Church finds herself. 'The liturgy', it is said, ' "through which the work of our redemption is accomplished"[1] . . . is the *outstanding means* whereby the faithful may express in their lives, and *manifest to others*, the mystery of Christ and the real nature of the true Church.' The Council sees the Church revealed in its most authentic light when she is gathered together in worship and engaged in what must be described as her most otherworldly activity. Here and at this moment 'the world' will see what the Church really is: the redeemed and redeeming community of Christ, gathered into one by his power, held together not so much by juridical bonds as by the love of Christ which is present and operative among his members. Here his saving word is proclaimed not as in a theological lecture room but simply and tellingly as to God's family here assembled. When those who are not in visible union with the Church make contact with her through her worship, it should be possible for them to say: 'Here is God's love and God's word made present' and we may pray that they will recognize the Lord here present in the breaking of bread.

Many private liturgists have written and spoken in this strain in recent years, but here we find it as the most formal and solemn statement of a General Council. Many are the

[1] Prayer over the offerings, IX Pentecost.

techniques and methods that have been discussed and adopted for the conversion of the modern world and they retain their validity, but the Council puts its finger on the central thing, worship, and this is to be the focal point of the Church's missionary effort. As we shall see later on, the Constitution assumes that this worship is going to be the worship of a community and this will normally be the parish. It implies then that in the future the parish must be an outward looking community, aware of the world in which it lives and concerned to bring Christ's love to it. Henceforth neither the Church nor the parish, which is its local manifestation, is to be regarded as a sacred enclave, much less as a protective ghetto. It lives in a dechristianized world which it is its function to bring back to Christ by living most intensely the mystery of Christ's redeeming work which lies at the heart of its existence.

All this is not a matter of inference. We find it expressed in the Constitution itself:

'While the liturgy daily builds up those who are within (the Church) into a holy temple of the Lord, into a dwelling place for God in the Spirit, to the mature measure of the fulness of Christ, at the same time *it marvellously strengthens their power to preach Christ*, and thus *shows forth the Church, to those who are outside*, as a sign lifted up among the nations under which the scattered children of God may be gathered together until there is one fold and one shepherd.'

It is in this way that the liturgy which lies at the heart of the Church's life will achieve a missionary dimension. The members of the Church formed by the liturgy and built up by it to make the Church the Lord's temple will move out to the world 'to preach Christ' and through their energetic spreading of Christ's love, derived from the liturgy, show forth the Church for what she is and so begin the slow and painful process of restoring all men to unity in Christ.

The Council has thus in a few words turned our attention away from an excessive concern with our own affairs and directed it to the situation in which we find ourselves. We are in a world which is receding from the Church. Already there are wide areas where Christ has been repudiated or is unknown. It is the vocation of the Church, and that means of its members both priests and people, to go out to that world and try to lead it back to Christ. The whole Church is in a missionary posture and even in our worship we cannot remain indifferent to that world. If 'the scattered children of God' are not yet with us, we must prepare the way to make their return the easier. Many already make contact with us, and often through our worship. If it is and must remain austere, concentrated on God and his glory, it must yet be welcoming, meaningful, so that those who come are made aware that here the authentic nature of the Church is being manifested and the mystery of Christ is available to them.

This, it seems, is how the Council would have us orientate our minds, this the way in which we should act. The sometimes stuffy cosiness of our worship will have to go, the oddities of our ways in church will have to be modified. If we are always at home, yet we have more or less permanent guests.

What then in fact is to be done? The Constitution immediately goes on to say that in the light of this situation the liturgy is to be 'promoted and reformed' (*fovenda atque instauranda*). The document then has two aims: first, the revision or reform of the liturgy and secondly, what it calls 'the fostering' of the liturgy. There is much in the document about both matters, but the latter has been less remarked upon. What it means is that there is now an *official* liturgical movement within the Church which must involve the whole Church, bishops, priests and lay-people, and at every level, diocese, parish and the houses of religious orders. As we shall see, various practical means are laid down, but the all-important thing is that *everyone* will be affected. No doubt this will mean much painful change of mind and habit, but here we have the clearest expression of the mind of the Church. Nothing could be more formal, nothing more emphatic, and for members of the Church many things that have been permissive for some years will sooner or later become obligatory. Some of the changes remain within the competency of the local hierarchies, but it is the intention of the Council that all the directives of the Constitution shall pass into the practice of all Catholics throughout the Church. There would seem to be no escaping this conclusion, and if people have spoken about a revolution within the Church in connection with the Council, it is clear that this revolution is already taking place, even if its pace will be slower in some places than others. But it is to be hoped that those who do their best, under the authority of their bishops, to implement the directives of the Council will henceforth be spared the indifference and even scorn with which they have been met for too many years now.

In what is not much more than a brief note (4),[1] the Council declares its mind that, in accordance with tradition, the Church acknowledges that other rites than the Roman have equality of right and dignity. The Holy See has often made similar declarations in the past which have not always been respected by lesser authorities in the Church. Now the situation is very different and the presence of so many bishops of the eastern churches at the Council has revealed their importance in the life of the whole Church. Not only should the eastern rites be respected, but it will be necessary to look to them for inspiration in the adaptation of our own rite of the west.

[1] Throughout, the numerals in brackets refer to articles of the Constitution.

General Principles for the Restoration and Promotion of the Sacred Liturgy

I. THE NATURE OF THE SACRED LITURGY AND ITS IMPORTANCE IN THE CHURCH'S LIFE.

5   God who 'wills that all men be saved and come to the knowledge of the truth' (1 Tim. 2:4), 'who in divers manners spoke in times past to the fathers by the prophets' (Heb. 1:1), when the fulness of time had come, sent his Son, the Word made flesh, anointed by the Holy Spirit, to preach the gospel to the poor, to heal the contrite of heart, to be a 'bodily and spiritual medicine', the Mediator between God and man. For his humanity, united with the person of the Word, was the instrument of our salvation. Therefore in Christ 'the perfect achievement of our reconciliation came forth, and the fulness of divine worship was given to us'.

The wonderful works of God among the people of the Old Testament were but a prelude to the work of Christ the Lord in redeeming mankind and giving perfect glory to God. He achieved his task principally by the paschal mystery of his blessed passion, resurrection from the dead and glorious ascension, whereby 'dying, he destroyed our death and rising, he restored our life'. For it was from the side of Christ as he slept the sleep of death upon the cross that there came forth 'the wondrous sacrament of the whole Church'.

6.   Just as Christ was sent by the Father, so also he sent the apostles, filled with the Holy Spirit. This he did that, by preaching the gospel to every creature, they might proclaim that the Son of God, by his death and resurrection, had freed us from the power of Satan and from death, and brought us into the kingdom of his Father. His purpose also was that they might accomplish the work of salvation which they had proclaimed, by means of sacrifice and sacraments, around which the entire liturgical life revolves. Thus by baptism men are plunged into the paschal mystery of Christ; they die with him, are buried with him and rise with him; they receive the spirit of adoption as sons 'in which we cry: Abba, Father' (Rom. 8:15), and thus become true adorers whom the Father seeks. In like manner, as often as they eat the supper of the Lord they proclaim the death of the Lord until he comes. For that reason, on the very day of Pentecost when the Church appeared before the world, 'those who received the word' of Peter 'were baptized'. And 'they continued steadfastly in the teaching of the apostles and in the communion of the breaking of bread and in prayers . . . praising God and being in favour with all the people' (Acts 2:41–47). From that time onwards the Church has never failed to come together to celebrate the paschal mystery; reading those things 'which were in all the scriptures concerning him' (Luke 24:27), celebrating the eucharist in which 'the victory and triumph of his death are again made present' and at the same time giving 'thanks to God for his unspeakable gift' (2 Cor. 9:15) in Christ Jesus, 'in praise of his glory' (Eph. 1:12), through the power of the Holy Spirit.

7.   To accomplish so great a work, Christ is always present in his Church, especially in her liturgical actions. He is present in the sacrifice of the Mass, not only in the person of his minister, 'the same now offering, through the ministry of priests, who formerly offered himself on the cross', but especially under the eucharistic species. By his power he is present in the sacraments, so that when a man baptizes it is really Christ himself who baptizes. He is present in his word, since it is he himself who speaks when the holy scriptures are read in church. He is present, lastly, when the Church prays and sings, for he prom-

ised: 'Where two or three are gathered together in my name, there am I in the midst of them' (Matt. 18:20).

Christ indeed always associates the Church with himself in this great work wherein God is perfectly glorified and men are sanctified. The Church is his beloved Bride who calls to her Lord, and through him offers worship to the Eternal Father.

Rightly, then, the liturgy is considered as an exercise of the priestly office of Jesus Christ. In the liturgy the sanctification of man is signified by signs perceptible to the senses, and is effected in a way which corresponds with each of these signs; in the liturgy the whole public worship is performed by the mystical body of Jesus Christ, that is, by the head and his members.

From this it follows that every liturgical celebration, because it is an action of Christ the priest and of his body which is the Church, is a sacred action surpassing all others; no other action of the Church can equal its efficacy by the same title and to the same degree.

8.   In the earthly liturgy we take part in a foretaste of that heavenly liturgy which is celebrated in the holy city of Jerusalem towards which we journey as pilgrims, where Christ is sitting at the right hand of God, a minister of the holies and of the true tabernacle; we sing a hymn to the Lord's glory with all the warriors of the heavenly army; venerating the memory of the saints, we hope for some part and fellowship with them; we eagerly await our Saviour, the Lord Jesus Christ, until he, our life, shall appear and we too will appear with him in glory.

9.   The sacred liturgy does not exhaust the entire activity of the Church. Before men can come to the liturgy they must be called to faith and to conversion: 'How then are they to call upon him in whom they have not yet believed? But how are they to believe him whom they have not heard? And how are they to hear if no one preaches? And how are men to preach unless they be sent?' (Rom. 10:14–15).

Therefore the Church announces the good tidings of salvation to those who do not believe, so that all men may know the true God and Jesus Christ whom he has sent, and may be converted from their ways, doing penance. To believers also the Church must ever preach faith and penance; she must prepare them for the sacraments, teach them to observe all that Christ has commanded, and invite them to all the works of charity, piety and the apostolate. For all these works make it clear that Christ's faithful, though not of this world, are to be the light of the world and to glorify the Father before men.

10. Nevertheless the liturgy is the summit towards which the activity of the Church is directed; at the same time it is the fount from which all her power flows. For the aim and object of apostolic works is that all who are made sons of God by faith and baptism should come together to praise God in the midst of his Church, to take part in the sacrifice and to eat the Lord's supper.

The liturgy in its turn moves the faithful, filled with 'the paschal sacraments', to be 'one in holiness'; it prays that 'they may hold fast in their lives to what they have grasped by their faith'; the renewal in the eucharist of the covenant between God and man draws the faithful into the compelling love of Christ and sets them on fire. From the liturgy, therefore, and especially from the eucharist as from a fount, grace is poured forth upon us; and the sanctification of men in Christ and the glorification of God, to which all other activities of the Church are directed as towards their end, is achieved in the most efficacious possible way.

11. But in order that the liturgy may be able to produce its full effects, it is necessary that the faithful come to it with proper dispositions, that their minds should be attuned to their voices, and that they should co-operate with divine grace lest they receive it in vain. Pastors of souls must therefore realize that, when the liturgy is celebrated, something more is required than the mere observation of the laws governing valid and licit celebration; it is their duty also to ensure that the faithful take part fully aware of what they are doing, actively engaged in the rite, and enriched by its effects.

12. The spiritual life, however, is not by any means limited solely to participation in the liturgy. The Christian is indeed

called to pray with his brethren, but he must also enter into his chamber to pray to the Father in secret; yet more, according to the teaching of the apostle, he should pray without ceasing. We learn from the same apostle that we must always bear about in our body the dying of Jesus, so that the life also of Jesus may be made manifest in our bodily frame. This is why we ask the Lord in the sacrifice of the Mass that, 'receiving the offering of the spiritual victim', he may fashion us for himself 'as an eternal gift'.

13. Popular devotions of the Christian people are to be highly commended, provided they accord with the laws and norms of the Church, above all when they are ordered by the Holy See.

Devotions proper to individual churches have a special dignity if they are undertaken by mandate of the bishops according to customs or books lawfully approved.

But these devotions should be so drawn up that they harmonize with the liturgical seasons, accord with the sacred liturgy, are in some fashion derived from it and lead the people to it, since, in fact, the liturgy by its very nature far surpasses any of them.

II. The Promotion of Liturgical Instruction and Active Participation.

14. Mother Church earnestly desires that all the faithful should be led to that full, conscious and active participation in liturgical celebrations which is demanded by the very nature of liturgy. Such participation by the Christian people as a 'chosen race, a royal priesthood, a holy nation, a redeemed people' (1 Pet. 2:9; cf. 2:4-5), is their right and duty by reason of their baptism.

In the restoration and promotion of the sacred liturgy, this full and active participation by all the people is the aim to be considered before all else; for it is the primary and indispensable source from which the faithful are to derive the true Christian spirit; and therefore pastors of souls must zealously strive to achieve it, by means of the necessary instruction, in all their pastoral work.

Yet it would be futile to entertain any hopes of realizing this unless the pastors themselves, in the first place, become thoroughly imbued with the spirit and power of the liturgy, and undertake to give instruction about it. A prime need, therefore, is that attention be directed to the liturgical instruction of the clergy. Wherefore the sacred Council has decided to enact as follows:

15. Professors who are appointed to teach liturgy in seminaries, religious houses of study and theological faculties must be properly trained for their work in institutes which specialize in this subject.

16. The study of sacred liturgy is to be ranked among the compulsory and major courses in seminaries and religious houses of studies; in theological faculties it is to rank among the main courses. It is to be taught under its theological, historical, ascetical, pastoral and juridical aspects. Moreover other professors, while striving to expound the mystery of Christ and the history of salvation from the angle proper to each of their own subjects, must nevertheless do so in a way which will clearly bring out the connection between their subjects and the liturgy, as also the unity which underlies all priestly training. This consideration is specially important for professors of dogmatic, ascetical and pastoral theology and for those of holy scripture.

17. In seminaries and houses of religious, clerics shall be given a liturgical formation in their spiritual life. For this they will need proper direction, so that they may be able to understand the sacred rites and take part in them whole-heartedly; they will need personally to celebrate the liturgical rites, but also should take part in popular devotions which are imbued with the spirit of the liturgy. In addition they must learn how to observe the liturgical laws, so that life in seminaries and religious houses of study may be thoroughly influenced by the spirit of the liturgy.

18. Priests, both secular and religious, who are already working in the Lord's vineyard are to be helped by every

suitable means to understand ever more fully what it is that they are doing when they perform sacred rites; they are to be aided to live the liturgical life and to share it with the faithful entrusted to their care.

19. With zeal and patience, pastors of souls must promote the liturgical instruction of their people, and also their active participation in the liturgy both internally and externally, taking into account their age and condition, their way of life and standard of religious culture. By so doing, pastors will be fulfilling one of the chief duties of a faithful dispenser of the mysteries of God; and in this matter they must lead their flock not only in word but also by example.

20. Transmissions of the sacred rites by radio and television shall be done with discretion and dignity, under the leadership and direction of a suitable person appointed for this office by the bishops. This is especially important when the service to be broadcast is the Mass.

III. THE REFORM OF THE SACRED LITURGY.

21. In order that the Christian people may more certainly derive an abundance of graces from celebrating the liturgy, holy Mother Church desires to undertake with great care a general restoration of the liturgy itself. For the liturgy is made up of immutable elements divinely instituted, and of elements subject to change. These not only may but ought to be changed with the passage of time if they have suffered from the intrusion of anything out of harmony with the inner nature of the liturgy or have become unsuited to it.

In this restoration, both texts and rites should be drawn up so that they express more clearly the holy things which they signify; the Christian people, so far as possible, should be enabled to understand them with ease and to take part in them fully, actively and as befits a community.

Wherefore the sacred Council establishes the following general principles:

(A) *General Principles*

22. (i) Regulation of the sacred liturgy depends solely on the authority of the Church—which means on the Apostolic See and, as laws may determine, on the bishop.

(ii) In virtue of authority conceded by the law, the regulation of the liturgy within certain defined limits belongs also to various kinds of local bishops' conferences legitimately established.

(iii) Therefore no other person, even if he be a priest, may add, remove or change anything in the liturgy on his own authority.

23. That sound tradition may be retained, and yet the way remain open to legitimate progress, a careful investigation is always to be made into each part of the liturgy which is to be revised. This investigation should be theological, historical and pastoral. Also the general laws governing the structure and meaning of the liturgy must be studied in conjunction with the experience derived from recent liturgical reforms and from the indults conceded to various places. Finally, there must be no innovations unless the good of the Church genuinely and certainly requires them; and care must be taken that any new forms adopted should in some way grow organically from forms already existing.

As far as possible, notable differences between the rites used in adjacent regions must be carefully avoided.

24. Sacred scripture is of the greatest importance in the celebration of the liturgy. For it is from holy scripture that lessons are read and explained in the homily, and psalms are sung; the prayers, collects and liturgical songs are scriptural in their inspiration; and it is from the scriptures that actions and signs derive their meaning. Thus to achieve the restoration, progress and adaptation of the sacred liturgy, it is essential to promote that warm and living love for scripture to which the venerable tradition of both eastern and western rites gives testimony.

25. The liturgical books are to be revised as soon as possible; experts are to be employed on the task and bishops from various parts of the world are to be consulted.

(B) *Principles drawn from the Hierarchic and Communal Nature of the Liturgy*

26. Liturgical services are not private functions, but are celebrations of the Church, which is the 'sacrament of unity' —namely the holy people united and ordered under their bishops.

Therefore liturgical services pertain to the whole body of the Church; they manifest it and have effects upon it; but they concern the individual members of the Church in different ways, according to their different rank, office and activity.

27. It is to be stressed that whenever rites, according to their specific nature, make provision for communal celebration involving the presence and active participation of the people, this way of celebrating them is to be preferred, so far as possible, to a celebration that is individual and quasi-private.

This applies with especial force to the celebration of Mass and the administration of the sacraments, even though every Mass has of itself a public and social nature.

28. In liturgical celebrations each person, minister or layman, who has an office to perform, should do all of, but only, those parts which pertain to his office by the nature of the rite and the principles of liturgy.

29. Servers, lectors, commentators and members of the choir also exercise a genuine liturgical function. They ought, therefore, to discharge their office with the sincere piety and decorum demanded by so exalted a ministry and rightly expected of them by God's people.

Consequently they must all be deeply imbued with the spirit of the liturgy, each in his own measure, and they must be trained to perform their functions in a correct and orderly manner.

30.   To promote active participation, the people should be encouraged to take part by means of acclamations, responses, psalmody, antiphons and hymns, as well as by actions, gestures and bodily attitudes. And at the proper times all should observe a reverent silence.

31.   The revision of the liturgical books must carefully attend to the provision of rubrics also for the people's parts.

32.   The liturgy makes distinctions between persons according to their liturgical function and clerical rank, and there are liturgical laws providing for due honours to be given to civil authorities. Apart from these instances, no special honours are to be paid in the liturgy to any private persons or classes of persons, whether in the ceremonies or by external display.

(C) *Principles based upon the Didactic and Pastoral Nature of the Liturgy*

33.   Although the sacred liturgy is above all things the worship of the Divine Majesty, it nevertheless contains much instruction for the faithful. For in the liturgy God speaks to his people and Christ is still proclaiming his gospel. And the people reply to God by both song and prayer.

Moreover the prayers addressed to God by the priest who presides over the assembly in the person of Christ are said in the name of the entire holy people and of all present. And the visible signs used by the liturgy to signify invisible divine things have been chosen by Christ or his Church. Thus not only when things are read 'which were written for our instruction' (Rom. 15:4), but also when the Church prays or sings or acts, the faith of those taking part is nourished and their minds are raised to God, so that they may offer him their rational service and more abundantly receive his grace.

This leads to the conclusion that, in revision of the liturgy, the following principles should be observed:

34.   The rites should be distinguished by a noble simplicity; they should be short, clear and unencumbered by any useless repetitions; they should be within the people's powers of com-

prehension, and normally should not require much explanation.

35. That the intimate connection between words and rites may be apparent in the liturgy:

(1) In sacred celebrations there is to be more reading from holy scripture, and it is to be more varied and suitable.

(2) Because the sermon is part of the liturgical service, the best place for it is to be indicated even in the rubrics, as far as the nature of the rite will allow; the ministry of preaching is to be fulfilled with exactitude and fidelity. The sermon, moreover, should draw its content mainly from scriptural and liturgical sources, and its character should be that of a proclamation of God's wonderful works in the history of salvation or in the mystery of Christ ever made present and active within us, especially in the celebration of the liturgy.

(3) Instruction which is more explicitly liturgical should also be given in a variety of ways; if necessary, short directives to be spoken by the priest or competent minister should be provided within the rites themselves. But they should occur only at the more suitable moments, and be in prescribed or similar words.

(4) Bible services should be encouraged, especially on the vigils of the more solemn feasts, on some week-days in Advent and Lent, and on Sundays and feast days. They are particularly to be commended in places where no priest is available; when this is so, a deacon or some other person authorized by the bishop should preside over the celebration.

36. (i) Though existing special exemptions are to remain in force, the use of the Latin language is to be preserved in the Latin rites.

(ii) But since the use of the mother tongue is frequently of great advantage to the people in the Mass, the administration of sacraments and other parts of the liturgy, the limits of its employment may be extended. This will apply in the first place to the readings and directives, and to some of the prayers and chants, according to the regulations on this matter to be laid down separately in subsequent chapters.

(iii) These norms being observed, it is for the competent ecclesiastical authority mentioned in art. 22 (ii) to decide whether, and to what extent, the vernacular language is to be used; their decrees are to be approved, that is, confirmed, by the Holy See. And whenever it seems to be called for, they are to consult with bishops of neighbouring territories which have the same language.

(iv) Translations from the Latin text intended for use in the liturgy must be approved by the competent local authority mentioned above.

(D) *Principles for Adapting the Liturgy to the Culture and Traditions of Nations*

37. Even in the liturgy, the Church has no wish to impose a rigid uniformity in matters which do not implicate the faith or the good of the whole community; rather does she respect and foster the genius and talents of the various races and nations. Anything in these peoples' way of life which is not indissolubly bound up with superstition and error she studies with sympathy and, if possible, preserves intact. Sometimes she even admits such things into the liturgy itself, so long as they harmonize with its true and authentic spirit.

38. Provision is to be made, when revising the liturgical books, for the legitimate variations and adaptations to different groups, regions and peoples, especially in the missions, provided always that the substantial unity of the Roman rite is preserved; and this should be borne in mind when drawing up the rites and devising rubrics for them.

39. Within the limits set by the typical editions of the liturgical books, it shall be for the competent local ecclesiastical authorities mentioned in art. 22 (ii) to specify adaptations of sacramentals, processions, liturgical language, sacred music and the arts—but according to the fundamental principles laid down in this Constitution. Above all this is to apply to the administration of the sacraments.

40. In some places and circumstances, however, an even more radical adaptation of the liturgy is needed, and this entails even greater difficulties.

Wherefore:

(1) The competent local ecclesiastical authority mentioned in art. 22 (ii) must, in this matter, carefully and prudently consider which elements from the traditions and culture of each of these peoples might appropriately be admitted into the liturgy. Adaptations which seem useful or necessary should then be submitted to the Holy See, by whose consent they may be introduced.

(2) To ensure that adaptations may be made with all the circumspection which they demand, the Holy See will grant power to this same authority to permit and direct, over a determined period of time and among certain groups specially suited for the purpose, whatever preliminary experiments may be deemed necessary.

(3) Because liturgical laws are wont to involve special difficulties when applied to adaptations, particularly in the missions, men who are experts in these matters must be employed to formulate them.

IV. PROMOTION OF LITURGICAL LIFE IN DIOCESE AND PARISH.

41. The bishop is to be considered as the high priest of his flock, from whom the life in Christ of his faithful is in some way derived and dependent.

Therefore all should hold in great esteem the liturgical life of the diocese centred around the bishop, especially in his cathedral church; they must be convinced that the pre-eminent manifestation of the Church consists in the full active participation of all God's holy people in the same liturgical celebrations, especially in the same eucharist, in a single prayer at one altar, at which there presides the bishop surrounded by his college of priests and ministers.

42. But because it is impossible for the bishop always and everywhere to preside over his whole flock in his cathedral, he cannot do other than establish lesser groupings of the faithful. Among these the parishes, set up locally under a pastor who takes the place of the bishop, are the most important; for in some manner they represent the visible Church constituted throughout the world.

And therefore the liturgical life of the parish and its relationship to the bishop must be fostered theoretically and practically among the faithful and clergy; efforts also must be made to encourage a sense of community within the parish, above all in the communal celebration of the Sunday Mass.

V. The Promotion of Pastoral-Liturgical Action.

43. Zeal for the promotion and restoration of the liturgy is rightly held to be a sign of the providential dispositions of God in our time, as a movement of the Holy Spirit in his Church. It is today a distinguishing mark of the Church's life, indeed of the whole tenor of contemporary religious thought and action.

So that this pastoral-liturgical action may become even more vigorous in the Church, the sacred Council decrees:

44. Each of the competent local ecclesiastical authorities mentioned in art. 22 (ii) is to set up a liturgical commission to be assisted by experts in liturgical science, sacred music, art and pastoral practice. So far as possible the commission should be aided by some kind of Institute for Pastoral Liturgy consisting of persons who are eminent in these subjects, and including laymen when appropriate. Under the guidance of the above-mentioned local ecclesiastical authority the commission is to regulate pastoral liturgical action throughout the territory, and to promote studies and necessary experiments whenever it seems that adaptations ought to be proposed to the Holy See.

45. For the same reason every diocese is to have a liturgical commission under the direction of the bishop, for promoting the liturgical apostolate.

Sometimes it may be expedient that several dioceses should form between them one single commission which will be able to promote the liturgy by mutual consultation.

46. Besides these liturgical commissions, every diocese, as far as possible, should have commissions for sacred music and sacred art.

These three commissions must work in closest collaboration; indeed it will often be best to fuse the three of them into one single commission.

I

General Principles for the Restoration and Promotion of the Sacred Liturgy

(5-46)

I. THE NATURE OF THE SACRED LITURGY

The pastoral liturgical movement as we now know it is rather more than fifty years old and during that time there has been a great deal of research on and theological exploration of the nature of the liturgy. In that time too there have been massive changes in scripture scholarship and in theology. In all this work it has been possible to observe certain converging points of view and the influence of one discipline upon another. Thus, the theological reflection on the Church as the body of Christ was originally prompted by a more developed liturgical practice and by certain social movements in the Church. Dom Odo Casel's investigations of forty years ago into the mystery of Christ turned the minds of theologians and scripture scholars to this matter. Beyond doubt, what has helped towards a deeper appreciation of the liturgy in recent years has been the advance and peculiar orientation of scripture studies. The mystery of Christ, the history of salvation and terms like 'the people of God' are heard equally on the lips of theologians, scripture scholars and liturgists. All this language and its underlying theology are to be found in the first part of Chapter I of the Constitution. All this 'new' theology is condensed into

23

less than four pages which present a richness that is wholly admirable, but which provides some difficulty to those who are not familiar with the language. The subject-matter is of the very first importance. The whole document is built up on what is written here, and if it is to make its proper impact on the Christian life of the people, it is essential to understand it. If the Constitution were thought to be just a series of rather tiresome 'reforms', mostly of ritual detail, it would have little value for the Church's life. Such details could have been enacted by the permanent officials of the Church. But it is not so and this rich theological introduction forms the background of the whole Constitution, conditioning all that it has to say about liturgical reform and practice.

Since this part of the Constitution is so important, an attempt is made here to give briefly some exposition of its main themes.

The Mystery of Christ

The first term we meet is that of the 'Mystery of Christ', a term that has become very familiar with theologians, scripture scholars and liturgists in recent years.

We are all familiar with the term 'mystery' in the context of 'mysteries of faith', that is doctrines we believe on the authority of God who reveals them. The term as it is used in this new context is nearer to that of the 'mysteries of the Rosary' when we meditate on certain sacred *events* of the life of Christ, though 'mystery' as used in the Bible and the liturgy goes much deeper than that. The mystery we are concerned with can be seen to exist on three levels:

(1) There is first the mystery of God himself dwelling in light inaccessible and hidden from the gaze of men from the beginning of time.

(2) There is the mystery of Christ which is the mystery that *is* Christ who is the manifestation of God, the only-begotten of the Father whose glory John and the other

apostles witnessed. He came at the 'fulness of time' and
summed up the long history of salvation that had gone
before him. Indeed, by his life and teaching he showed what
was the meaning of that history, embodying as he did God's
redeeming love and eventually making it possible for men
through him to express their love of God in return, to
respond to God's love which is poured out upon us by Christ
and in his Church. The mystery of Christ is not just the fact
of his taking flesh and becoming one of us; it is an active
thing. It is the expression in deeds, and above all in his
sacrificial death, of God's love towards men. That is why
the Constitution can say, 'His humanity, united with the
person of the Word, was the instrument of our salvation.
Therefore in Christ "the perfect achievement of our reconciliation came forth, and the fulness of divine worship was
given to us" ' (5).[1]

At this second level, mystery is essentially an *event*, something God did, or a series of events; in the concrete, the
history of salvation as it is set forth in the Old Testament,
in the life of Christ and finally in the Church. The truth
that is contained in this teaching is that God *has* intervened
in our history and that through this intervention we are
saved.

(3) The third level at which the mystery exists is the
liturgy. In other words, the liturgy itself is 'mystery', as the
missal says so frequently, especially in its prayers. On the
Wednesday in Holy Week we ask that what we are doing *in
mysterio*, in the mystery, *of* the Lord's Son, we may lay hold
of in reality. The Latin genitive indicates identity between
the passion of Christ in the historical order and the liturgical
mystery which is being celebrated. This is more explicit in
the second prayer at the end of the Good Friday service:
'Almighty and merciful God, you have *renewed us by the
blessed passion and death of your Christ*; preserve in us *the*

---

[1] The quotation is from the *Sacramentarium Veronense*, n. 1265
(ed. Mohlberg).

work of your redemption (operis misericordiae) that by our partaking of this *mystery* we may always live devoted to your service.' We are renewed by the passion and death of Christ, the work of redemption, which we make contact with by the liturgical mystery we celebrate. As the Constitution says elsewhere, the liturgical celebration makes present the redeeming mystery of Christ.

It has a second function too. The mystery was hidden, 'it was never made known to any human being in past ages' (Eph. 3:5), but it was revealed by Christ and preached by the apostles. So far as it is possible, Christ revealed the mystery of the Father, made known the 'hidden purpose of his will' (Eph. 1:9). So the liturgical mystery has the function of revealing God's redeeming purpose, his love for all men. It manifests the Church, to the eye of faith it shows more clearly than anything else what the Church really is and ultimately leads men back to Christ from whom came the Church and the Church's liturgy. But the Church is its members, the priests and laity who belong to it and the mystery of the Church is mediated to the world by those same members. It is through them who, as the liturgy prays over and over again, carry over into their lives what they celebrate, that people outside the Church will be able to see it for what it is. It is of this that the Constitution speaks (2) when it says that the liturgy is the outstanding means whereby the faithful will be able to express in their lives and so manifest to others the mystery of Christ.

That there can be no doubt that this is the mind of the Council is shown by the words that follow immediately: 'and manifest the *real nature* of the *true Church*'. These words may come as a surprise to those who have been brought up to think that the *only* way to manifest the Church was by apologetics, by, for instance, an exposition of the Four Marks or the infallibility of the pope. In the mind of the Council, the Church is above all Mystery, the great mystery spoken of by St Paul (Eph. 5:32), which is the

Bride of Christ, holy and the source of holiness, the meeting place of man with God. It is this Church that is revealed by the sign of the liturgy and this is one of the main reasons why the liturgy is in the order of sign. It is totally sacramental, it is mystery. It contains, conveys but also manifests the mystery of Christ.

The History of Salvation

Inseparably connected with the Church is the history of salvation of which it is part. If the Church is 'a sign lifted up among the nations' (2), it is, with its head and founder, the climax of that self-revealing by which God made himself known to those people he would make his own and to whom throughout the ages he was offering his redeeming love.

The Constitution refers only quite briefly to the history of salvation: 'The wonderful works of God among the people of the Old Testament . . .' (5) and that is all. But it indicates in the following words how we are to understand it: the wonderful works of God '. . . were but a prelude to the work of Christ the Lord in redeeming mankind and giving perfect glory to God'. Thus is recalled the saving history which is not a mere record of events which we may read for our edification (and some of it is far from edifying). It is a whole process by which God redeemed his people, ultimately only through the passion, death and resurrection of his own Son, a process that continues and especially in the liturgy. The history of salvation enters into the very substance of the liturgy; its climax is the centre of the chief liturgical action, the Mass, in which is made present the paschal sacrifice of the Saviour. The events of the whole history are recalled, celebrated, in the Church's year and thereby become the sources of grace. A recent writer can say that in the liturgy the history of salvation is actualized.[1] It is not merely a series of events existing in the past. It is brought into the present. The same love that

[1] C. Vagaggini, *Il Senso Theologico della Liturgia* (Rome, 1958).

God poured out on the people of the Old Testament, that love that was embodied in the God-made-man, is made present and offered to man now. Through this approach of God to him, man can make his return and embody his response of faith and love precisely in the liturgy that God has provided for him.

The different phases of the history of salvation are well enough known, but it may be helpful to recall the main ones here and to point out something of their essential significance. The Old Testament is the record of the events by which God revealed himself to the Israelites and, but more important, sought to bring them nearer to himself, to make them his own people and to bind them to himself by a covenant which was the expression of his love. He called Abraham who responded with faith and entered upon an unknown and unsuspected destiny. God saved his descendants by leading them away from famine into Egypt and through his servant Moses rescued them from slavery and destruction when he revealed that he was God the 're-deemer', the one who would strike off their bonds and lead them into the promised land. There was the revelation in the desert when the great word was uttered, 'I am who am'. The sense of this utterance and of all that followed is given by Père Congar in the magnificent passage that follows:

'The third way in which we can translate the phrase ("I am who am") is this. We find precisely the same verb in verse 14: "I will be with you." It is in the future tense and therefore we can translate, "I will be who I will be." What does that mean? You ask me what is my name and this is what I reply: "I am he who will bring you out of Egypt, who will lead you across the Red Sea and into the desert. I am he who will nourish you there when you are in want. I am he who will lead you to Sinai and there will make a covenant with you on the basis of my Law. I am he who will give you my Law. I am he who will bring

you to the promised land and will lead you into it. I am
he who will live in the midst of you, setting up my
dwelling in your midst, abiding in the Temple. I am he
who will chastise you for your sins, who on account of
those sins will let Jerusalem be taken and destroyed. I am
he who will lead out the chosen ones into the captivity of
Babylon. But I am also he who will be with you in captivity, who will lead you back from it. I will be Saviour."

It is this that is sacred history. His name, what he is in
himself, this God does not reveal in the Old Testament.
In the New Testament we know that he is Father, Son
and Holy Spirit, but in the Old Testament God does not
reveal what he is in himself. Rather, all through the ages
he gives himself so that men may know him as the One
who can be called upon in prayer, as the God who judges,
who chastises, as the God who forgives. Lastly, "I will be
God-with-you up to the point where I take human flesh.
I will be Saviour, I will be Jesus Christ, I will be my
Holy Spirit, I will be Eucharist. . . ."

Such is God, such is the God of the Bible. He is the
living God, the God who acts."[1]

God, then, showed his love for his people in the saving
events of the passover, in the rescue from Egypt, in the
passage through the Red Sea, but above all in the covenant
which the later writers of the Old Testament could call the
marriage union or even the love match between God and
the Israelites. When faith was growing dim God sent his
prophets to recall to the people what he had done for them
in the past—the *mirabilia Dei*, referred to in the Constitution—and to deepen their understanding of these events
so that they should see God loved them, and to turn their
minds to the future when a Messiah would come to deliver
them finally from sin.

[1] *Les Voies du Dieu Vivant*, in the essay 'Action et Foi', p. 400
(Paris, 1962).

When the voices of the prophets were stilled, as the official priesthood became discredited, there remained 'the poor ones' (the 'poor in spirit' of the beatitudes) who were ever awaiting the 'redemption of Israel'. It was they who remained true to the promises, it was they who kept faith with God, and it was to them the Messiah came at the end. For among them were to be found Mary, Joseph and Simeon who thanked God that he was able to hold in his arms the 'salvation' which had been prepared throughout the ages in the sight of the people.

They were the faithful 'remnant' and they formed the bridge between the old and the new. It was from among them that Jesus went out to proclaim the Good News and by his life, teaching, death and resurrection to bring the salvation so long desired. Here in him and in all he did we have the 'revelation' of God, the unveiling of his face; it is in Jesus and in him alone that we become able to understand that love of God which he had been offering to them from the beginning. Here was salvation no longer in hope but in fact and it is to this that men must be brought in every succeeding age.

The Paschal Mystery (5)

The heart of the history of salvation is the paschal mystery, and so we read in the next sentence of the Constitution: '(Christ the Lord) achieved his task (of redeeming mankind and giving perfect glory to God) principally by the paschal mystery of his blessed passion, resurrection from the dead and glorious ascension, whereby "dying he destroyed our death and rising, restored our life".'[1] The paschal mystery too takes us back to the past and to see it in perspective it will be as well to set it out in its various phases. Like mystery itself, it exists on three levels:

(1) The great saving event of the Old Testament, one to

[1] Preface of Easter.

which its writers and prophets returned incessantly, was preceded by the passover, the domestic sacrifice which the Israelites prepared and ate at God's command the night before they escaped from Egypt. Rather as the eucharist explained in advance what our Lord was to do on the cross, so the passover interpreted the meaning of the saving events that were to take place immediately afterwards. It was to be a memorial festival which the people were to keep annually for ever, and when they had passed into the Promised Land they would recall its meaning to their children and tell them that it was a sacrifice of the Lord's passover, marking their deliverance from the bondage of Egypt and from God's wrath that might otherwise have fallen on them. Obscurely it was a token of his love.[1] So it happened, and the passover remained the principal festival throughout Israel's history. Just as Easter is the central festival of the year for Christians, so was (and is) the passover the central festival for Jews.

(2) The passover sacrifice of the New Testament which fulfilled that of the Old Testament is nothing other than the passion, death, resurrection and ascension of Jesus Christ in which he offered himself as the true Lamb of God and took away the sins of the world.

This can most clearly be seen from St John's gospel. Deliberately he sets the saving events of Christ's redeeming work in the context of the passover feast: 'Before the *paschal feast* began, Jesus already knew that the time had come for his *passage* from this world to the Father . . .' (13:1). In loving obedience to his Father, Jesus was to make his 'passover' from this world to the next and through offering himself in sacrifice would redeem the world. He would pass through the suffering of the passion and the ultimate pain of death, he would rise again the third day and would be exalted in glory with his Father. Thus constituted Lord

[1] Exod. 12 : 14, 24–27.

of all men, he would send his Spirit upon the Church who would become the source of life to all who through baptism and repentance would give their allegiance to him (Acts 2:22–36).

As the passover of the Israelites was associated with a sacrificial meal, so was Jesus' passover, and in it he declared the meaning of what was to happen from the agony in the garden to the cross and indeed on to the resurrection and ascension: 'He still loved those who were his own . . . and he would give them the uttermost proof of his love' (John 13:1). The meal, the new rite he instituted at the Last Supper was the first token of this perfect love: 'Take and eat. This is my body. Take and drink. This is the cup of my blood.' . . . 'He who eats my flesh, and drinks my blood, lives continually in me, and I in him' (John 6:57). At this Last Supper he dedicated himself to his sacrifice (John 17:19) and as he held out to his apostles the bread that had become his body, he told them that it was already made over to his Father as victim: 'This is my body, given for you', given over already to death for you. The blood in the cup which is to be poured out would establish the new covenant based on Christ's love and would bring about an infinitely deeper union between God and man than that of the Old Testament, for it would really take away sins (Luke 22:19–20 and Matt. 26:28). This covenant was to be kept alive in the Church through the repeated doing of what Christ told his apostles to do at the Last Supper: 'Do this for a commemoration of me.'

All that happened from the Last Supper to the resurrection and exaltation of Christ was the Lord's paschal mystery, and just as the old passover formed the centre of Old Testament religion, so does Christ's passover for Christians.

(3) Faithful to the Lord's last commands, the Church through the centuries has celebrated in her liturgy the

paschal mystery. For now this mystery exists in a new way, no longer in the historical order but under signs and symbols which yet convey the reality of what Christ did long ago. Every time the Church celebrates the Mass she *recalls*, as Christ bade her, 'the blessed passion of Christ the Son, our Lord, his resurrection from the shades of death and his ascension to glory'[1] and makes present to men here and now the saving power of his redeeming work. We may recall the prayer over the offerings which the Constitution has quoted in almost its first words: the liturgy, and especially the divine sacrifice of the eucharist, is the means by which 'the work of our redemption is accomplished'. This is the paschal mystery of the Church which is intended through the liturgical celebration to become the paschal mystery of every Christian who, once incorporated into Christ's body, is destined to live out in his life the dying to self and the rising with Christ which is the essence of Christianity.

It is this same paschal mystery which the Church celebrates at Easter time, from Maundy Thursday to Easter Sunday morning, and this she does with an especial effectiveness through a rich variety of rite and symbol and through the solemn proclamation of God's word in lesson and sermon. Indeed in one service, the Easter Vigil, the whole redeeming work of Christ is celebrated and made present and that is why the Church can call it the 'mother of all vigils' in which Jesus who 'died, was buried and rose again' is made present to the Christian people with all his power and love.[2]

Christ's Redeeming Work: the Exercise of his Priesthood

The Constitution sees the paschal mystery as the exercise of Christ's priesthood (5 and 7), though the doctrine is not

[1] Translation from *The Layman's Missal* (London and Baltimore, 1962).
[2] The two quotations are from the introduction to the decree of 1955 restoring the Holy Week liturgy.

given so fully as in Pius XII's *Mediator Dei* (1–3; 14–18)[1] to which however it clearly refers. There we are taught that Jesus Christ, the one mediator between God and man (1 Tim. 2:5) is the high priest 'who has passed right up through the heavens' (Heb. 4:14) after completing the work of his redemption. The high priest of the New Testament, he offered to his Father the worship that was foreshadowed in the Old Testament but which remained without effect until his coming into this world. At his incarnation he was made a priest 'in the line of Melchisedech', exercised his priestly office throughout his life and completed it in the sacrifice of the cross. Jesus Christ was priest and the supreme act of his life was a priestly act, the offering of himself in sacrifice, and thus 'the perfect achievement of our reconciliation came forth, and the fulness of divine worship was given to us'.[2]

This doctrine is of immense importance for an understanding of the liturgy, as the Constitution makes clear later on. Here it is concerned to put a rather different point of view. Its intention is to expound more fully the mystery of Christ which it has but mentioned in its second paragraph.

It begins with the statement from St Paul to Timothy (1 Tim. 2–4) that it is God's will that all men should be saved, and goes on to speak of the sending of the Son who is the Word made flesh, 'anointed by the Holy Spirit, to preach the gospel to the poor, to heal the contrite of heart, to be a "bodily and spiritual medicine", the Mediator between God and man'.[3] This sums up what *Mediator Dei* had described as his 'priestly' activity during his life and

---

[1] Paragraph references to *Mediator Dei* are to the English translation, C.T.S., London, 1947.

[2] Constitution 5, and *Sacramentarium Veronense* (usually called the Leonine Sacramentary), n. 1265 (ed. Mohlberg).

[3] The first series of quotations is from Luke 4:18 (cf. Isa. 61:1); the last from 1 Tim. 2:5; and the 'medicine' one from Ignatius of Antioch, *Ad Ephes.* 7, 2.

perhaps the Constitution wished to emphasize Christ's ministry of the word as it does elsewhere (e.g. 7). But its quotation of Hebrews 1:1 (not given above) would seem to indicate that it was the intention of the Constitution to consider the Word made flesh as the manifestation of the Godhead and this in an active way. The Son of God by becoming man revealed something of what God is like, brought him close to us so that we can grasp him as a concrete reality. This he did by the very act of taking flesh in the womb of the Blessed Virgin Mary. He, though man, was God and his very coming among us is a proof of God's love for us. These truths are so well known to Christians that there is no need to say more. But the Constitution is concerned to say something else: the Son of God revealed God by his actions, by his preaching to the poor, by his forgiveness of the repentant sinner and, above all, by being the mediator between God and man in his redeeming sacrifice.

In the Constitution is found a significant phrase which is not in *Mediator Dei* and which would seem to be intended to show that the Word-made-flesh is not just a static symbol of God's love for man but a dynamic one. And this is what we mean by 'mystery': it is an event, a sacred action, an action done by God for the salvation of man which at the same time reveals God. The phrase is: 'His humanity, united with the person of the Word, was the instrument of our salvation.'[1]

At first sight this phrase seems uninteresting enough, a mere commonplace of conventional theology. In fact it is one of the many rapid references made by the Constitution to broad theological ideas that everywhere underlie the document. For St Thomas, Christ's soul and body joined to the Word are the instrument by which he was able to produce all those miraculous effects that could serve

---

[1] The references given are to St Thomas, *S.T.* III, 48, 6 and 56, 1. To this may be added what is the foundation article: 13, 2. It is interesting to find St Thomas's doctrine appearing naturally and as of right amidst all the biblical theology.

(*ordinabiles*) the purpose of the incarnation which is to 'restore all things whether in heaven or on earth'.[1] Even, we are told, his very flesh was the instrument of the divine power which vanquished sin,[2] so that all he did and suffered contributed to man's salvation. This is true of the passion, but also of the resurrection and ascension which are described as the efficient causes of our resurrection and eventual ascension. What this means is that Christ's human nature was *operative*; as man through and in his human nature he actually wrought our redemption. There was a real effect and a real operation that must be attributed to the human nature united to the Godhead. And when we consider St Thomas's perspective we see that it is not so very different from that of the scriptural and liturgical scholars of today. He too was thinking of the mystery of Christ, his life, death, resurrection and ascension, all of which effected man's salvation, and in all these saving acts he manifested the mercy of God who is 'the lover of mankind' (Titus 3:4).

There is a further reason why this teaching of the saving power of Christ's human nature is introduced here. Theologians call the human nature the 'conjoined instrument' of Christ by which he saved us. Later we shall find that the liturgy is called 'an action of Christ' (7) and that in the sacraments Christ's power is operative (they are what modern theologians describe as 'actions of Christ'). We may conclude that the Constitution wanted to point the contrast between the sacraments which are 'separated instruments' of salvation and the human nature of the Word which is united with him. From this latter the sacraments derive all their power.

What, then, the Constitution has done here is to put before us the picture of the Christ of mystery, the 'sacra-

---

[1] This quotation from Ephesians 1 shows that Aquinas's mind too was running on the mystery of which St Paul there speaks.
[2] III, 49, 1.

mental Christ', who shows forth his Father love and conveys it to man, and also of the priestly Christ, because it
was through the exercise of his priestly power that he
actually redeemed us.

The Church: the Great Mystery

Closely, indeed one may say inseparably, connected with the
mystery of Christ and his priesthood is the Church. They
are so seen in the Constitution.

In an effort to make things clear I have treated separately
the matter of the mystery of Christ and the Church, but
in the Constitution they are fused into a very close synthesis
and one realizes that articles 6 and 7 are a condensed treatment of the priestly Church. It is this we will try and deal
with now.

After speaking of the 'paschal mystery of his blessed
passion', the Constitution goes on immediately to speak of
Christ's work in his Church, drawing what might be called
a liturgico-theological picture of the early Church.

First came, it insists, the proclamation, the *kerygma*, of
the paschal mystery, Christ's death and resurrection, by the
apostles who had been sent by Christ (John 20:21) who first
had been sent by his Father (John 3:17). This was the first
work he had sent them to do, but it was 'his purpose also
. . . that they might accomplish the work of salvation
which they had proclaimed, by means of sacrifice and sacraments, around which the entire liturgical life revolves' (6).
Thus, very emphatically, the Constitution endorses the
theological thinking that has gone to build up the teaching
that the liturgy makes present the saving events of Christ's
redeeming work: what Jesus had done, what the apostles
proclaimed, *that* was and is effected (*exercerent*) in and by
the liturgy. Naturally, the Constitution is not endorsing any
particular theology of 'mystery-presence', such as that of
the late Dom Odo Casel, but it does affirm the presence
in some way of the saving events of Christ's passion. In the

liturgy we are not merely recalling past events, we are not simply contemplating them or thinking *about* them. We are brought into contact with them; as theologians say nowadays, we make a real encounter with the redeeming Christ. This is what the Council is teaching, as becomes very clear when we read the rest of the passage. First, baptism 'plunges' men into the paschal mystery of Christ so that they die, are buried and rise again with and in him. Secondly, when they eat the Lord's supper, they proclaim the Lord's death until he comes again.

Both these activities are shown in the earliest days of the Church: the apostles preached, the people repented and were baptized and they all continued in the teaching of the apostles, in fellowship and in the breaking of bread and in prayer (Acts 2:41–47).

Then comes the conclusion, putting the eucharist at the centre of things:

'From that time onwards the Church has never failed to come together to celebrate the paschal mystery; reading those things "which were in all the scriptures concerning him" (Luke 24:27), celebrating the eucharist in which "the victory and triumph of his death are again made present" and at the same time giving "thanks to God for his unspeakable gift" (2 Cor. 9:15) in Christ Jesus, "in praise of his glory" (Eph. 1:12), through the power of the Holy Spirit.'

Here we find the eucharist identified as the paschal mystery 'making present' the victory and triumph of the Lord. Through the words of scripture (from 2 Corinthians and Ephesians) it is suggested that the eucharist is, too, the sacrifice of thanksgiving (precisely *eucharistia*) and the sacrifice of praise, as we find it called in the Canon of the Mass. Finally, the ministry of the word within the eucharist is indicated by the phrase 'reading those things . . .' which recalls the preaching of the apostles mentioned in the first part of the passage.[1]

All these activities belong to the Church and, of course, as much now as in the beginning. They *manifest* the Church and should be seen against the background of the Church as Mystery which has been sketched out in an earlier article (2) to which we will now turn. The Word of God manifested, showed forth to men, in the flesh he took from the Blessed Virgin Mary, the mystery of God's redeeming love and that same flesh was the instrument of salvation. The physical and tangible human nature of the Son of God was the means by which the divine life was conveyed to mankind. The invisible became palpable through the visible —a theme the Fathers were never tired of speaking about and one that significantly is found in the Preface of Christmas:[2] 'The light of your glory (the Father's glory) has flooded the eyes of our mind anew in the mystery of the Word made flesh, and through him whom we recognize as God made visible, may we be caught up into a love of things unseen.'

From the side of Christ who was both God and man, as he slept the sleep of death upon the cross, there came forth 'the wondrous sacrament of the whole Church' (5)[3] and this Church has the same qualities as its head: 'It is of the essence of the Church that she be both human and divine, visible and yet invisibly equipped, eager to act and yet intent on contemplation, present in the world and yet not at home in it; and she is all these things in such wise that in her the human is directed and subordinated to the divine, the visible likewise to the invisible . . .' (2). The Church, 'a sign lifted up among the nations', is in the same

[1] The phrase 'the victory and triumph . . .' comes from the Council of Trent. Sess. XIII. Perhaps it has an even earlier origin; it has a strongly liturgical tone.

[2] Probably the work of St Gregory the Great.

[3] This phrase comes from the second collect of Holy Saturday before the reform of 1955.

order as the incarnation—visible and invisible—which it exists to prolong in time and space. The Church as 'sacrament' or 'mystery' (and it is hardly possible to say that the one word differs in meaning from the other) is the sign of the encounter between God and man that has taken place in Jesus Christ. As a modern writer has put it quite simply:

> 'As the body is animated by the soul and makes it visible and expresses it in manifold activities, so the Church is animated by Christ, makes him visible and expresses him in manifold activities. . . . It is the visible and tangible expression of Christ, it is a "Christophany", the visible body of his Spirit.'[1]

We may ask exactly *how* the Church manifests Christ? To this there are many answers. The very visible structure of the Church that makes it a visible institution in this world is one way in which Christ is shown, though if the emphasis falls too heavily on organization, the 'sacrament', the symbol will become opaque and it cannot be said that that danger has been avoided in the last hundred years. Yet on the other hand, it does show that this sheer visibility is an essential part of the Church and therefore essential to its nature. It makes the Church tangible, graspable and corresponds to man's nature. It fulfils a need. Next, the Church is shown forth in the life of its members. They mediate the mystery of the Church to the world and especially by their faith and charity. The Church becomes, or should become, tangible to the world through the living faith and charity

---

[1] Yves Congar, *Esquisses du Mystère de l'Eglise*, p. 26 (Paris, 1941; cf. Eng. trans., *The Mystery of the Church*, London and Baltimore, 1960, p. 70). Congar goes on, 'The Church is the fulness of Christ and in realizing itself is destined to realize Christ "until we reach the mature measure of the fulness of Christ"', thus supplying a commentary on this part of the Constitution (2) where it speaks of the Church as mystery. St Paul is referring to the *pleroma* which is at once the place where the fulness of the divine life dwells and where it is also active. The quotation is from Ephesians 4:13.

of its members. They are in the fact the community of the Church immersed in the world, making the Church 'present' in the world, as the Constitution observes (2). There is the word of God which the Church proclaims and must proclaim before ever men can be brought into the Church; and this word, which is an invitation from God, a word in which a life-giving grace is contained, must meet with a response from man. Otherwise it remains dead. But above and beyond all else, it is through the liturgy that the Church is seen as the sacrament of Christ's redeeming activity. If the Church could be thought of in abstraction from what it does, *as if* for instance the sacraments did not exist, it would appear as a sort of static symbol of Christ. But since the sacraments are an essential part of the Church's structure, since it is the source of the whole sacramental system (what modern theologians call the '*Ursakrament*' (Semmelroth) or the '*sacramentum radicale*' (K. Rahner)), it is through the sacraments, and indeed through the whole liturgy, that the mystery of the Church is expressed and made known at least to the eye of faith.[1] As the Constitution has already said, 'the liturgy daily builds up those within (the Church) into a holy Temple of the Lord . . . *and* shows forth the Church, even to those outside through the life and worship of its members.

The Liturgy, the Action of the Priestly Church

But we can and indeed must go further, as the Constitution itself does (7). Just as Christ was the 'sacrament' of God in his redeeming activity, so is the Church which exists to continue it. Christ lived among men, preached the good news to them, worked miracles for them and founded the Church for them. But his whole life was summed up in the final act of his life, namely his offering of himself in sacrifice on the cross. This, the supreme act of his life by which he

[1] See O. Semmelroth in *Yearbook of Liturgical Studies* (Notre Dame, 1961).

consummated or achieved the work his Father had given him to do, was a priestly act. The salvation of mankind was accomplished by what was the essentially priestly act of the redeemer. And it was by this same priestly act that he brought the Church into existence, so that it is by its nature a priestly church,[1] a priestly community. We are made by baptism, said Pius XII,[2] members of Christ the priest who is head of the body. The same pope taught us that the liturgy is continuation of the priestly activity in the Church and by the Church, necessarily therefore the Church itself is a priestly body. This teaching is re-stated with a new force in the Constitution (7). It is given in three stages. First, it says that Christ is always present in his Church but especially in her liturgical actions, present in the priest who celebrates and acts *in persona Christi*,[3] present in a special way in the consecrated bread and wine and present by his power in the sacraments 'so that when a man is baptized it is really Christ himself who baptizes'. Thus is consecrated in an official document of the teaching Church a phrase that has been used now for some long time by theologians. Sacraments are gestures or acts of Christ in the Church which bring us into contact with his redeeming work. The Constitution goes on: 'He is present in his word, since it is he himself who speaks when the holy scriptures are read in Church.' Here too we find the Council endorsing what might be called a comparatively recent theology of the Word.[4] This understanding of the theological meaning of the proclamation of the word in the liturgical assembly is of crucial importance in the matter of the language in which they are read. Many people still do not seem to realize that the lessons in the Mass are not so much reading material which you can 'read out of a book' just as well as listening

---

[1] 'From the side of Christ . . . on the cross . . . came forth "the wondrous sacrament of the Church" ' (5).

[2] *Mediator Dei*, 90.

[3] *Mediator Dei*, 96.

[4] See C. Davis, *Clergy Review*, September, 1960 (45).

to it and, they say, often more easily and pleasurably. The reading of the lessons is a proclamation of *God's* word. It is an *action* that takes place and as the Constitution emphasizes elsewhere, one of the highest importance. As the theologians say nowadays, the proclamation is an *event* in which God is active. In this proclamation God is approaching us, God is offering us his grace and if we take it into ourselves, if we respond to it, then it is grace-bearing. Theologians even speak of a 'real presence' of God in his proclaimed word, though as the term is liable to misunderstanding it is better not used. But it does serve to emphasize the reality or even realism of what takes place.

Further, it is because the nature of the proclamation of the word is such that *normally* it is the function of the ordained minister, priest, deacon, etc. From Christ and through the Church he receives a *mission* to proclaim God's word not just at any time, not just to the 'heathen', but precisely and first of all in the liturgical assembly. In the Roman rite at High Mass the deacon receives this mission from the celebrant and the book is carried in solemn procession with lights and incense to the most honourable place on the right-hand side of the sanctuary.[1] And if the theology of the matter should seem new, let us remember the extraordinary words with which the people greet the gospel as it is announced: *Gloria tibi, Domine*; Glory to you, Lord, who are present in your word. In short, the whole ritual of the Mass teaches us, as it has always taught, that Christ is present in his word when it is announced and that in it he comes to us demanding our response and offering his grace.

It is for reasons such as these that liturgists and pastors have for so long been asking that at least the lessons of the Mass should be proclaimed in the language of the people. What is true of the lessons is true only in lesser degree of

---

[1] I.e. from the bishop's point of view who is considered to be presiding from behind the altar.

the other scriptural parts of the Mass, for in them too God's message is made known to us and in a form in which we are able to make a direct response, that of prayer.

Finally, and once again echoing *Mediator Dei*, the Constitution tells us that Christ is present when the Church prays and sings, 'for he promised "Where two or three are gathered together in my name, there I am in the midst of them"' (Matt. 18:20). The prayer of the 'gathered' Church (*ecclesia*) is the prayer of Christ which again was a priestly activity which he continues in heaven where 'he is ever living to make intercession for us'.[1] Of this more will be said later on, but it may be remarked that one of the most devalued parts of the liturgy is the Divine Office.

The teaching is carried forward with the next statement which wishes to underline the close relationship between Christ and his Church: 'Christ indeed always associates the Church with himself in this great work (namely the liturgy) wherein God is perfectly glorified and men are sanctified.'[2] The basis of this close association between Christ and his Church is suggested by the use of the word 'Bride': 'The Church is his beloved Bride who calls to her Lord, and through him offers worship to the eternal Father.'

This notion of the bridal or marriage union between Christ and his Church is one of great richness and St Paul saw fit to make of it the great symbol of the Church. It is in relation to it that he calls the Church the 'great mystery' or sacrament and it has been said that it is permissible to see in it the final development of his thought on the Church as the body of Christ.[3] It is here better than anywhere else that we can see the Church as mystery. First, it takes up the ancient theme of the Old Testament that the Israelites are God's people, so much loved by him that he can call

[1] Heb. 7:25.
[2] Here is one of the many places in the Constitution where the twofold purpose of the liturgy is taught: the liturgy exists to give glory to God and to make men holy.
[3] P. Benoit, *Exégèse et Théologie*, Vol. II, p. 135 (Paris, 1961).

them his bride (Osee 2:14, 19-24). He had bound them to himself by the Covenant[1] in the desert when he offered his love and sought theirs in return. That love for the most part they repudiated and God's purpose seemed to be frustrated until there came the one who was a member of that same people, one who incarnated or embodied the necessary response of man to God[2] and who through his love for man and for his Father brought forth a new people out of the old. These now become his Bride in a new and deeper sense. Through the redeeming love of the Bridegroom a new relationship is established between God and man and it is expressed in an exchange of love between them that now becomes possible through a communication of Christ's life to them.

Secondly, this union between God and man was established by Jesus' sacrificial love and it is interesting to observe that precisely in the place where St Paul teaches that the Church is the Bride of Christ, he also speaks of Christ's priestly act: Christ showed his love for us 'when he gave himself up on our behalf, a sacrifice breathing out fragrance as he offered it to God'.[3] In the same place husbands are exhorted to love their wives as Christ loved the Church when he gave himself over to death for her so that she might be holy, without stain or wrinkle or any other disfigurement.[4] The *head* of the body who is the *husband* of the body becomes the *saviour* of the body.[5] Here all the great themes of St Paul's teaching on the nature of the Church come together and we see that the result is the ineffable union between Christ and his people. We are reminded once again that this union was established by the priestly act of Christ who brings into existence a church

[1] Mentioned only in 10 in the Constitution and then *en passant*.
[2] See E. Schillebeeckx, *Christianity Divided* (London and New York, 1961), pp. 245ff.
[3] Eph. 5:2.
[4] Eph. 5:25-27.
[5] 'As Christ the *head of the Church*, the same who is the *Saviour of the body*', *ibid.*, verse 23.

that is essentially a priestly body now permeated by his redeeming love. The two-in-oneness of human marriage is the symbol of union between Christ and his Church.

There is however a third element in this bridal symbol which the Constitution indicates and that has a special reference to the liturgy: 'The Church is his beloved Bride who calls to her Lord, and through him offers worship to the eternal Father.' A marriage can only be made between two people, two persons who, however close the union, can never be absorbed by one another. This is true even of God; even in the sublimest mystical union the human personality remains distinct and is not, as certain eastern philosophies would have it, absorbed into the Godhead. If then the figure of head-and-body emphasizes the *union* between Christ and his Church, the bridal figure suggests the inevitable *separateness* of the people who stand over against God with functions that in the present order cannot be performed directly by Christ their head. Among other things, this people has to make its response to God in faith and love and God seeks and wants that response. He never treats us as less than human and will have nothing to do with a mechanical or automatic salvation. Modern theologians are saying that this human response was seen at its highest in Our Lady who in her *Fiat* perfectly responded to God's love with her faith, trust and love. The Church (including Mary) is able to make this response to God over a whole range of activities but nowhere more effectively than in the liturgy. There is first the downward movement of God's saving grace to man which makes possible his response, and then the return movement of man to God through Jesus who is the head and husband of the body. This is in fact what the Church is doing in the liturgy or worship which, says the Constitution, she offers to the eternal Father through Christ.

It is against this vast background which resumes so much of the history of salvation that we can see the depth of meaning to be given to the definition of the liturgy in the next paragraph of the Constitution: 'Rightly, then, the liturgy is considered as an exercise of the priestly office of Jesus Christ', as we have seen, continued in the Church. And then, 'In the liturgy the sanctification of man is signified by signs perceptible to the senses, and is effected in a way that corresponds with each of these signs.' Without for the moment exhausting the full meaning of these words, we may say that here the *manner* in which Christ's priesthood is exercised in the Church is indicated: the liturgy is essentially *sacramental*, in the deepest and broadest sense. In the deepest sense, meaning the way in which the sacraments as such operate, that is with an effectiveness which is the result of Christ's continuing operation through them;[1] in the broadest sense, namely through the whole range of sacramental symbols which the Church itself has instituted and which has an effectiveness that comes of the Church being the Bride of Christ and that is only less than that of the sacraments themselves.[2] Briefly Christ acts as priest now through the sacramental liturgy which he himself instituted for the continuation of the 'work of our redemption' in time and space.

The whole doctrine is then summed up in two sentences that provide a definition of the Church's worship: 'In the liturgy the whole public worship is performed by the mystical body of Jesus Christ, that is, by the head and his members.'[3] It is hardly necessary to insist that here we have the formal teaching of the Church on the nature of the

---

[1] Cf. 'When a man is baptized it is really Christ himself who baptizes'; in a word, *ex opere operato*.

[2] In a word, *ex opere operantis Ecclesiae*, the teaching of *Mediator Dei*.

[3] This is very close to that of *Mediator Dei* (20), though we notice that the phrase 'to its Founder (Christ)' is omitted. Christ's function in the liturgy is essentially mediatorial or priestly and the liturgy *normally* addresses God through Jesus Christ. The compilers of the Constitution evidently thought it better to omit a phrase that would itself need a special explanation.

liturgy as the public worship done by the Church in and through Jesus Christ. But perhaps it is still necessary to insist that it is *public worship* and not private devotion, that the whole body as such is involved in its action and that, as the Constitution insists over and over again, *all* the members of the liturgical assembly are required by the very nature of the liturgy to take an active part.

Finally, the Constitution re-states the truth that the liturgy is an action of Christ the priest and sees in this the reason for its pre-eminent place in the life of the Church:

'From this it follows that every liturgical celebration, because it is an action of Christ the priest and of his body which is the Church, is a sacred action surpassing all others; no other action of the Church can equal its efficacy by the same title and to the same degree.'

The whole liturgy then, both Mass and sacraments and its other parts in differing ways, flows out of the Church, which is the primary sacrament and also the body of Christ in which his Spirit dwells. And we can go back further still. On earth Christ's physical body, united to his divine personality, was the instrument of his redeeming acts. The liturgy is the action of Christ in his Church and the Mass and the sacraments are the separated instruments of those same acts of redemption which are made ours through them. It is the one Christ, divine and human, acting in the one Church, visible and invisible and the place of encounter between God and man, through the liturgy, itself visible and invisible, that is sacramental, where in fact we meet the same redeeming Christ and are carried up into his eternal sacrifice in heaven where he is ever-living to make intercession for us. From the beginning to the end we see that it is the one paschal mystery that is the centre of Christ's life, the centre of the Church's life, and in her liturgical celebrations the climax of her saving activity among men: 'The liturgy is the summit towards which the activity of the Church is directed (and) at the same time the source from which all her power flows' (10).[1]

To sum up this first part of the Constitution: Christ is the mystery revealing the Father and his saving love. By the paschal mystery in which he summed up his whole life and exercised his high-priestly function, he brought forth the Church which is his body and Bride. To this sacramental and priestly Church he committed the power to continue *in mysterio* throughout the ages the priestly work of his redemption. The liturgy is that *mysterium* in which it continues Christ's priestly work and by which it is able to make present to the assembly (*ecclesia*) the whole paschal mystery of passion, death and resurrection.

The Heavenly Liturgy and the Second Coming (8)

The liturgy recalls (*anamnesis*) the past events of salvation, makes Christ present here and now and looks both upwards to heaven and on to the future.

The Constitution has dealt with the paschal mystery in its historical context and taught us that it is made present by the liturgy. Now very briefly it turns first to the heavenly liturgy and secondly to the *parousia*, Christ's second coming. Both these themes have come back into the forefront of theological and liturgical thinking no doubt because both of them play an important part in the theology of the New Testament.

The first theme is one that is particularly marked in the Byzantine liturgy, in which the liturgy celebrated in time by the Church is regarded as but the earthly reflection of the heavenly liturgy into which we are drawn by Christ the eternal high priest, the *leitourgos*, the liturgical minister of the heavenly temple.[2] It is a theme that is present in the

---

[1] I have ventured to alter the translation here slightly.
[2] Heb. 8:2.

Roman liturgy too. We are conscious of it in the Mass Prefaces where we pray that our voices may be joined to those of the angelic hosts who are ever crying out *Holy, holy, holy.* . . . And after the consecration we pray that our sacrifice, the sacrifice of the Church, may be carried up to the altar on high into the sight of God's majesty, there to be joined to Christ's through whom it becomes acceptable to the Father and from whom it receives its divine efficacy to nourish our bodies and souls.

All this is but part of the New Testament theology about the resurrection and lordship of Christ which is referred to here in the brief phrase, 'Christ is sitting at the right hand of God, a minister of the holies[1] and of the true tabernacle.' Christ by his triumphant death and resurrection earned the right, so to say, to enter into his glory and to be exalted ('sitting on God's right hand') and becomes in fact Lord, Lord of the Church and the whole world. He, as the New Testament says over and over again, is *Kyrios*, the Lord who 'by dying overcame death' and now rules from his place in heaven. With his resurrection and ascent to glory, he becomes too the source of the Spirit whom, with his Father, he sends upon the Church which can now become the Spirit-filled body of Christ and the source of all salvation to mankind. The Church, and the world in so far as it accepts Christ, now moves into a new era, the Last Days, the age of the Spirit, *Pneuma*, and it is the whole effort of the Church to eliminate the sinful condition of the world so that it may be transformed into the new kingdom in which sin has no part. In this slow process of winning the world to Christ and his Spirit the liturgy has a central part to play. The liturgy of Christ is a worship in Spirit and in truth (John 4:23), it is permeated by the Spirit, it is a spiritual worship, not in the sense that it is purely mental or a matter of private contemplation but because it is the place where man now, through the operation of the Holy Spirit, may

[1] This is the quotation from Heb. 8:2.

meet the Spirit-filled Christ and in and through him offer 'pneumatic', pure spiritual worship to the Father.[1]

Associated with Christ in his glory the Constitution sees the angels and the saints. The first are referred to, more clearly in the Latin, by the words *'cum omni militia caelestis exercitus hymnum gloriae Domino canimus'* which to all intents and purposes is a quotation from the Mass Preface.[2] The saints are referred to again with words from the Canon of the Mass, this time from the *Nobis quoque peccatoribus*, in which we pray that we may have some part with them and so one day be of their company.

In this simple way the place of the angels and saints in the economy of salvation is suggested and we are further reminded that at worship the whole Church in heaven and on earth is engaged. It reminds us of the Body of Christ in its fulness, of which the liturgy is the sacred action.

From our contemplation of heaven we are led on to think of Christ's second coming: 'We eagerly await our Saviour, the Lord Jesus Christ, until he, our life, shall appear and we too will appear with him in glory.' There is much that could be said of this aspect of things but one can do no more here than call attention to it. The Constitution resumes in a couple of phrases from St Paul (Phil. 3:20 and Col. 3:4) all the new emphasis of modern biblical theology on the *parousia*. By his resurrection Christ has inaugurated the Last Times and in this new order the wedding feast, that is the sacred meal of the eucharist, is central. It is principally through this that the new people of God make contact with the Risen Lord in the Holy Spirit. But this is no more than anticipation of the consummation of all things, when Christ will come again in glory to take to himself all those who have followed him in this life. This moment will mark the final passover towards which the whole of the Christian life and

[1] For this reason it is a pity that there is no *epiclesis* of the Holy heavenly army.'

[2] 'We sing a hymn to the Lord's glory with all the warriors of the Spirit in the Roman rite.

liturgy is orientated. Each time Christians, both priest and people, offer the Mass together they enter more deeply into Christ's paschal mystery. Each time they celebrate the paschal mystery at Easter time, the same thing takes place. But all this is directed to and makes possible the final passover when we shall go from this world with Christ to sit down with him at the feast of the Lamb for ever (Apoc. 19:9).

In the early Church the looking for the coming of Christ at the end was a joyful expectation, it was a consummation that all eagerly desired and one of the prayers that seems to have formed part of the early liturgies was 'Maranatha', 'Come, Lord', or as it is in almost the last words of that most 'liturgical' book, the Apocalypse (22:20), 'Come, Lord Jesus'. No doubt if we have not followed Jesus in this world, there will be an element of terror in our encounter with him at the end, but holy scripture and the early Church saw that event as a triumph of Christ when all his faithful ones would be gathered into his kingdom, when all wrongs would be righted and God's justice would be written out plain for all mankind to see. Through the biblical and liturgical revivals in the Church, Christians are once again coming to have a similar expectation and to find in it a source of comfort and hope.

It would not be difficult to point out that this is the constant teaching of the liturgy, but it must be sufficient to say that it is to this that the Constitution is referring in this brief statement.

A Pastoral Liturgy

It will have been clear from all that has gone before that the liturgy has a twofold aim: to give glory to God and to sanctify man. This is written into the Constitution in many places (e.g. 7) and is indeed its constant theme. In this the Council has taken over the insights of the modern liturgical movement which has its origins in the seminal statement of Pius X who said that active participation in the liturgy is the primary and indispensable source of the Christian spirit and in the work of Dom Lambert Beauduin who nearly sixty years ago first put it into effect in Belgium. A pastoral liturgy is simply what has been stated above: one that is the means by which men may give God the glory that is his due and at the same time is the source of their sanctification. But it is not always realized that the glory must be given by *man* and that mere ritual is not enough. The most imposing High Mass that leaves out the people is doing only half its work, if that. It is for these reasons that throughout the Constitution insists, almost to wearisomeness, on the essential part the people have in the whole range of the liturgy, in the Mass, in the sacraments and sacramentals, in the Divine Office and in the liturgical year. Even musicians are bidden to take them into account in their composition of music for the liturgy and artists and architects are told they are to work for the Christian community. It must indeed be said to be one of the leading and most important themes of the Constitution. It is not surprising, then, that immediately after laying down the theological foundations, it goes on to speak of the liturgical formation of the people.

The Liturgy in the Life of the Church and in the Life of the People (8-13)

The Constitution now breaks away from its theological consideration to deal with more practical matters, though these are seen as consequences of the doctrine already given.

Both in *Mediator Dei* (30-41) and now here there is detectable a certain anxiety that people should not have exaggerated notions of the liturgy even if and perhaps because it is of such surpassing importance. There were slight tendencies to what has inelegantly been called 'pan-liturgism' that, it was said, wished to eliminate from the life of Christians all 'private' devotions and to underestimate mental prayer, retreats and similar exercises. At no time, I think, was the danger very great and such statements on these matters as were made were nearly always called forth in reaction against the undoubtedly undue emphasis that had come to be put on personal, interior religion at the expense of the Church's worship.[1] It remains true however there is always a danger of exaggeration in these delicate matters and the Constitution achieves a very sane balance in its statements on them.

In any case, the Church has other functions than that of worship and the first of these is preaching the gospel:

'The sacred liturgy does not exhaust the entire activity of the Church. Before men can come to the liturgy they must be called to faith and conversion: "How then are they to call upon him (in worship and prayer) in whom they have not yet believed? . . . and how are they to hear if no one preaches? . . ."' (9).[2]

Here we encounter once again the noble pastoral outlook of the Council which never forgets the great world outside the Church and which it is its ardent desire to bring to Christ. A shut-in Church with an esoteric liturgy is far from the vision of the Council Fathers and, as we have said, this outlook must be allowed to condition all our thinking, even about liturgy itself.

'Therefore', the Constitution continues, 'the Church announces the good tidings of salvation to those who do not believe, so that all men may know the true God and Jesus Christ whom he has sent[3] and may be converted from their ways, doing penance' (9).

It will be useful to remark that the Council insists on the preaching of the gospel which is called 'the good news of

---

[1] I have rapidly traced the history of the post-Tridentine tradition in this matter in 'A Historical Sketch of the Roman Liturgy' in *True Worship*, ed. L. Sheppard, pp. 72–81 (London, 1963 and Baltimore, 1964).
[2] Rom. 10:14, 15.   [3] John 17:3; Luke 24:27; Acts 2:38.

salvation' and which should be not presented as if it were bad news,[1] *as well as* on the need for conversion. The preaching is not to be a mere 'explanation' of doctrines (though that has its place) but is to be an urgent proclamation, concrete and existential, of what God has done for man, leading him to an encounter with Christ through which he will be able to turn away from his old ways back to God. Preaching and teaching with a view to a complete turning of mind and heart to God (*metanoia*) is what is envisaged by the Council. The preaching is to lead to conversion. One does not know whether the Council in the future will have more to say about this all-important matter, but in this brief statement it can be said to have laid down a programme for the missionary work of the Church which should reach right down to pulpit and class-room catechetics.

For, surprisingly, the Constitution goes on to say the same about the members of the Church in words that frankly are found more often in works of Protestant theology: the Church must preach faith and repentance even to believers. Catholics might be a little shocked to be told that the Church must preach *faith* even to them. Have we not the faith already? Yes, but faith is not like a nugget, even of gold, embedded once for all in our hearts. It is more like a seed which is meant to grow into an ever richer and fuller knowledge of God and which should lead to an ever deeper commitment to Jesus Christ. There is no doubt that this is the perspective of the Council, as can be seen from what follows: the faithful are to be taught to observe all that Christ has commanded[2] and exhorted to all the works of charity, piety and the apostolate. These are precisely the marks of a 'committed' Christian who, because he has given himself as completely as possible to Christ, can give himself to his neighbour.

Secondly, even believers need constantly to be 'converted',

---

[1] To borrow a phrase from Canon F. H. Drinkwater.
[2] Matt. 28:20.

turned back to God, and so one of the permanent themes
of Christian preaching must be repentance. This is a more
familiar notion, but unhappily the *way* repentance is often
preached falls short of what the gospel requires. There are
the old-fashioned 'terror' sermons mainly concerned with
hell fire and eternal loss and there are the more emotional
ones, which might be described as 'tear-jerking'. Both are
inadequate and without lasting result because they are not
based on God's word and remain on the periphery of Christian truth. In the last resort we can only be converted by
God's word which it is the function of the Christian preacher
to plant in our hearts and then we can make our response
to God, turn back to him and be saved. And the heart of
this word is nothing other than the paschal mystery of which
the Constitution has spoken earlier. If you like, in the
broadest and deepest sense, the centre of the preaching of
conversion is nothing other than Christ in his redeeming
activity.

Although the Constitution does not say so here,[1] it must
be said that this sort of preaching should take place in the
liturgical assembly although it is not confined to it. Every
occasion and opportunity is to be taken to deepen the faith
of the people and to turn them back to God. In parish life
there will be many such opportunities and the directives of
the Constitution are there to remind pastors that this is
what should be done.

The third element in this outlook is that of the apostolate,
meaning the share of the laity in the missionary work of
the Church. They are not only to be taught to keep Christ's
commandments, they are to be invited to go out to the
world to help their neighbours by the service of charity, to
do what they can to permeate society with the spirit of
Christ and to 'redeem' or bring it back to him. Here in a
phrase is concentrated all the Church has been saying about
the role of lay-people in the life of the Church and it is very

[1] But cf. II, pp. 61 ff. below.

significant that it is said here in the context of the liturgy. This last is seen as the source of all this apostolic activity and we may say that experience shows that the activity of the layman in the liturgy is the correlative of his activity in the world. If he has learned to take an active part in the Mass, he will naturally go on to take an active part as a Christian in the society in which he lives. If he is active in the world, he will not be satisfied with being passive in the Church. It is not without its importance that one of the factors in the promotion of the liturgical movement just before the war, as well as since, was the experience of the Young Christian Workers.

It is in this context, too, that one of the Constitution's great statements, already much quoted and destined to be quoted often in the future, is made:

'The liturgy is the summit towards which the activity of the Church is directed; at the same time it is the fount from which all her power flows. For *the aim and object of apostolic works* is that all who are made sons of God by faith and baptism[1] should be gathered together into one body (*in unum conveniunt*),[2] that they may praise God in the midst of the Church, take part in the sacrifice and eat the Lord's supper' (10).

The perspective here and in the following paragraph is that of the spiritual formation of the laity of which the centre is to be the liturgy and their participation in it. It fills them with 'the paschal sacraments' so that they be 'united in love'[3] and prays that 'they may lead lives in keep-

---

[1] This inclusion of 'faith' here should be noted. Formerly it might very well have been omitted, not because the Church does not believe that we can be saved without faith or that baptism is a substitute for it, but because there is now a keener awareness of the role of faith along with the sacraments in the process of Christian initiation and conversion.
[2] I have altered the translation here a little.
[3] Prayer after Communion, Easter Vigil and Easter Day Mass.

ing with what they received by faith'[1] so that, as St Benedict
said, their lives may be in harmony with what they profess
by their voice. The message is clear: liturgical worship
that is not translated into life and action is vain and incurs
the strictures of Christ upon the Pharisees (and so upon us).
The danger of hypocrisy is always with us.

The liturgy, and especially the eucharist, renews the
covenant between God and man for it makes present that
sacred meal of the new and eternal covenant, fulfilling the
old, which Christ made with his Church at the Last Supper
and sealed with his blood the next day. Through contact
with the Lord men are drawn into the compelling love of
Christ so that the liturgy, with the eucharist at its centre,
is to be seen as the main source of man's sanctification and
the means by which he gives glory to God.

This is the main teaching given in this place about the
relationship of the liturgy first to the apostolate and then
to the interior spiritual formation of Christians. Simply, it
is central. There follows an interlude about the priest's
responsibility in this regard to which we shall return in a
moment. Then comes a final section (12) which speaks of
the other aspects of the interior life with the purpose of
stressing, just as *Mediator Dei* did, that other spiritual
activities are indispensable to any healthy Christian life.
First are listed practically in the words of the New Testament[2] the necessity of private prayer (we are to pray in
private and without ceasing) and of self-denial or mortifica-
tion so that bearing in our bodies the dying of Jesus Christ,
his life may be made manifest in our bodily frame.[3] These
have a value of their own and it is certain that if they are
absent from the life of any Christian, he cannot be called
a sincere follower of Christ. But what is remarkable is that
the Constitution links the matter of self-denial directly with
worship, recalling in a brief phrase all that St Paul had to

[1] Collect, Tuesday of Easter Week.
[2] Matt. 6:6 and 1 Thess. 5:17.   [3] 2 Cor. 4:10–11.

say about our lives being a spiritual sacrifice[1] which we must offer constantly to God. What we do in our daily lives becomes matter for offering at Mass and the Mass in turn takes up this offering and joins it to Christ's so that it becomes a source of holiness for us. All indeed leads to the summit of the Church's activity, namely the liturgy, and from it receives its power to sanctify. If one may say so, it is this kind of teaching that makes sense of the spiritual life and draws it into a unity. The Christian life is seen to be all of a piece with the liturgy at its centre.

The same is to be said of the next article (13) which speaks of 'popular devotions'.[2] These are highly commended so long as they are in accord with the laws of the Church and especially when they are ordered by the Holy See. The same is to be said of devotions proper to individual churches when they are celebrated by order of the bishop and according to customs and books that are lawfully approved.

What these devotions are is well enough known and *Mediator Dei*[3] specified those to Our Lady in the month of May (and some countries have particular customs in this matter which are not necessarily appropriate to other countries) and those to the Sacred Heart of Jesus in June. These are to be preserved, though the Constitution does not make mention of any of them in particular. What it does say, as in connection with the practices of the interior life, is that

---

[1] E.g. Rom. 12:1. It is all the more significant that this place in Romans is recalled via a missal prayer (offertory prayer, Monday after Pentecost): 'Hostiae spiritualis *oblatione suscepta nosmetipsos sibi perficiat munus aeternum*'; 'accept this spiritual sacrifice and make *us* an eternal offering to you'.

[2] *Pia exercitia*. We have no very satisfactory term for these 'acts of piety'. They cannot be called 'private' simply, as they are frequently very public, involving the presence and active participation of thousands of people. Even the term 'non-liturgical' is not wholly satisfactory for such public services are in some sense 'of the Church'. 'Popular devotions' which Fr Howell has used here is probably as good as any other term.

[3] 194.

they should be harmonized with the liturgy in three ways.
(1) They should not conflict with the liturgical seasons (thus
to obliterate Lent in favour of the 'Month of St Joseph'
would be wrong). (2) They should accord with the liturgy
itself and in some ways be derived from it. By this standard
many of those devotions which are regarded as the people's
favourites are in need of radical reform, perhaps especially
in being more closely related to holy scripture (e.g. a greater
use of psalms) and in a development of a more classical form
of intercession. 'Three Hail Marys' seems hardly adequate
to meet the need of, say, a national calamity. (3) Perhaps
more important than all, though obviously dependent on
what is done under (2), these devotions should be so
fashioned and of such character as to lead the people into
liturgical worship which 'by its nature far surpasses them
all'.[1]

Even, then, in this more intimate aspect of the people's
religion, the liturgy is still to have a pre-eminent and central
place and all practices of whatever kind are intended to
ensure a more active, fuller participation in it. This has not
always been seen even in the more recent past and devotions
at the practical level have often shouldered out of the
centre the official worship of the Church, even to the
extent of making the Mass seem to be no more than one
devotion among others. Yet, it can hardly be denied that
the reason for this was that the ritual of the Mass and of
other parts of the liturgy was so rigid and its language so
incomprehensible that God's ordinary people failed to find
in it what was necessary for their spiritual lives. This is
but another reason why, with the Council, we can hail the
reform of the liturgy, which will make it more understandable to simple folk.

[1] This recalls the Instruction attached to the decree on the reform
of the Holy Week rites in 1955 which states that the people are to be
instructed that the liturgy far surpasses any other devotions and
customs however excellent they may be.

II. PRACTICAL MEASURES (14-20; 41-46)
THE PROMOTION OF THE LITURGY IN
DIOCESE AND PARISH

The Constitution is pre-eminently a practical document and it is not its first aim to expound at length the theology of the liturgy, though we have seen that in its first paragraphs it has done this succinctly and with a remarkable economy of words. But it is necessary to recall that it is very definitely its intention to promote liturgical practice all over the Church (1, 3). Accordingly, we find throughout the document urgent recommendations to prompt a sane liturgical practice. It will be convenient to group them here although they are concerned with a variety of subjects. The two main sections are 14-20 (liturgical instruction and active participation) and 41-46, the organizations (national and diocesan commissions) which are to be set up for the promotion of the liturgy. With these we may take one or two observations on music (115) and art (126-127).

Before the principal directives on the promotion of the people's participation in the liturgy, there is a single paragraph in the context of the interior life which is not without its importance by reason of its position. The Constitution throughout shows a concern for true worship which shall be both interior and exterior and seems to be directly addressing itself to those who even to this day talk glibly of the people's participation in the liturgy as if it were no more than reciting words parrotwise, whether in Latin or in English. This they seem to think is a decisive criticism against such practices, little realizing that the same charge can be brought against *any* public prayer, including the Rosary to which they would have us think they are very attached. In fact the Free Church tradition has made this reproach for some hundreds of years and the logical conclusion of it is the silent worship of the Society of Friends. *All* public worship, of whatever kind, can become formalistic, mechanical and dead and it has been the Church's constant concern for the last fifty years to avert this danger. Almost every pope since Pius X has spoken of this matter and every papal document on liturgy since *Mediator Dei* (1947), which has a long passage on the matter, has spoken of the fundamental need that the people's public worship should in the first place be from their hearts.

This is the burden of this article (11) which requires that if the liturgy is to produce its proper effects in the people they should come to it 'with the proper dispositions', and that what they express by their voices should be reflected in their lives. The very liturgy itself, that part of it which is sometimes called pejoratively 'ritual', is designed to evoke these dispositions and, as we have already seen, the ministry of the word has a decisive part to play in this respect. The readings and sermon offer a grace, they are intended to renew faith and charity in the listener, and the Constitution is perfectly aware of this. It says that if the right dispositions are not present, the people will receive divine grace in vain (*ibid.*). It is accordingly the duty of pastors to see that their people may have the right dispositions. They are told that a mere correct performance of the liturgy according to 'the laws governing valid and licit celebration' is not enough. They have an obligation to see 'that the faithful take part fully aware of what they are doing, actively engaged in the rite, and enriched by its effects' (*ibid.*). That is pretty inclusive and implies that the days of an 'unconscious' worship are over. Both priests and people must now make efforts to understand this infinitely holy thing that is put into their hands and must engage in the celebration of the liturgy with minds informed and hearts alive. If this seems a heavy price to pay, it is only at this cost that our worship will be saved from the Pharisaism so severely condemned by Christ.

The People's Share in Christ's Priesthood (14)

As so often in the Constitution, a practical section is introduced by a theological one. This explains the summary reference to the priesthood of the laity in the midst of practical matters that is found in article 14:

'Mother Church earnestly desires that all the faithful should be led to that full, conscious and active participation in liturgical celebrations which is demanded by the very nature of the liturgy.[1] Such participation by the Christian people as a "chosen race, a royal priesthood, a holy nation, a redeemed people" (1 Pet. 2:9 and cf. 2:4–5) is their right and duty by reason of their baptism.'

This is the only reference to the people's share in Christ's priesthood in the whole document and it sums up not only the statement of the matter in *Mediator Dei* (84–110), but a great deal of the theological investigation that has been going on for over thirty years. Something must be said about it here, for it is the basis of that 'active participation' urged by Pius X and practised by great numbers in the Church since then.

The Church is the people of God, as they are called many times in the liturgy, and the legatees through Christ of the chosen people of the Old Testament. They were a priestly people: they had first the tabernacle, then the Temple, a priesthood 'set apart' and a liturgy laid down by God himself. They were the called and gathered 'church', God's assembly, *Qehal Javé*, which becomes in the New Testament *ecclesia*. They were chosen by God, called by him into a people, and in the very moment of their calling they were told they were to be priestly people: 'Listen to my voice, and keep your covenant with me; and I, to whom all the

---

[1] For a similar expression, cf. *An Instruction by the Sacred Congregation of Rites on Sacred Music and the Liturgy*, 3 September 1958, para. 22 (Eng. trans. C. Howell, S.J., London, 1959). Hereafter referred to simply as Instruction.

earth belongs, will single you out among its peoples to be
my own. You will serve me as a royal priesthood, as a consecrated nation' (Exod. 19:5-6). Through Christ, who sums
up in himself this chosen people and indeed is head of all
the redeemed of whatever nation, Christians become the
new people of God, what St Paul called 'the Israel of God'
(Gal. 6:16).[1]

However difficult it may be to discern the exact significance of the Exodus text, it was destined to have a long
history. It was taken up by St John in the Apocalypse (1:5-6)
and by St Peter in the two texts (1 Pet. 2:9, cf. 2:4-5) cited
in the Constitution:

> 'Draw near to him (the Lord); he is the living antitype
> of that stone which men rejected, which God has chosen
> and prized; you too must be built up on him, stones that
> live and breathe, into a spiritual fabric; you must be a
> holy priesthood, to offer up that spiritual sacrifice (lit.
> "spiritual sacrifices") which God accepts through Jesus
> Christ.'

St Peter's thought is dominated by the notion that the
people are not only a people but a holy people. He is recalling another Old Testament passage (Lev. 20:7-8) where
the people are described as 'holy' and this word, we are
told, always has a cultic or liturgical significance. So Peter
tells his Christian hearers to 'draw near' (another liturgical
expression) to Christ who is the new Temple (John 2:18
and parallels in the synoptic gospels) into which they are to
be built so that they may become a 'spiritual fabric'. St Paul
is even more explicit: the people are like a temple in-
dwelt by the Holy Spirit: 'In him (Christ) the whole fabric
is bound together, as it grows into a temple, dedicated to
the Lord . . .' (Eph. 2:19-22); and the people *are* this
temple: 'Do you not know that you are God's temple and

---

[1] It should be noted that he does not say the 'new' Israel of God,
though that is what he means.

that God's Spirit has his dwelling in you. If anyone dese-
crates the temple of God, God will bring him to ruin. It is
a *holy* thing, this temple of God which is nothing other than
yourselves' (1 Cor. 3:9-17).

It should be noted that both Peter and Paul are envisaging the *whole* of the community to which they are writing
They are not addressing 'bishops' or 'priests' in this community. For them the whole body is a priestly people,
dedicated to God, destined to worship him *as a people*.
And it is against this background that we should see Peter's
statements about the people and their primary functions.
Echoing Exodus he says, 'You are a chosen race, a royal
priesthood, a consecrated nation, a people God means to
have for himself (i.e. a redeemed people). . . . Time was
when you were not a people at all (before the redemption),
now you are God's people; once you were unpitied, and
now his pity is yours' (and here he is thinking of Osee 2:24,
1:10, passages to which St Paul refers in Romans 9:24-27).
Further, it has been suggested that the whole of this passage
from verse 2 to verse 9 has a strongly liturgical flavour.[1]
'You are children new-born (neophytes, as they were called
in the early Church), and all your craving must be for the
soul's pure milk, that will nurture you into salvation, once
you have tasted, *as you have surely tasted*, the goodness of
the Lord. Draw near to him. . . .' Here we have a fairly
complete quotation from Psalm 33 which was the usual
communion psalm in the earliest days of the Church. It is
in this context that Peter calls the people 'a royal priesthood' and tells them that it is their function to offer up
spiritual sacrifices that are acceptable to God through Jesus
Christ. It would not seem then to do justice to St Peter's
thought to say that he was speaking of merely moral sacrifices (though they are not excluded) and the very adjective
'spiritual' (*pneumatikas*) indicates that they were not the
the gross material sacrifices of paganism he was speaking of

[1] See F. L. Cross, *I Peter, A Paschal Liturgy* (London, 1954).

but the 'pneumatic' sacrifice of the kingdom of the Spirit (*Pneuma*) which had come into existence with Christ's death and resurrection. They are then a people called by God to offer sacrifice, that is, they are a priestly people. But they had as their second function to proclaim the mighty deeds of salvation wrought by God (verse 9). They are also essentially a missionary people; worship and apostolate go together.

If all is not absolutely certain in this interpretation, it is how the Fathers of the Church interpreted this passage from St Justin the Martyr onwards. Naturally, there has been development and it has been seen in the course of centuries that it was necessary to distinguish certain functions within the one priesthood of the Church which is nothing other than that of Jesus Christ. By the end of the first century the functions of the bishop, the 'president' of the eucharist, of the priest and of the deacon had become clear. Later still, it has been necessary to insist that the priesthood of the ordained minister is specifically different from that of the people[1] but, as we can see from the teaching of Pius XII, this does not destroy the priesthood of the laity. The same pope after saying that the very structure of the Mass shows that the people have their part in offering it (91), continues, 'And there is no wonder that the faithful are accorded this privilege: by reason of their baptism Christians are in the mystical Body and become by a common title members of Christ the Priest; by the character that is graven upon their souls they are appointed to the worship of God, and therefore, according to their condition, they share in the priesthood of Christ himself' (92).[2] The following paragraphs of the encyclical set out the means by which this priesthood is exercised. The people offer through the priest who acts *in persona Christi*, as Christ's representative,

[1] *Mediator Dei*, 88.
[2] This is to all intents and purposes the teaching of St Thomas, III, 53 (the whole question).

no longer using words of merely human composition but the
very words of Christ, as St Ambrose said, and uniting the
whole community present to Christ's eternal sacrifice. They
offer with the priest, both interiorly by uniting their senti-
ments of praise, thanksgiving, entreaty and expiation with
those of the priest and through him with Christ, and externally by taking an active part in the Mass according to
the approved methods of the Church (*Mediator Dei*, 97–
112). The teaching of the encyclical was carried forward a
considerable way by the Instruction of 1958 in which a wide
variety of ways were laid down by which the people might
exercise their priesthood. Its suggestions have for the most
part not been taken up in English speaking countries.

Perhaps I may be allowed to sum up this matter in words
that have appeared elsewhere: 'The people take part in
the Mass not just by some sort of permission. Their function
is based on something that is given them by God, something
that is rooted in them as Christians. . . . The people have
a duty to take part in the offering of the Mass not merely
because they are called to do so by the Church; they are
called to do so by the Church because they *are* something
that implies it. By baptism we are made members of Christ's
body . . . and this means that in the depths of our being
we are made like him, we are 'conformed' to him. But
what was he? Was he, is he, just some sort of undefined
head of the Church, like a chairman or schoolmaster? Christ
our Lord is head of the Church primarily as *Priest*, for he
called it into existence by the supreme act of his priesthood,
namely the offering of himself in sacrifice on the cross:
"Christ loved the Church and delivered himself up for it"
(Eph. 5:25). So when we are baptized, by the character of
that sacrament *we are made like* Christ the Priest'[1] and
must therefore have a priestly function to perform. Since
then the Mass is the common public act of the Church and
of Christ, its head, he is the principal offerer, the priest

[1] *Life of the Spirit*, June 1957, No. 132, pp. 552–3.

being his earthly representative, but the people as members of that body and sharers in Christ's priesthood offer with him and his representative. Just as the priest's action is public, so is theirs. Assistance at Mass is not a private devotion but, whether we like it or not, the most public act that the layman or laywoman ever engages in.[1] If, then, we are to be faithful to the nature of the Mass as the common act of the Church, if we are to express its sacramental nature as a visible sign of the unity of the body (as the Constitution says we should), the people's priestly activity must be made manifest. It is in fact through their visible and active participation that the sign of the Mass as the sacrificial act of the Church is constructed and made known. Although a Mass celebrated with great devotion by a priest before a completely silent crowd is entirely valid, it is not expressing the liturgy of the Mass, it is not manifesting the nature of the Church.

With this theological background, however lightly sketched in, we may now go on to consider the main practical recommendations of the Constitution.

Once again the Constitution enunciates its aim in the restoration and promotion of the liturgy: the full and active participation by all the people in it. 'This is the aim to be considered *before all else*' (14). And the reason is, in the words of Pius X (so long ago!), that it (active participation) 'is the primary and indispensable source from which the faithful are to derive the true Christian spirit'. This too is why pastors must make every effort to achieve it, and especially by instruction. Evidently, this instruction is not just a matter of telling them 'how to do it', but of conveying to them the teaching of the Constitution and indeed of all that popes have said in the last sixty years.

The kind and quality of participation is also emphasized

[1] The more devotion they bring to their offering the better, but it must be subordinated to the action of the Mass.

not only here but throughout the document and it will be worth while examining this matter for a moment. It has been said in the recent past that the people can take their part, as they do and have been accustomed to do, silently. They can offer themselves wordlessly at the consecration. They can unite themselves silently with the offering the priest makes. They can meditate on the passion and say private prayers and, indeed, *Mediator Dei* mentioned most of these things (115). But it has not always been observed that this is a less perfect way of taking part in the Mass, as the Instruction of 1958 made clear (22, 4) and that *it is only justifiable if it does in fact lead people into an active offering of the Mass.* In any case, since the liturgy is by its nature a sacramental thing, both visible and invisible, involving external action as well as internal offering, it must be said that *normally* the external action of the people is required. So the 'full' of the Constitution means the external activity of the people, that is, *their* words, actions and gestures. The Instruction indeed spoke of the 'fuller' participation of the people in the context of the sung and dialogue Mass. This is supported by the use of the word 'active', in Latin *actuosa*, and it is difficult to know what that means if it does not mean external activity. But the Council is not satisfied with that. It speaks of the 'conscious' participation of the people. It is not to be a mere parrot-like uttering of words whether in Latin or English. The rite should *not* appear to them as some 'mysterious' action that proceeds at the altar without reference to them and their condition. They are to understand the liturgy, they are to be taught what it means so that they can give an intelligent assent to what is done and make the fruits of the sacred action their own. In short, the activity of mind and will is an essential part of active participation. It is precisely for this reason that the Constitution goes on to speak of the priest's responsibility in all this and to lay down practical measures to make it possible.

'It would be *futile* to entertain hopes of realizing this unless pastors themselves, in the first place, become thoroughly imbued with the spirit and power of the liturgy and undertake to give instruction about it. A prime need, therefore, is some reflection upon the liturgical instruction of the clergy' (14).

A three-pronged attack is therefore planned by the Constitution, directed to teachers ('professors'), seminarists and priests already engaged in pastoral work.

(1) Professors of liturgy are to be appointed in seminaries forthwith and the *Motu proprio* of 25 January orders that bishops shall choose them at once and see that they are prepared to teach in September of this year.

(2) Liturgy is to have a central place in the scheme of seminary studies. It is to be principal subject ranking 'among the compulsory and major courses in seminaries and religious houses of studies' (16).

Nor is any doubt left as to the content of the course. It is to be concerned with the mystery of Christ, and teachers of other courses in scripture, theology, ascetical theology and pastoral theology, are to throw light on it and on the history of salvation. This of course implies a revolution in the plan of seminary studies and echoes a bold article of Archbishop Hurley (Durban, S.A.) on the subject which appeared in *The Furrow* some short time ago.[1] Not only will the Christian mystery have a central place in all studies but it will mean that those studies themselves will have to be related to each other in a way that has not been customary since the thirteenth century. Fortunately all the tendencies in theology have been in this direction for some years and already in some places a large measure of synthesis has been achieved. It will now be easier and will have to be started in those places where it is as yet unknown.

At the level of the students' spiritual life there is to be a

[1] January 1962.

more effective liturgical formation. This too implies a revolution. Not that students, in the best seminaries at any rate, have not had a liturgical formation, mostly by their practice of the liturgy, but too often it has been secondary and apart from what was regarded 'properly spiritual', i.e. individualistic and largely monastic. The liturgy, then, is to become the centre of the student's spiritual life too and it should be observed that this will in effect mean the working out in the terms of prayer and moral effort of all the implications of the paschal mystery. This is in fact all-inclusive, demanding not only the practice of self-denial of a very searching sort (dying with Christ), but also an attempt to share in the triumph of Christ, which is hardly less difficult. At any rate, in future it will be possible for students to see the whole of the Christian life, worship, apostolate, personal religion, all as aspects of the one reality, and this will make sense to them and give them a measure of peace and tranquillity they have often needed in the past.

They are of course to practise the liturgy, i.e. celebrate it in their houses of study, but this is not regarded as enough. They, like the people, must be taught to understand the liturgy so that they can 'take part in it wholeheartedly'. But there is something that is new. Many priests engaged in pastoral work have for long complained that the liturgy they celebrated in the seminary, a liturgy which most celebrated with joy and appreciation, was an almost entirely monastic one: High Masses, Vespers and the rest, all in Latin. Yet when they moved out to pastoral work, they found it largely irrelevant. In Britain and the United States, High Mass and Vespers have for years been very rare events and utterly unknown in a great number of smaller parishes which in fact are the most numerous. Students had no training in the organization and planning of popular devotions, no training in even the techniques of the parish dialogue Mass with all that goes with it nowadays. To this extent they were unfitted for the tasks of the ministry, tasks which would be

a life-long obligation. The Constitution wishes to put an
end to this state of affairs and we find written into it the
injunction that students are to take part 'in popular devotions which are imbued with the spirit of the liturgy' (17).
This has already been done in some places and students
not only take part in such devotions but themselves arrange
and organize them. The Constitution does not specify what
they are to be, but we may take it for certain that it has in
mind 'biblical devotions' or vigils, as they are called in
Europe, which consist of psalms, readings, homilies and
prayers of intercession. But the whole matter of presenting
and arranging the more popular religious acts of parish life
is raised too, and it must be said that if students are to be
fitted for that life they will have to learn a number of things
that have hitherto been entirely overlooked. For instance,
if they are well taught to sing plainsong, the same cannot
be said about the singing of hymns. In French seminaries
years ago many a student would teach himself or get himself
taught sufficient music to enable him to play the harmonium
so that when he was ordained he could teach his people to
sing. One would like to see a much greater measure of
encouragement to students that they should do likewise and
the means to do it provided for them.[1] Then there is the
question of constructing devotional acts. How many students know how to build up a prayer of intercession, for
instance? Do we not even now usually have resort to 'Three
Hail Marys' for this and that?

These and a great number of other matters will have to
find a place in the seminary course and it may be suggested
that it would be a very good thing (for both parties) if there
were a much closer contact between the seminary and the
parish clergy.

(3) It is these in fact who next come in for attention.
Priests, both diocesan and religious, who are already en-

---

[1] The harmonium may be thought to be an instrument of the
devil, but some skill with it is at least a start.

gaged in pastoral work, are themselves to be instructed and 'helped by every suitable means to understand ever more fully what it is that they are doing when they perform the sacred rites; they are to be aided to live the liturgical life and to share it with the faithful entrusted to their care' (18). If the Constitution is to enter into the life of the Church, if the liturgical movement is really to move at parish level, then it will depend on what is done for the parish clergy. Various means suggest themselves as to how this help may be given, but whatever they are, they will require the fullest support of the bishops if they are to be effective. We have a lot of leeway to make up, and the level of liturgical practice in English speaking countries is generally very low.

Perhaps the most suitable means of initiating the clergy into liturgical practice is the deanery conference which priests are bound to attend and which occur about six times a year. Here, it may be thought, the bishop could, by means of letters each time, address his clergy and express his mind to them about the new liturgical situation. If these could be followed up by a series of conferences totally devoted to the content of the Constitution, then in a comparatively short space of time its main teachings would have been conveyed to the clergy. If, combined with this, there were practical demonstrations of, for instance, a dialogue Mass with hymns and similar techniques (which, alas, are still largely unknown to parish clergy), there would be some chance of the directives of the Constitution being implemented in parishes within a reasonable space of time. In addition, it should be possible to call together small groups of priests in different parts of a diocese for a one- or two-day conference in which the same things could be done. But such conferences will need to be called by the bishop and given his support if they are to make any impact. All this would in fact be but a beginning. Other long-term measures are spoken of elsewhere in the Constitution.

If in addition a 'Directory' for England (and likewise for

U.S.A.) were issued, such as has been in use for some years in France, Germany, Belgium and a number of other countries, the desire of the Constitution that the liturgical movement should be effective at parish level would be achieved. The directories, prepared by liturgists (both scholars and pastors), are issued with the full authority of local hierarchies.[1] They contain a background of doctrine, setting out the ideals of liturgical practice. They then lay down certain practical rules as to what may be done in different kinds of liturgical celebration and they usually indicate how to do them. As well as setting up an ideal, these booklets secure a certain degree of uniformity within a given region and protect the people from fantasies of individual priests. Within the ambit of the Roman rite they are normative. Experience has shown that in a developing liturgical situation, such as that that now faces us, they are indispensable.

This section, then, concludes with an urgent appeal to pastoral priests to promote the liturgical instruction and practice of their people: they are to do so 'with zeal and patience' (it is something that will not be achieved overnight). They are to secure the people's active participation 'both internally and externally' (there we have it: 'silent' participation is not enough). And this instruction is to be adapted to the age, condition, way of life and standard of religious culture of the people they are in charge of. This introduces an important catechetical principle: the instruction is to be adapted to the people to whom it is to be given. With less educated people we must be content with less, though it does not follow that they are to be excluded from a proper instruction, much less from liturgical participation. On the other hand, it would be wrong to harass older people who cannot be expected to change their ways and we can leave them to their own practices. Yet if a parish offers

[1] See, for example, *Directoire pour la Pastorale de la Messe à l'usage des diocèses de France* (Éditions Notre-Dame, Coutances, 1956). This followed an earlier *Directoire pour la Pastorale des Sacrements*.

the Mass as a community, and with the help that will come from the use of English, even these will be drawn into the liturgical action. Further, although children are not mentioned (and it is a pity they are not mentioned throughout the document except in connection with choirs), they must be said to be included. An adapted liturgical initiation is a fundamental requirement of any parish worship. Lay-teachers know a good deal about this and have often been frustrated by their parish clergy in implementing what they know to be right in principle. It is to be hoped that teachers will be given greater liberty in these matters and that priests will give them a willing co-operation, which of course is indispensable. In fact, the whole relationship between school and parish especially in this matter of worship needs to be thought out afresh.

The last word to priests here is to assure them that in carrying out this liturgical programme 'they will be ful-filling one of the chief duties of a faithful dispenser of the mysteries of God' and that such duties, since they are so important, must be given priority in the priest's pastoral work. Finally, they must practise what they preach: 'They must lead their flock not only in word but also by example' (19).

(In one brief sentence the Constitution directs that trans-missions of liturgical services shall always be done 'with discretion and dignity' by a suitable person appointed by the bishop. In England this is very well looked after by the Catholic priests in charge of radio and television, and in the U.S.A. by the N.C.W.C., and we must be grateful that we have, thanks to them, so very high a standard.)

The Bishop and the Liturgy

The next group of practical directives (41–46) is again prefaced by a theological statement the full development of which would take us very far. What in fact the Constitution does at this point is to set out the fundamental structure of the Church. It deals first with the position of the bishop in the Church. He is the high priest of the whole flock committed to his care and from him the people derive in some way the divine life of Christ. This is a very strong statement and with it we return to the teaching of the earliest days of the Church on the episcopate. Further, the Constitution states that the whole liturgical life of the diocese is centred upon the bishop. The doctrine that is implied here is that the episcopate is the first and principal participation in the priesthood of Christ. The question, long debated but less so recently, whether the episcopate is a sacrament or not is really decided, though not formally, by this passage.

The bishop has sometimes been thought of as a 'blown up' priest, or as the more respectful language of the text-books had it, as receiving a 'completion' of the priesthood. It is perhaps for this reason that the episcopate has been thought of as primarily a dignity, honourable and honoured and because of this surrounded by certain ceremonial signs and gestures. The truth of the matter is that the different ranks of the hierarchy are to be distinguished not by dignity but by function. A cardinal, for instance, has a higher dignity than a simple bishop but not a higher function. The bishop shares more fully in Christ's priesthood than any other member of the Church. He is in fact the *typical* priest and in the early Church the word *'sacerdos'* meant simply 'bishop'. His function in the Church is essentially an active one. He is the vital link geographically, since it is he who maintains contact with the visible head of the Church, the pope. He is the vital link chronologically in the sense that he maintains the priestly succession, for it is through him that holy order has been handed down from the time of the apostles. He is the direct representative of Christ in the diocese over which he rules. He is its chief pastor, its chief teacher of the faith and the principal guardian of that same faith.[1] He is too the principal witness of the faith in the diocese and that is why his other active and sacramental function is to send out into his diocese lay-apostles to spread the faith. This he does by confirmation. But above all he is the chief liturgist of the diocese and priests 'of the second rank' even in this are his delegates, his co-operators, exercising all their functions in dependence upon him. In the early Church bishops baptized, confirmed, forgave sins, did *all* the preaching and celebrated the eucharist. This was the vision of St Ignatius of Antioch at the end of the first century. He could speak of there being but one Christ and one eucharist, one altar and one bishop, together with the presbyters and deacons, and exhorted the Christian people to do nothing apart from the bishop or someone delegated by him, for without him (the bishop) there was no valid eucharist or baptism either.[2]

In the course of time the bishop had to delegate many of his functions to priests and they still normally exercise them only with permission from the bishop and in dependence upon him. Even the eucharist, celebrated by the priest in his parish, is done by way of supplying for what the bishop cannot do physically himself. But in the mind of the Council the bishop still remains the chief liturgist of the diocese and his liturgy the chief liturgy. This, says the Constitution, is the principal manifestation of the Church when the people with their bishop take a full and active part in the one liturgical celebration of the bishop, saying the same prayers at one altar, at which the bishop presides, surrounded by his college of priests and ministers.[3]

But although the bishop cannot be physically everywhere, the people must be taught that he is their principal priest

---

[1] As we say at the end of the first prayer of the Canon of the Mass.

[2] Letter to the Philadelphians, 4, and to the Smyrneans, 8.

[3] We hear the echo of St Ignatius' language and if the 'collegiality' of the bishops gave the Council a good deal of trouble, that of the priests with their bishop did not!

and ways and means must be found to foster the link between the people in the parish and the bishop in the diocese. In France and other places since the war, the solemn carrying of the Holy Oils, consecrated on Maundy Thursday by the bishop with the college of his priests, has been instituted as a way of establishing the link. Other ways could be thought of. With a simplification of pontifical ceremonial, it would be much easier for a bishop to celebrate the eucharist in a parish church on any ordinary Sunday morning and at the same time he could exercise his function of being the chief teacher of the people. Now that confirmation may be celebrated within the Mass, the occasion when the bishop comes to confer this sacrament would seem to be a very appropriate one for this common celebration of the Mass with the local clergy and people.

Inevitably when the Constitution comes to speak of the diocese it must speak also of the parish which, it says, is the most important of all the local groupings within the diocese. The expression 'theology of the parish' is somewhat equivocal and the Constitution is properly reserved in its language on the subject. But it does say three things about it that are important. It calls them 'local' groupings of the people and thus emphasizes the normal structure of the parish and diocese. The parish is the local 'expression' of the diocese. It is here that it is tangible and it is this aspect of locality that more than anything else defines its nature. Secondly, it is said to 'manifest the visible Church constituted throughout the world'. Not only the diocese but also the whole Church is made tangible and concrete through the parish and it is here that the Church normally and territorially exists. Thirdly, it is called a community. It is not just a haphazard collection of individuals who by accident live in one place (though it often looks like that), but it is in miniature the body of Christ into which men are incorporated by baptism, confirmation and the eucharist and all these acts take place in the parish. The Constitution goes on to suggest that it is precisely by the eucharist that the community of the parish is created and insists that it must form the centre of its life:

'Therefore the liturgical life of the parish and its relationship to the bishop must be fostered theoretically (*in mente*; in the people's minds and so obviously through teaching) and practically among the faithful and clergy; efforts too must be made to encourage a sense of community within the parish, *above all in the communal celebration of the Sunday Mass*' (42).

This emphasis on the community aspect of the parish as on the communal nature of the principal liturgical act of the parish, the Sunday eucharist, is very encouraging. Once again, one finds reflected here what theologians and pastors have been teaching for some long time. But it cannot be disguised that there is still an enormous task before us to re-orientate people's mind so that they see their parish as a community. Most are almost completely indifferent to it. They think of it as a sort of service station where they can get Masses 'laid on' according to need and inclination, or as a first-aid post where sundry repairs can be effected. Many are still resistant to the notion that they are a people, a community gathered in one place, where they should express what they *are*, first in their celebration of the common act of the Church, the Mass, and then by their service in charity of the community in which they live. No doubt they, and all of us, are victims of the atomized society of our day. No doubt the purely territorial parish is not going to meet all the pastoral needs of our time (and a good deal of investigation about this would seem to be indicated), but parish communities still exist, often held together by nothing more vital than bingo and such-like activities, and the task that lies before priests and people is to understand the nature of the community in which they live and seek to revitalize it.

Liturgical Commissions (44–46)

It is against this background that the Constitution considers the practical measures that are to be taken for the advancement of the liturgical movement, remarking (43), in the words of Pius XII to the International Liturgical Congress of Assisi, that

> 'zeal for the promotion and restoration of the liturgy is rightly held to be a sign of the providential dispositions of God in our time, as a movement of the Holy Spirit in his Church. It is today a distinguishing mark of the Church's life, indeed of the whole tenor of contemporary thought and action.'

This in itself is a remarkable statement and should put an end once for all to the carping criticisms of those who for far too long have resisted the obvious desire of the Church that the liturgy should be improved so that the people may have a fuller part in it. Concern for the liturgy can no longer be regarded as a peripheral activity, something on the border-line of pastoral practice which the 'realistic' priest can very well ignore. If the liturgical movement is a sign of the action of the Holy Spirit in the Church, is it not a grave matter to resist it?

Therefore, so that 'this pastoral-liturgical action may become *even more vigorous* in the Church, the sacred Council decrees' the following:

(1) Local conferences of bishops are to set up liturgical commissions for the territories which they govern. These will be coterminous with that territory. Thus, if the regional episcopal conference covers one nation, the commission will be a national one. But it may also be smaller or bigger. Most countries now have such conferences, though their juridical nature and status have yet to be determined by the Council. Meanwhile, such conferences are already acting and almost every hierarchy in Europe

has already extended a measure of the vernacular in the liturgy. Active liturgical commissions have been established in France, Germany and Belgium, not to mention other countries, for some years now and have done very good work from which indeed the Council itself has profited.

(2) The commissions are episcopal, that is, with at least an episcopal chairman or president, but they are to consist of experts in liturgical science, sacred music and art as well as in pastoral practice. They will reflect the pattern set by the Council for the promotion and reform of the liturgy which is to be based on a knowledge of tradition and pastoral experience. Ideally, parish priests should be in a position to make their views known about the practicality of what such commissions propose, and it should not be thought that because a man has no particular learning in the history of the liturgy he is thereby to be excluded from liturgical commissions. One would go further and say that, as has been done in some countries, certain parish priests should be given permission to carry out *ad experimentum* certain measures provisionally decided by the commission. Liturgy is a living thing and new rites cannot be devised in a sort of laboratory and then simply imposed. Certain less pastoral features of the Easter Vigil service, for instance, are the result of such procedures. On the other hand, the 'practical' man must be willing to listen to the experts, to the theologian and the historian. Otherwise there is a danger of treating the sacred liturgy as a pastoral gimmick. It would seem that the best way to use these commissions would be to give them a wide freedom of debate and a mandate to initiate programmes of action which should then be considered by the bishops and judged on their merits. It would be at this point that the authority of the bishops would come into play, rather than before. Certainly for some years to come priests will be feeling their way in the new world that is opening to them and there will be need for constant and perceptive guidance. The Constitu-

tion is aware of this. The function of the commissions is not to hand out rules or merely supervise the observance of the rubrics. They are to *guide* pastoral practice, under the bishops' authority, and to promote studies and even experiments whenever these would seem to be indicated. The Constitution in this last matter is, it is true, thinking about the 'adaptations' of the liturgy which it may be necessary to make in missionary territories, but the principle would seem to be valid for the whole Church. In any case, it is an indication that the Council does not envisage these commissions as being merely guardians of the rubrics, but as active initiating bodies whose main duty is to promote liturgical worship throughout the territory with which they are concerned. To a certain extent they are even to be study groups; they are 'to promote studies'. This will be particularly necessary in two or three fields. There is the whole question of turning the Latin of the liturgy into the language of the people. Solutions will not be found immediately. We have no experience of a vernacular liturgy. We have not an instinctive 'feel' for English words in worship. Then there is the whole complex problem of marrying the words to music, and here a close collaboration between linguists, translators and musicians is indispensable. Again, there is the whole matter of constructing 'Bible devotions' and other popular devotions which shall bear the mark of the liturgy, according to the requirements of 13, as they have not in the recent past. In fact, the whole area of pastoral parochial worship should come under the supervision of such commissions.

Finally, it should be possible for the liturgical commissions to train a number of priests in the necessary techniques so that they can go about the diocese helping other priests and teachers to implement the decrees of the Council.

(3) But the Constitution is aware that the commissions cannot do everything and it recommends that 'so far as possible' Institutes of Pastoral Liturgy should be set up.

These are to consist of 'persons who are eminent for these subjects, and including laymen when appropriate'. Institutes of this kind have long been in existence in France and Germany and more recently Rome, and it is not too much to say that the Centre de Pastorale Liturgique in France, the later Institut supérieure de liturgie and the Liturgisches Institut of Trier have not only been the mainspring of the marvellous advance in liturgical studies and practice since the war but have a reputation for scholarship and practical experience which have been of the greatest value to liturgists everywhere. Their work has indeed changed the face of the Church. It is urgent that some such institute should be set up in this country and that some priests should be able to devote the whole of their time to the study of the liturgy with a view to pastoral practice. Without it, liturgical practice will always be in danger of being superficial.

It is surprising that it is only in connection with liturgical institutes that the Constitution mentions the laity. One would have thought that they had a place on the commissions too. Not only are there very large numbers of laypeople, both men and women, of great scholarly attainments, but they after all are the chief 'consumers' of the liturgy, just as they may be the chief victims of clerical shortcomings in the matter. They have a contribution to make in the framing of liturgical worship that is quite invaluable and fortunately there is nothing in the Constitution to exclude them.

(4) Not only are national commissions to be set up, but there are to be diocesan commissions under the direction of the bishop 'for promoting the liturgical apostolate' (45). The words are to be noted. The diocesan liturgical commission is to be a centre for the promotion of liturgical practice and it should be able to provide the sort of help and guidance that is required by priests in their parishes. Its function, in other words, is to be positive and not repres-

sive or merely regulatory. It is to be a centre of apostolate. Normally, it will take in the whole range of activities that are connected with worship, including music, church architecture and art (46).[1]

Not everyone will greet this injunction with enthusiasm. In the past diocesan commissions on architecture and art have been ultra-conservative and have blocked many an imaginative project. It is to be hoped that liturgical commissions will not go the same way. Too often they have been staffed by older or even old priests whose ideas have been those of a former generation. They have had a *horror novi*. One way to avoid this sort of thing would be to have a changing personnel with, say, one-third retiring every five years or so. If in addition lay-people, architects, artists and musicians were given a proper status on these committees, then the danger of stagnation would be largely averted.

The practical measures for the advance of the liturgy receive further notice in the chapters on music and church architecture and art (VI and VII). In the first we find that church music is to be taught and practised in seminaries, novitiates and houses of study as well as in Catholic schools and institutions. The teachers are to be competent and carefully trained. Institutes of sacred music should be set up wherever possible and no doubt they would form a department of the liturgical institute. Composers, singers and choir boys are to be given an adequate liturgical formation. Composers are to be encouraged to write music for the liturgy but they are not to confine their attention merely to composing for choirs. They should provide for the needs of the people who are to be enabled to take their part in the singing of the liturgy:

'Bishops and other pastors of souls are to ensure that whenever the sacred liturgy is to be solemnized with

[1] For a sketch of a possible diocesan liturgical commission, see 'The Diocesan Liturgical Commission' by J. C. Buckley in *Liturgy*, January 1960, No. 121, vol. xxix.

song, *the whole body of the faithful* may be able to contribute *that active participation which is rightly theirs* as laid down in articles 28 and 30.'

Native music in missionary territories is to be given a suitable place in the liturgy (119).

The care of liturgical objects is imposed on bishops who are asked to encourage artistic activity:

'Ordinaries, by the encouragement and favour they show to art which is truly sacred, should strive after noble beauty rather than sumptuous display.'

These then are the principal measures the Council has decreed for the promotion of the liturgy. Doubtless, no practical measures will be effective unless those with the duty of carrying them out are filled with the spirit of the liturgy. This is demanded with great vigour throughout the Constitution and it is only this spirit that will turn dead directives into living principles of action.

III. THE PRINCIPLES OF REFORM

So far the Constitution has done no more than set out the theological basis of the liturgy and given certain directives for its promotion in diocese and parish. Now it turns to the question of reform, or as it prefers to call it, the restoration (*instauratio*) of the liturgy. It is this part of the document that has raised the highest hopes and the greatest fears. But it must be said that the aim of the Council has also been widely misunderstood. Some seem to have thought that the Council was going to 'wreck' the ancient liturgy by which the Church has lived for two thousand years, that everything was to be turned upside down for no very obvious reason, and that when they go to church in the near future, they will not recognize the services at all. There are others who think that the liturgy is more or less perfect as it is and that no change is necessary. This is probably the commonest view and shows itself particularly in those who still write to the Catholic press against any extension of English in the liturgy. Some of these, well-educated people with a knowledge of Latin, may very well feel that its suppression or diminution will be a great cultural loss, but they have no idea at all of the pastoral situation in which most priests and laity are involved. One would have a little more patience with this point of view if our Catholic schools had succeeded in teaching Latin as a usable instrument in worship. But for the most part they have failed, or even never attempted it. Connected with this view is another that somehow or other the liturgy will be removed from the world of sacred and exposed to the profane world. This, which overlooks the hieratic beauty of the Anglican liturgy, is to turn Christian worship precisely into a mystery cult which has nothing at all to do with the Christian mystery. Viewing the situation as a priest (one had almost said, as a mere priest), one is struck by the highly individualistic and subjective attitude many of the laity have to pastoral work in general and the liturgy in particular. They seem to think that if something is all right for *them*, then it must be all right for everyone else.

But there is another mistaken view about the liturgy. Some think that the Mass, for instance, has always been as it is now. They are completely ignorant of liturgical history or indeed of the history of the Church altogether. They cannot distinguish essentials from accidentals. To these the Constitution has some pertinent remarks to make. In the opening paragraph of this section on reform it states (and repeats what Pius XII said in 1947[1]) that there is an unchangeable part of the liturgy which was instituted by Christ, but also that there is a changeable part which it is within the competence of the Church to vary as the needs of the Church in different ages require.[2] It is this variable

[1] *Mediator Dei*, 54.
[2] A similar statement was made as long ago as the Council of Trent, Sess. XXI, c. 2.

part of the liturgy that the Council now proposes to examine and where necessary change. These variable parts, it says, not only may but *ought* to be changed 'if they have suffered from the intrusion of anything out of harmony with the inner nature of the liturgy or have become unsuited to it'.

Change then there is to be and it is important to understand how the Church proposes to tackle it. In more than one place the Constitution states that there are to be two principles or criteria of liturgical reform. The first may be summed up in one word, tradition, and this surely should give comfort to the timid who fear that tradition is going to be thrown out of the window: 'That *sound tradition may be retained*, and yet the way remain open to legitimate progress, a careful investigation is always to be made into each part of the liturgy which is to be revised' (23). This passage perfectly expresses what was the state of affairs in an earlier age: respect for tradition and the willingness to effect such changes as the needs of the Church indicated. In the earliest days indeed the *only* part that was 'traditional' was what Christ himself had instituted; in the case of the Mass, the simple rite of the Last Supper. To this before the end of the first century was added the ministry of the word, which was substantially the synagogue service with which the apostles and many of the early Christians were familiar. It is to this nucleus that has been added in the course of ages the complexus of rites that we now know as the Mass of the Roman rite. In the first centuries, up to the middle of the fifth, the development was organic, no more than the emphasizing of elements that were implicit in the traditional form. A more solemn way of presenting the bread and wine became a rite of offertory and later, since priests and people had to walk in procession to a church or inside it, certain chants were added as accompaniments to these liturgical actions. Later on the development became more haphazard and many things were added which, as the

Constitution says here and elsewhere, were out of harmony with the nature of the liturgical action.

A return to tradition, then, means a scientific investigation, based on our present theological and historical knowledge of the liturgy (which is far greater now than it has ever been before) so that its organic structure can be discerned and essentials can be separated from unessentials. This was the approach made to the reform of the Holy Week rites, and after 1955 we saw the disappearance of the long fore-Mass of the palms on Palm Sunday and of the triple candle (which no one could explain) on Holy Saturday. The ancient liturgical books will be examined and no doubt a picture will be formed of what the Roman rite once was. Not that the investigation will stop there, as we shall see in a moment, for liturgy is a living thing and a mere archaeologism was repudiated by *Mediator Dei* (5). Nonetheless this is the first basic requirement, for if we do not understand our rite in the various phases of its historical development, we shall not be in a position to propose changes that will be in harmony with its nature.

It may be asked, however, what phase of the historical development is going to be taken as normative. This we do not know, but there has been a tendency to say that the liturgy of the book usually called the Gregorian Sacramentary is to be the norm. This may be all very well, but one disadvantage is that this was a papal book and its liturgy was not even practised at first in the titular churches of Rome. Moreover, by the time it came to be compiled (somewhere in the early seventh century) one or two less fortunate changes had been made. In the fourth and fifth centuries there had been the great prayer of intercession, the Prayer of the Faithful, which survives in our rite now only on Good Friday. This was first moved to the beginning of the Mass (where the *Kyrie*, which indeed is a vestigial relic of it, now is) and then by St Gregory the Great drastically shortened, at least on some occasions. After his time it was reduced to

no more than the people's answer, namely *Kyrie*, etc. That
the Church is not going to allow itself to be limited by any
one book, however venerable, is indicated by the fact that
almost the only ritual change in the Mass mentioned in the
Constitution is the restoration of the Prayer of the Faithful
in its ancient form and in the place, after the Gospel (or
sermon), it once had.

No doubt it is chimerical to suggest, as Dr Hans Küng
has, that we should revert to what is to all intents and purposes a first-century liturgy. Life has moved on, the people
of the twentieth century have, if not different, then certainly
additional, needs to those of the early Christians. On the
other hand, the greater the simplicity of the liturgy and
the more closely it reflects the New Testament, the more
likely we are to have a rite that will in fact speak to ordinary
Christians. What is very marked in the Constitution is its
concern for ordinary people, and this matter in fact introduces the second principle of reform. Already in article 23
it is stated that the investigation into the liturgy should be
not only theological and historical but pastoral, and it is
implied that the reform is not to be archaeological: 'The
general laws governing the structure and meaning of the
liturgy must be studied in conjunction with *the experience
derived from recent liturgical reforms* and from the indults
conceded to various places.' The very considerable experience gained by the liturgical movement will not be excluded from consideration and this means an extensive
pastoral experience will be drawn on. The weaknesses of
the existing Roman rite have in fact been discovered in the
very process of making it more available to the people, and
not only do we know a great deal about these defects, but
we know a good deal more about the needs of the people.

But the Constitution goes a good deal further than this.
If one takes all the statements of the Constitution into
account, one is forced to the conclusion that the *dominant*
principle of liturgical reform is the good of the people. The

texts and rites are to be restored so that they express more clearly the holy things they signify, and that *the Christian people may be able 'to understand* them with ease and take their part in them fully, actively and as befits a community' (21). With this we may take one of the most moving sentences of the Constitution (34) which is set in the context of the didactic nature of the liturgy:

> 'The rites should be distinguished by a noble simplicity; they should be short, clear and unencumbered by any useless repetitions; they should be within the people's powers of comprehension, and normally should not require much explanation.'

This, as Dom Vagaggini commenting on it after the first session said,[1] is the principle of principles of liturgical reform. The criterion of the intelligibility of the liturgy is not to be the recondite information of liturgical scholars, nor the fuller knowledge of the rites that might be expected of the clergy, but precisely the 'powers of comprehension' of the people. If this principle is really carried through in the whole range of liturgical reform, then we may look for a liturgy that will indeed make its proper impact upon the people and draw them into taking their full part in it. That this is the determination of the Council can be seen from similar statements, with which we will deal later, made in connection with the Mass and the sacraments.

Is it of any use to speculate what line the post-conciliar commission will take? In matters of detail, perhaps not, but the Constitution itself invites a further consideration of what has been called the 'transparency' of sacramental signs. In a former passage which we did not comment on when dealing with other matters mentioned in it, there are to be found the words:

> 'In the liturgy the sanctification of man is signified by

[1] *L'Osservatore Romano*, 8 December 1962.

signs perceptible to the senses, and is effected in a way which corresponds with each of these signs' (7).

This, that might seem no more than an anodyne commonplace of sacramental theology, is taken further in 21 and 34. These passages which we have quoted above are in fact the interpretation of this principle. It is the nature of signs to signify. It is their function to convey, at the first level, a message, a teaching, and if they do not do this they are precisely *as signs* ineffective. That does not mean, for instance, that where people do not understand the rite of a sacrament it is invalid. That is altogether another question and it is unfortunate that a minimizing sacramental casuistry has affected the celebration of the holy mysteries of the liturgy. If *all* that is important is whether a sacramental administration has been valid or not, and if all that one had to worry about was that the 'matter' and the 'form' were duly present and properly used, then the total significance of the sacramental action becomes a matter of secondary importance. It is for this reason that in recent centuries there has been a steady devaluation of sacramental symbolism and even the rites in the official books of the Church have too often been regarded as just so much material to be got through. Words have been mumbled, gestures have been no more than sketchy and the symbols themselves reduced literally to insignificance. What *is* the symbolism of oil whose sole function seems to be to impregnate cotton wool? Why *should* we put a smear of oil on a forehead only to rub it off immediately? Is *any* message conveyed? Why is the water of baptism sometimes reduced to the tiny trickle that the moral theologians say is 'sufficient for validity'? And why anyway lock up the living water in a font where it corrupts month after month?[1]

If we are going to retain symbolism in our liturgy it must be meaningful and meaningful to the people. Otherwise it

---

[1] This is now to be changed; cf. 70.

has no *raison d'être* at all. So the first task will be to revalidate the symbolism that already exists in the liturgy and to examine carefully if there is any of it that is no longer valid. For instance, is there any good case for retaining the anointing with the oil of catechumens in infant baptism? The smear we put on chest and back in no way conveys the truth that the candidate is being prepared for the struggle with Satan. Either the baby should be anointed all over (and that one imagines would be unpopular) or the rite should be abolished. The anointing with spittle has already to all intents and purposes disappeared.

Nor is this matter of symbolism confined to things or to the gestures of the clergy at the liturgy. The Constitution insists over and over again that the liturgy is the celebration of a community, and as modern theologians have said for some time, the very community is part of the liturgical sign. How is the fellowship of the eucharist which, the Constitution says, is a manifestation of the Church, made plain if the people never do anything, never say anything? Not only, then, must the rites themselves be understandable to the people but they must be such that the people can use them, can enter into them, in a word, take an active part in them. That this is the intention of the Council can hardly be doubted, for every time that the significance of the liturgy is discussed in the Constitution the need of the people to understand is mentioned.

But in that phrase, 'that in the liturgy the sanctification of man is signified by signs perceptible to the senses, and is effected in a way that corresponds with each of these signs' (7), there are three further truths that may be considered. One is that the liturgy is essentially sacramental, that is, it corresponds to the nature of man, and we are reminded of the words of the Council of Trent about the Mass, that Christ left to his Church a visible sacrifice because the nature of man demands it. God *could* have arranged a purely spiritual form of salvation and sanctification. He could have accepted the inner movements of our heart as all-sufficient, he could have accepted a simply interior repentance as sufficient for our salvation. But in fact he did not. Christ knew 'what was in man' and he himself instituted signs and symbols by which man might approach God, signs and symbols that are in some sense the extension of his own human nature. Therefore, not only is God's approach to us 'concretized' in the sacramental encounter in which is embodied Christ's redeeming love, but we too make our response to him through signs and symbols. The interior movements of our soul, adoration, thanksgiving, praise and the rest, are embodied in the uttered words (prayers, hymns, chants), in the gestures and actions of the Church's worship; our interior repentance in confession is taken over by Christ himself and permeated with his love so that we can be forgiven. All this is as much a human necessity as is God's approach to us through signs and symbols.

Secondly, these words make plain that the liturgy is made up of different kinds of symbols with different effects. We are familiar enough with this doctrine when it is applied to the seven sacraments each of which is designed to make us Christ-like in different ways (the conformity to Christ intended by marriage is different from that intended—signified—by Holy Order). But perhaps we give less attention to the truth that within the liturgy itself there are symbols of varying significance and so of efficaciousness. The rites surrounding every liturgical act are means by which we are brought to make a closer encounter with Christ. They are not matters of indifference. They are not just there for 'ceremonial' reasons (and how unfortunate is the expression 'ceremonies' for the sacred liturgy). Nor are they just a 'playing before God'. They are purposive, and if we learn their language, they convey God's message, they activate the soul and they in their own way effect within us God's grace. If the external part of the liturgy is called 'sacred', this is the reason for it.

Thirdly, this statement of the Constitution clearly teaches what is the nature of the liturgy. It is sacramental, existing in a world of its own, real yet not of the historical order, but rather providing a link with the past, with what happened historically, the redeeming events of Christ's life, and the present. It is because it is of this sort that it can be called 'mystery'. In its own way it recalls and makes present what Christ once did and to the eye of faith reveals the meaning of what he did. As the Constitution has said in more than one place the liturgy, which is the exercise of Christ's priesthood by the Church, manifests the Church and makes it known.

We have not yet finished with this paragraph 23. It has two final observations of a general nature on the principles of liturgical reform. Its ultimate justification is said to be the good of the Church: 'There must be no innovations unless the good of the Church genuinely and certainly requires them.' This is wise and sane and removes the possibility of merely fantastic changes of which nowadays however there would seem to be little danger. If we look back to the peculiar changes that were sometimes made in the eighteenth century in France and some of the suggestions that were made at the same time in Germany, then some caution would be necessary. But anyway, we can be sure that the liturgy is not to be turned upside down for reasons that would be frivolous. This principle is interpreted and reinforced by the next: 'Care must be taken that any new forms adopted should in some way grow organically from forms already existing.' This is a very interesting observation. It has been said that the only genuine liturgies are those that grew (an organic process) and were not made. In our own age when we are very conscious of the weight of history and are psychologically so sophisticated that we find it difficult to be natural and simple, there is in all this question of liturgical reform a danger of producing results that will painfully reveal that they have been fabricated for the occasion. If then there is, as the Constitution desires, a deep understanding of the liturgy, of its historical development and what can be called its 'laws', this danger will be averted. What the Constitution seems to have in mind is the mere juxtaposition of 'ceremonies' which might be eye-catching at first but would soon be seen for what they were, mere gimmicks *ad captandum vulgus*. On the positive side, one can see that, for instance, the restoration of an offertory procession would not be a mere piece of archaeologism but would express what is undoubtedly a need, that the people should in some way externalize their interior offering. How this is to be arranged is altogether another matter.

A short note adds that notable differences between the rites of places that are close to one another are undesirable and are to be avoided. Evidently the Church does envisage a rather different situation in the future. Since the Council of Trent the Roman rite has been imposed throughout the western world and the territories that were evangelized from the west. It is foreseen that that era is now ended (and compare 37–40). Even the introduction of the vernacular will produce striking differences between one region and another, and in a country like Belgium it is difficult to see how these differences can be avoided. In addition to that, the Constitution itself gives reason to suppose that in the coming decades there will be a development of rites, perhaps not very radical, and that in the interests of good order these should not be allowed to proliferate to the possible confusion of the people. It is to be presumed that there will be a certain uniformity within the British Isles where there is a good deal of movement of population, but it is hardly to be expected that even here there will be a rigid uniformity if only because this will be difficult to achieve. England, Scotland and Ireland, as well as Wales, with their very different traditions, are almost certain to develop different 'accents', different emphases which will eventually solidify into different 'uses' or observances. These could not be described as 'notable ; with a more adequate liturgical formation, people will not bt 'scandalized' by such variations. In U.S.A., different regions and ethnic groups may do likewise.

In article 24 that follows, we have the second urgent recommendation of the Constitution about the importance of God's word and its ministry. Its purpose is to establish in the minds of pastors and people that Bible and liturgy go hand in hand. The cultivation of the first will promote the well-being of the second and the Constitution insists in a way that is evidently meant to be pastoral and catechetical on the scriptural content of the liturgy:

> 'It is from holy scripture that lessons are read and explained in the homily, and psalms are sung; the prayers, collects and liturgical songs are scriptural in their inspiration; and it is from the scriptures that actions and signs derive their meaning.'

Therefore 'sacred scripture is of the greatest importance in the celebration of the liturgy', and in the restoration, progress and adaptation of the liturgy, 'it is essential to promote that warm and living love for scripture to which the venerable tradition of both eastern and western rites gives testimony'. We may say, then, that if the words of the liturgy are to be properly understood, the scriptures must be known and this has been the universal experience of the liturgical movement in the last twenty years. That is why the two movements, the biblical and liturgical revivals, are regarded as indissolubly bound up with each other. In the near future this should mean that at the level of parish life there will have to be a much more intensive study of the Bible, and if Bible study groups which have already been started in many places could become universal, a large part of the Christian people could receive the necessary initiation. Schools too will have to take up the matter with a new seriousness and this should lead to new developments that will be not at all burdensome. Much of our so-called 'religious instruction' is like an arid desert waiting for the dew of God's word to fertilize it.[1]

Then we note that the Constitution says that 'the words and actions' of the liturgy derive from the scriptures. This is an important clue for the interpretation of liturgical actions (which as we have seen are part of the symbolism of the liturgy) and the use of things which also are symbols. If we read the Bible we have no difficulty in understanding the meaning of, for instance, prostrations (Moses in the presence of God) or the raising of the hands in supplication (again as Moses on the mountain, Exod. 17:11-12). As for things, the liturgy itself usually gives their interpretation through scripture. One has only to think of the water symbol of the Easter Vigil and the lessons and preface that accompany its blessing to see where the key to an understanding is to be found. Oil, the most 'opaque' of symbols for the western world or at least that part of it that is not Mediterranean, can be made significant if we use the examples given throughout the Bible concerning it.

Competent Authority (22, i, ii, iii)

Before embarking upon a more detailed consideration of the principles of liturgical reform, the Constitution sets out the authority which alone is competent in the matter. This is the Holy See with which however are associated, 'as laws may determine', the bishops. This is a re-affirmation of canon 1257, though it is interesting to note that the phrase about the bishops (in matter of fact, 'bishop', in the singular) is an addition to the canon of the Code. Paragraph 2 of the same article recalls another canon (1261) and states that 'in virtue of authority conceded by the law, the regulation of the liturgy within certain defined limits belongs to various kinds of local bishops' conferences legitimately established'. The wording is very careful and does not prejudice the

---

[1] It is still possible to hear of children at our Catholic schools who have never read through one gospel from beginning to end.

Council's eventual decision on local conferences of bishops, but already in the Constitution they are given certain powers that previously they did not possess, e.g. in the matter of the language of the liturgy (36, iii and iv). If the bishops' conferences do achieve recognized status as part of the structure of the Church, it can be said with some certainty that their powers in this matter of liturgy will grow. Already in the large and important document on the restoration of the catechumenate, certain powers of adaptation were granted to episcopal conferences in missionary territories.

It follows therefore that no one else, whether priest or layman, may change the rites in any way whatsoever.

The Proximate Principles of Reform (26–36)

However much new life may be injected into liturgical practice, in the last resort we have to face the question of reform, and that means a change of rites. It has been found that our present Roman rite, which hardly ever mentions the people and which is so rigid that it makes their participation more difficult than it ought to be, was not well adapted to the new pastoral vision that has opened up for the Church in recent years. Moreover, it perhaps still needs to be said that since the Council of Trent we have, in the matter of liturgy, been living an unnatural liturgical life. The Church is a living body, the liturgy is the 'manifestation' or expression of that body, and for centuries the liturgy was growing, taking on new forms and meeting the needs of the people. With the reform of the liturgy in the sixteenth century all this stopped. The liturgy was rigidly fixed by rubric and so it has remained for four hundred years. That it was necessary to do so, that it saved the liturgy from irremediable corruption in the most unliturgical epoch that ran from 1570 until the beginning of this century, may be granted, but now the Church has decided that the time has come for reform and for a greater flexibility in the liturgical rites. It cannot be said that such reform is premature.[1]

If the rites are to be reformed, then the first thing that needs attention is the liturgical books in which the rites are enshrined, and this is to be done: 'The liturgical books are to be revised *as soon as possible*; experts are to be employed on the task and bishops from various parts of the world are to be consulted' (25). We note that the revision is to be taken in hand as soon as possible, but it is generally thought that it will probably be five years before any new liturgical book is issued, with the possible exception of the Ritual. People in a hurry for results do not realize the complexities of the problems involved. Even the revision of the Ritual will have repercussions on the Missal. For example, the sacrament of matrimony which may already be celebrated within the Mass. Will the rite appear in the Ritual or in the Missal (and thus return to where it once was, that is, in the sacramentary), or in both? And the arrangement of the lectionary for the Missal is bound to affect what is done for the lectionary of the Breviary. Yet, it would seem that the Council has a sense of urgency about the matter and it is to be hoped it will be pursued in that spirit.

Experts are to be employed, no doubt those who worked on the pre-conciliar commission, most of whom have had a wide pastoral experience. But it is to be hoped that room will be found on the commission for pastors who know better than anyone the needs of the people and the limits of what is possible in parish life. In addition, bishops from the Catholic world are to be consulted, though it is generally supposed that some at least of them will be members of the commission. Their experience, combined with that of pastors, would ensure a liturgy that was really viable and would enable the people to worship as the Church wishes

---

[1] Some account of this period of liturgical history will be found in J. D. Crichton, 'An Historical Sketch of the Roman Liturgy', in *True Worship* (London, 1963 and Baltimore, 1964), pp. 72–82.

them to. No doubt during the period of revision bishops will consult their priests and it would be highly desirable that they should. Such a come-and-go between the central commission in Rome and diocesan bishops with their clergy at home will ensure that pastoral considerations, of which the Constitution speaks so strongly, will be kept well to the fore.

The Liturgy, Hierarchical and Communal

It might seem strange at first sight that what are in fact laws of liturgical celebration, I mean at the practical level, should be set down here as principles of liturgical reform. This but shows the strong pastoral sense of the Constitution. The Council Fathers were not at all content to project the construction of a liturgy that would be perfect from a merely academic point of view. Liturgy is not merely an object of study, whether historical or theological. It is a living thing. It is in the order of *action* and until it reaches that order it does not exist. It is, in short, something to be done and so the principles of reform must be found in the practical order of celebration. It is for this reason that in these articles from 26 to 32, which at first sight seem to be recommendations for active participation (and indeed reflect so much of what the Holy See has said for so long), we find stated the basic requirements of liturgical reform. They indicate that the Church is not going to be content merely to revise books or to express a few pious hopes. Just as in the case of the reform of the Holy Week rites, so here, the reform is going to be carried down to the level of practical action in parish churches.

The two principles insisted on here may be summed up as 'community' and 'hierarchy'. 'Liturgical services are not private functions, but are celebrations of the Church, which is "the sacrament of unity"—namely the holy people[1] united and ordered under their bishop' (26). This refers back to the

---

[1] Cf. *Unde et memores* of the Mass, '*Plebs tua sancta*'.

teaching of articles 2 and 7 where the liturgy is described as the action of the Church. Here it considers the same matter in the concrete circumstances of existence. Where does the Church exist? The answer is in the diocese and the parish, and the liturgy must be the expression or manifestation of *this* community which means that *these* people have to fulfil their function if the Church as community or fellowship, created and bound together by the one bread that makes them one body,[1] that is the 'sacrament of unity', is to be shown forth for what it is. The first place where this is done, or should be done, is in the celebration of the liturgy by the bishop with his people. Wherever the bishop is, there is the one altar and the one eucharist, as St Ignatius of Antioch said, and wherever in his diocese the bishop celebrates with his people, there is the centre of unity, there it is that the diocese is being built up into one body.

There is hierarchy, then, in the diocese, but there is hierarchy within the parish, and this should be expressed in its liturgical action:

'Liturgical services pertain to the *whole* body of the Church; they manifest it and have effects upon it; but they concern the individual members of the Church in different ways, according to their rank, office and activity' (26).

It is the mind of the Council that it is precisely this hierarchically ordered offering of the Mass, whether in diocese or parish, that expresses and makes plain the nature of the Church and reveals it, so far as that is possible, as the mystery of Christ here present in the world. Such a celebration of the Mass is in fact the sacramental and efficacious sign of Christ's redeeming work made present by the Church, i.e. the community of Christ's faithful under the presidency of the priests, in the world. St Thomas, sum-

[1] 1 Cor. 10:17.

ming up all the tradition of the Fathers, taught that the *res*, the final reality conveyed by the eucharist, is the unity of the mystical body.[1] By a harmonious and *functional* celebration of the eucharist, this is made plain for all to see. All are *visibly* united in the performance of the one sacred action, and when in their order they gather round the altar to receive the one bread that makes them one body, the inner effect and its outward expression coincide.

Hierarchy and community also coincide, for the community is an ordered one and each part of it has a function to perform. This the Constitution now deals with in various ways. The community nature of the liturgy is insisted upon:

> 'It is to be stressed that whenever rites, according to their specific nature, make provision for communal celebration involving the presence and active participation of the people, this way of celebrating them is to be preferred, so far as possible, to a celebration that is individual and quasi-private' (27).

What this means can be gathered from the next sentence: 'This applies *with special force* to the celebration of Mass and the administration of the sacraments' (*ibid.*). If these words mean anything at all, they mean that *whenever* people are present the 'communal' form of celebrating the Mass is to be used, that is, the people are to answer and pray with the priest. Week-day Masses in a parish church or convent should be of such sort that the people can take part actively. If this is likely to 'disturb' some priests and lay-people, let them reflect on the teaching of the Constitution that '*every* Mass has of itself a *public* and *social* nature' (*ibid.*). We have become so inured to the notion that the Mass is largely the private concern of the priest that both clergy and laity have found it difficult to adapt themselves to another and more fundamental view of it. Yet a moment's reflection should show that it is absurd for a priest to carry

[1] III, 73, 2, etc.

on a dialogue with himself (as he often does when there is no server) and to add an expression of agreement (Amen) to his own utterances.

It might be asked whether there are *any* liturgical actions that do not imply a 'communal celebration'. There is an idea abroad that the sacraments are somehow 'private' and this has no doubt led to the practice of baptizing children in a quasi-private way. All sacramental acts are public, they are acts of the Church through which the people make contact with Christ. This is true even of the Anointing of the Sick and the Communion of the Sick. The link between the church and the administration of these sacraments needs to be re-established. In a former age when the priest could go publicly with at least some of his people to the house of the sick person this was easier. But even in our day, if the priest could celebrate the votive Mass of the Sick and go straight from the church to the sick-bed, something would have been done to establish that this is a liturgical act in which the whole local community is involved. In any case, where there is a family and/or relations, they should be instructed to be present at the administration of the sacrament, as in fact the Ritual requires. Then a mere 'administration' becomes a celebration.

Within the liturgical celebration there is distinction of functions and each person or group should perform their and only their parts:

'In liturgical celebrations each person, minister or layman, who has an office to perform, should do all of, but only, those parts which pertain to his office by the nature of the rite and the principles of the liturgy' (28).

This mention here and in 29 of lay-people is interesting. In 28 they are said to have 'a genuine liturgical function'. If they are not clerics they are, it is implied, sharers in Christ's priesthood, for the whole liturgy is an action of Christ the Priest in his Church. It would seem that it is no longer correct to think of 'servers' as mere substitutes for the clergy, as present legislation has it. In other words, the theology of the priesthood of the laity is here expressed in the practical order of liturgical celebration. What can be said of servers applies equally to the choir, which has been regarded by the rubrics since 1570 (and indeed long before that) as supernumerary to the liturgical 'choir', the only body of which the rubrics took cognizance and which indeed had long ago abdicated its function.

Who the 'celebrants' of the liturgy are is specified in 28: servers, lectors, commentators and members of the choir who all 'exercise a genuine liturgical function', and lower down the people themselves are mentioned. 'Lectors and commentators' appeared for the first time in a Roman document in the Instruction of 1958 and now they are recognized as a normal part of any liturgical celebration. That same Instruction states that the office of commentator, who may also be the lector or reader, may be performed by a layman (95, a). Although the Constitution does not particularize, it must be said to include him too.

Since the role of the commentator and the rules about him and the reader are given in the Instruction (96, a–f), there is no need to say more about the matter here.[1] It will be sufficient to say that the commentator, whether clerical or lay, is in fact fulfilling the role of the deacon in an earlier age of the Church and provides the link that is often necessary between the people in the nave and the priest in the sanctuary. Even in a reformed liturgy where the rites 'normally should not require much explanation', he will still have a useful function. As the Instruction remarks, he may direct and encourage the people's answering and singing.

Of all these participants in the liturgy, the Constitution

[1] A complete account of the matter will be found in Clifford Howell, S.J., *Commentaries at Mass* (London, 1961), pp. 3–25. The rest of that book gives commentaries to be used for all Sundays and greater feasts.

enjoins that they should be thoroughly imbued with the spirit of the liturgy and properly trained for their functions (29).

Finally, the Constitution speaks of the specific part the people are to play in the liturgy. They are to be encouraged to make the acclamations and responses, to sing the psalms, antiphons and hymns that form part of the liturgy, and they are to take part by their actions, gestures and bodily attitudes (30). Although brief, this injunction sums up the vast quantity of exhortation and practical direction in the matter that has come from the Holy See since the time of Pius X. If there are still those who do not follow out these directives, one can only suppose that it is because they have no intention of doing what the Church so obviously requires them to do.

In this short statement we find actually more than in any previous document. Acclamations (e.g. *Gloria tibi, Domine,* before the gospel), responses, all those answers the people make during the course of the Mass, these are common form and everyone knows about them. Obviously included is the *Gloria in Excelsis,* the creed, the *Sanctus,* etc., which for many years now have been regarded as the people's prayers. But 'psalms, antiphons and hymns'? True, in theory these have always belonged to the people, even entrance psalms and so on. Now it is envisaged that the people *shall* in fact sing these chants and that in turn assumes they are going to be in the language of the people, for everyone knows that whatever you can do with the common chants of the Mass, it is vain to expect people to sing long tracts of Latin that differ from week to week. It is encouraging to find that these parts of the Mass, which for centuries the people have not been able to sing, are now restored to them, and we can begin to see the far-reaching nature of some of these simple and apparently innocuous statements of the Constitution. This is in fact why they are 'principles of liturgical reform'.

This is driven home in the next statement, where we are told that in the revision of the liturgical books the revisers must give careful attention *in the rubrics* to the people's parts. Whereas the rubric of the sixteenth-century Missal mentions the people only twice in its whole vast mass of legislation, now they are to receive their proper place in the liturgical books. Thus is reversed a tendency to treat the liturgy as a clerical affair that goes back over a thousand years.

If we consider this part of the Constitution, covering no more than six articles, we must come to the conclusion that the low Mass, and to some extent the High Mass, *as we have known it*, is a thing of the past. Nothing can ever be the same again. Whatever arrangements are made for the 'private' celebration of the priest, whenever the Mass is celebrated with the people present, it will be a communal activity in which all will have to take their several parts. The priest will not monopolize the rites as he has done for so long. Psalms, hymns, prayers of various kinds will be said or sung by those to whom they properly belong and these in ordinary parish churches will be almost wholly lay-people. A celebration of the Mass will in fact convey a vision of the whole church gathered in one place to give glory to God and to achieve holiness for itself.

In Great Britain, where the level of liturgical participation is so low, this will take some time but it is to be hoped that those who have been dragging their feet for so long and holding on to any specious excuse not to do what the Church wants will at last respond to the Church's injunctions.

In what appears to be not much more than a note, article 32 lays down that in the celebration of liturgical actions there is to be no distinction of persons, no distinction between rich and poor. England and America, by historical accident rather than innate virtue, have escaped the dreadful conventions that have afflicted the Church in other places.

We have never had 'classified' funerals and weddings, even if there has been a certain pressure from the laity in that direction from time to time. And one reflects that even fifty years ago a Nuptial Mass and a funeral with Requiem Mass were regarded as the perquisites of the rich. That has now all gone, and the Council can be said to have buried it. But it would help if all 'fees' or other expected offerings on these occasions disappeared too. If people supported their parish properly there would be no need for them, as there is no place for them anyway.

In the case of certain civil authorities, liturgical honours (unspecified) may still be given to them.

The Liturgy is Didactic and Pastoral (33-35)

The liturgy is hierarchical and communal. It is also didactic and pastoral. If 'it is above all things the worship of the Divine Majesty, it nevertheless contains much instruction for the faithful. For in the liturgy God speaks to his people and *Christ is still proclaiming his gospel*. And the people reply to God by both song and prayer.' In addition, the very signs of the liturgy convey teaching of the invisible things of God. So throughout its whole range the liturgy teaches. This is a particularly condensed piece of writing. Most people would say, 'Yes, of course the liturgy teaches. That is what the lessons are for.' But the vision of the Church goes deeper. While affirming with great force that what the people hear in the liturgy is God's word, no less, and that in the gospel they hear Christ himself, yet it goes on to say that the people's prayers and chants contain a message. And how could they not since they too for the most part are God's words? Implicit in this statement is the sound catechetical principle that people learn about God through prayers and hymns. It goes further. They learn about him through the signs of the liturgy and through their own gestures. These could be said to translate into the concrete order what they profess with their lips. For is not Holy Communion an action? So one could say that the liturgy is not only informative but formative, as indeed it is.

It is against this background that the Constitution speaks of the ministry of the word in the liturgy. There are three things: the readings or lessons, the sermon and other kinds of liturgical instruction.

We have already observed (pp. 42-3) that the proclamation of the word in the liturgy is an event in which we make an encounter with God. Readings in the liturgy are not just the perusing of a page. Liturgical reading, which the Constitution itself calls a 'proclamation', is a sacred and, in the broadest sense, a sacramental thing. Through that most tenuous but most powerful of means, the word, God makes himself present to his people. All this is of the highest importance for the spiritual life of the people, and the Council accordingly takes measures to ensure that they are provided with what they need.

It will be convenient to take together here the directives given in connection with the lectionary of the Mass (51, 52).

In 35 it is said that there are to be more readings, that they are to be more varied and more apt or better adapted (to the liturgical service or feast). For the Mass we are told that this means that over a number of years a more considerable portion of the Bible will be read to the people.[1] The lectionary of the Missal, not to mention here that of the Breviary, is one of the least satisfactory parts of our liturgy. Only a very small portion of the Bible is covered in the course of a year and everyone is aware of the lack of variety in the readings of the Sundays after Pentecost. The Council, then, has accepted a very important principle: that the reading of the Bible is to be spread over a number of years. This is a notion that has long been canvassed in

---

[1] This could mean the greater part of the Bible. The word is 'praestantior' which the French translate 'la partie la plus importante' (La Maison-Dieu, 76, p. 85). 'Important' in French can be interpreted both quantitatively and qualitatively. The Latin is patient of the same interpretation.

the Church and various schemes have been drawn up, most of which have been based on the existing lectionary. This would seem to be the way in which the reform will have to be achieved though it will be undesirable to leave the readings of the Sundays after Pentecost as they are. Epistle rarely corresponds with gospel and this makes preaching all the more difficult. On the other hand, the older and greater feasts such as Easter, Christmas and Pentecost do not need any change. Their lessons form a pattern and it is easy to discern their significance. But even here, it might be a very good thing if an Old Testament lesson were included. Whether or not such lessons are to be inserted here or elsewhere is not clear from the Constitution, which does not go into details. But it can be assumed that if a more considerable part of the Bible is to be used in the Mass, it will be necessary to insert readings from the Old Testament. In spite of the need not to make the Mass too long, there is everything to be said for this from a homiletic point of view. It will mean that every Sunday and feast day, a part at least of the history of salvation will be brought to the notice of the people, and it will make the task of the preacher all the lighter if the texts are before them.

As to what is more or less apt, this will be a more difficult matter which cannot be decided by the people's *present* biblical culture. For instance, some object very fiercely to the difficult epistle of the Fourth Sunday of Lent and, certainly, it cannot be said to be easy to expound to the people in the few minutes available. But a great deal of the difficulty comes from the fact that one cannot be *sure* that the people know who Sarah and Agar and the rest were and the word 'Jerusalem' awakes no echoes in their minds. In any case this Mass is all so much of a piece that it is difficult to imagine a text that would be more appropriate to the occasion.

What we may suppose, then, is that the greater feasts will remain as they are, with the possible addition of an Old

Testament reading. Some (few) readings will be suppressed in favour of others that are liturgically more apt, and for the Sundays after Pentecost it is conceivable that we shall have two or even three parallel sets of lessons which will be read out in different years.

There remains the matter of week-day Masses which in turn raises the question of whether we are going to have entirely new sets of texts for ferial Masses throughout the year. On the supposition that at least some days will have their own Mass texts,[1] here is another place where there could be a more extensive reading of the Bible which might well be co-ordinated with the lectionary of the Breviary. As will be seen, the matter is of some complexity and it cannot be supposed that the solutions first found will be entirely satisfactory. The Church of England has long sought a more satisfactory lectionary and no one solution has yet been agreed upon.

There is nothing in the chapter on the sacraments about the possible use of scripture readings on the occasion of their celebration. One can but hope that further thought will be given to the matter. Words of Christ included in the poor little rite of the Communion of the Sick would give much consolation. Scripture passages from which the priest might select according to circumstances would be very appropriate when the Anointing of the Sick is administered. Such passages are to be found in the Visitation of the Sick, but they and others might well be transferred to the Anointing of the Sick and made an official part of the rite. And one cannot but feel that even in baptism it would be a good thing to read the words of our Lord about this sacrament either before or during its administration. If, as article 72 says, the rite of penance is to be revised, there would be a place in it, and an abundance of biblical material, for such readings.

[1] The Sarum Missal, as well as others, provided lessons for Wednesdays and Fridays.

Immediately connected with the matter of the biblical lessons is that of the sermon or homily. Even the use of the term 'homily' which is more often found than 'sermon' in the Constitution, is significant. As opposed to the sermon, which is more formal, the homily is a familiar discourse of the sort that St Augustine usually preached to his people. He is very evidently speaking to them, he rallies them from time to time, he asks questions that were by no means purely rhetorical, and the people often enough answered him and expressed their feelings in other ways. No doubt we could hardly bear this way of going on now and, in any case, more important than the style is the content. The patristic homily was nearly always a familiar treatment of the texts read in the liturgy, and we have those of St Ambrose and St Leo in the West and of St Cyril of Jerusalem in the East (to mention no others) to show us what this kind of sermon could be. If it was familiar, it was often profound and, more important still, moved from the texts of the Bible to a veritable introduction or initiation into the holy mystery being celebrated. It was a mystagogy.

It is of this sort of sermon that the Constitution speaks. First, the sermon is a part of the liturgy and accordingly its place in the liturgical service must be indicated by the rubrics: 'It is to be highly esteemed as part of the liturgy itself' (52). It is well enough known that in the course of time the sermon has been regarded as a separate element which had no necessary connection with the Mass. Years ago some even expressed the view that a sermon 'interfered' with the sacred, hieratic action of a High Mass which was better without it. That is because the nature of the liturgical sermon was unknown or misconceived. Most preachers thought they were little Bossuets. The sermon was a literary exercise, an uttered essay on religious topics. The Constitution is in no doubt about the nature of the liturgical sermon. It should draw its content from liturgical and scriptural sources, evidently first those that form the Mass of the day.

It should be a proclamation of the wonderful works of God in the history of salvation. This means not a mere recounting of the facts of sacred history but a penetration of their meaning, derived from a theological reflection on them. The main means to assist such reflection will be a study of biblical theology and of the liturgy itself. Finally, since the mystery of Christ is in one way or another recounted in the history of salvation and forms its very heart, and since it is this same mystery that is made present by the liturgical action, it is the preacher's duty before all else to throw light on the mystery and on that aspect of it that is being celebrated in the liturgy of the day.

That this return to an earlier and more fundamentally Christian form of preaching will cause something of a revolution can hardly be denied. Nor can it be supposed that many of the clergy will find it easy. Yet sooner or later this is what must be done. Fortunately there is an abundance of material, both scriptural and liturgical, available nowadays that will assist the preacher.[1] Granted the good will of preachers, we shall need a radical re-shaping of the courses of catechism that are ordered in most dioceses in England now. They are no longer in line with the best catechetical thinking of our day and they hardly ever meet the liturgy at all. They have often not been intelligently arranged[2] and sometimes they have been repeated without revision year after year. The fear is expressed that if we do not have these catechism courses, the people will not know the Faith. What seems to be necessary is some re-thinking of exactly what is the faith, or at any rate what are the most important parts of it. It is these that need repetition, though in no wooden way, and with floating populations

---

[1] Pius Parsch's 'The Church's Year of Grace', Eng. trans., five vols. (Liturgical Press, Collegeville, Minn.), is helpful, if getting a little old-fashioned now. In an article in the Clergy Review, December 1960, I attempted to give an introduction to 'Liturgical Preaching'.

[2] Fancy having to preach on the Seventh Commandment on Easter Day!

we cannot be too ambitious. Does it really matter if people do not know all the conditions for gaining indulgences? What of course is required is a re-orientation of catechetics. This has proceeded apace in Europe for some years now, but as yet has not reached clerical education in all countries. It will be interesting to see what the Council has to say both about the latter and about catechetics.

In any case the Council in the liturgical Constitution has made its mind clear about the nature of the homily at Mass and we can at once begin by putting it into practice.

The next point taken up is what the Constitution explicitly calls liturgical instruction, which is envisaged as taking place within the liturgical action. It should be remarked that it is not talking about sermons on liturgical matters, such as the history of the Mass. Such instruction is nowhere mentioned in the whole document. It is in fact thinking of the content of what the commentator might say in his interventions at various points of a service. It speaks of 'short directives spoken by the priest or competent minister (deacon?)' and it is thinking first of such interventions as might be written into the liturgy itself[1] and then of comments made by the commentator himself. These should only occur at the more suitable moments. What we may conclude from this is that such directives are to be written into the liturgy and will supplement those already there, although they have unhappily become fossilized. Examples are the *Flectamus genua* of Ember Days and certain days in Lent and certain phrases in the rite of ordination. If these are to be increased, it will mean that the diaconal function in the liturgy will become more prominent, and that there will be much more 'dialogue' in the sense of a continuous contact between the celebrant and the people. In itself this would help to keep worship alive. But—and this should

[1] As has been done for the sacraments in the *Manuale Parvum* of the diocese of Strasbourg (Colmar, 1954).

be noted—this procedure is placed in the context of the didactic nature of the liturgy. Although such interventions are not normally instructional in the sense of giving information (and no document of the Church has ever envisaged quite that sort of commentary), it implies that in a broad and general way the people will be helped to an understanding of the rite they are taking part in and so will be able the better to appreciate its meaning.

Outside the liturgy proper, it is 'Bible services' that come in for recommendation. This is in fact the endorsement by the Council of a practice that has grown up in the last twenty years, first I think in France, where it was really made possible by vernacular psalm-singing, and later in various parts of the Church. Such services consist of psalms, readings from holy scripture, homily (or homilies), prayers of intercession or a collect. They are at once thoroughly biblical (and their biblical content requires a biblical homily) and popular. It is probably the most successful liturgical form that has emerged in modern times. These are now recommended on the vigils of more solemn feasts (evidently as a preparation for them), during Advent and Lent, and on Sundays and feast days themselves.

The practical requirement now is texts that can be used in parishes. It is quite feasible to do one or two biblical services, but to use them as a regular practice is burdensome as all the psalms and other texts have to be duplicated in one form or another and in a short time one can accumulate a formidable amount of paper. One book, covering the main seasons of the year, with a selection of psalms and suggested readings, would do the work quite adequately.

The Constitution, mindful of the situation of the Church in many places, suggests that these Bible services should be used where there is no priest available and that they might be led by a deacon or some other person authorized by the bishop.

The Question of Language

No matter has been debated with such heat and acrimony as that of the use of vernacular languages in the Roman liturgy. It would serve no purpose to try and resume the main points of the debate, even if it were possible. Judging by the correspondence columns of the Catholic Press, there are still far too many people who do not understand what the Church has said on the matter. It is necessary then to state as clearly as possible what is the mind of the Council on it. It should be observed that the Constitution is very tightly constructed. There is not one waste word and it proceeds with an almost remorseless logic. It has stated that the liturgy is communal, hierarchical and didactic. In addition it has said that the liturgy is made up of visible signs which must be understood by the people. They must be transparent. It is not until all this has been expounded that it goes on to the question of language, for all these factors come into play at this point. The Constitution has made it clear that the whole purpose and tendency of liturgical reform is that the people may be able to take a full, conscious and active part in the communal action of the Church. The liturgy, both in itself and in the process of celebration, must be understandable by the people. They must be able to read the signs of the liturgy without difficulty and the very place where the matter of the use of the vernacular is put in the Constitution shows that it is the Council's intention and concern that this shall be achieved. The use of the people's language is a quasi-necessity if they are to understand the liturgy as they ought. More than anything else, the use of the vernacular will reveal the significance of the sacramental signs and show what the whole liturgical celebration in which they are taking part means.

It is against this background that the Constitution legislates about the use of the people's language in the liturgy.

(1) In principle, the use of the Latin language is to be preserved in the Latin rites. This means that the books of the Roman rite are to be regarded as the *editiones typicae* or even the source books in which will be contained the liturgy of the Roman rite. They will remain always as criteria of what the Roman rite is and it will be to them that scholars and pastors will always have to return in their study and practice of the liturgy. A knowledge of the Roman liturgy in Latin must be regarded as a necessity at least for clerics and priests, not merely for practical purposes so that they may celebrate Mass without difficulty wherever they may go, but so that they may penetrate more deeply into its meaning and so be able to expound it to their people. The language of the Latin liturgy is a very subtle instrument, with nuances of meaning which translation does not readily yield, and some understanding of this will be necessary if the priest is to serve his people as is required by the nature of the pastoral office.

(2) Some Latin will always remain as part of the Roman rite. It may be preserved in cathedral worship or in monastic worship, it will be useful in great international congresses and, as we have said, it will serve the priest who has to move from one country to another. It is for reasons such as these that the Council asks that the people shall be taught to sing 'also in Latin, those parts of the Ordinary of the Mass which are rightfully theirs' (54). In spite of great efforts in the past, made with the full encouragement of the Holy See, it cannot be said that any very wide measure of success in this matter has been achieved. Whether a greater success is likely in the future will depend on a revitalization of liturgical practice among priests and people and perhaps a new seriousness in trying to teach Latin in our schools.

It is interesting to observe that the Constitution does not repeat the statement of *Mediator Dei* (64) that the use of Latin is a sign of the Church's unity. This is presumably intentional, as another part of the same statement appears in the next paragraph.

What may be regarded as the principal statement on the use of the people's language in the liturgy is to be found in article 36, ii:

'But since the use of the mother tongue is frequently of great advantage to the people in the Mass, the administration of the sacraments and other parts of the liturgy, the limits of its employment may be extended. This will apply in the first place to the readings, and directives, and to some of the prayers and chants, according to the prescriptions to be laid down separately in subsequent chapters.'

The first part of the statement is in fact a quotation from that in *Mediator Dei*, where however 'the parts of the liturgy' were not specified. Here they are, though not exclusively: the Mass, the sacraments, to which we may add the divine office in certain circumstances (101). What is new and of the greatest interest is that the statement of *Mediator Dei* which had usually been interpreted as applying exclusively to the sacraments and a number of blessings, is here extended to the Mass. Thus is ended a long and sometimes tedious controversy about the permissibility and propriety of admitting the people's language into the Mass. What however is of even greater importance is that no part of the liturgy is excluded by this statement. While the Constitution does specify certain texts belonging to different liturgical services, it leaves the door open for further extensions of the use of the vernacular. Whether or not such extensions will be made will depend on the action of local hierarchies. Machinery for doing so is provided under article 40.

The statement, it is interesting to note, *assumes* a use of vernacular languages; it is to be extended. This refers to the many local rituals issued in more recent years[1] which have a larger or smaller proportion of the people's languages in them. It should be observed too that the use of vernaculars has been permitted in the renewal of the baptismal promises at the Easter Vigil and in low Mass, according to the various regulations of the Instruction of 1958. The Church is not without experience of the vernacular and knows something of its advantages for the people. This justifies the procedures used by a great number of priests for some years in having the lessons read to the people in their own language. It is only if trial is made of the vernacular that the Church itself can be in a position to know whether or not it is profitable. Yet there has been a good deal of reluctance in English speaking countries to use the permissions given by the Holy See.

The Constitution then goes on to say in what parts of the liturgy *in general* a use of the vernacular is indicated. These are 'above all'[2] the readings, the directives and 'some' of the prayers and chants, 'according to the regulations on this matter to be laid down separately in subsequent chapters'. There can be no question about the readings. Of their nature they demand the vernacular, and this will apply *whenever* there are readings in any part of the liturgy. For example, if any part of the Office for the Dead is recited in a parish church, as it is on the death of a priest, it should be established that at least the lessons should be read out to the people in English. The same must be said of *all* the Holy Week lessons. 'Directives' pose some pretty problems unless, for instance, the *whole* of the first part of the Mass and the people's prayers and responses in its second part are to be in their language. '*Oremus, Dominus vobiscum*', though invitations, must be said to fall into the category of 'directives', and there can be no doubt at all about *Flectamus genua* which has no reason for existence if it is

---

[1] Though the first one, for Austria, dates from as long ago as 1935.
[2] Rather than, 'in the first place'. The French translate '*imprimis*' by '*surtout*', I think correctly.

not a directive to the people to kneel (even if, alas, they are usually already kneeling!). It would be odd, to say the least, that the celebrant (or deacon) should address the people in English and then go on to pray in Latin. This is particularly acute in the matter of the *Pater noster*. Here is a directive if ever there was one: 'We have been directed by our Saviour's word . . . so we make bold to say.' It would be hardly tolerable that the people should be required to say the Lord's Prayer in Latin following a directive in English. These are indeed matters which local bishops' conferences may decide and no doubt the incongruity of having English directives (and, I repeat, there is no point in having them in Latin) followed by Latin prayers will be appreciated. The problem is likely to be greater rather than smaller when the liturgy is reformed, as we may expect more directives rather than fewer.

Nothing in detail is said at this point of what prayers and chants are to be in the vernacular. We are referred to other parts of the document which will be considered in due course. But undoubtedly *the principle* is established that prayers (e.g. collects) and chants (e.g. introits) *may* be in the language of the people.

All things considered, the Constitution envisages that a great part of the liturgy will eventually be in the language of the people and it does not make the distinction between the parts that belong to the priest and those that belong to the people, as Pius XII did in his address to the members of the Assisi Conference in 1956. Here, then, there is nothing *in principle* to exclude the Canon, for instance, from being in the vernacular.

As for the implementation of these decrees, the Constitution states that the proper authority is the local bishops' conferences (cf. 22, 2) who are to decide *whether* and to what extent the vernacular language is to be used. It is within the competence of conferences of bishops (but not individual bishops) to ban all use of the vernacular. That seems to be plain reading of the Constitution and it is possible to envisage situations, where, for instance, there is communal strife over language in a single country, where it would be inadvisable to permit one or other vernacular. This happily does not apply to Britain or U.S.A., and it is to be hoped that the Church in Wales will get its own vernacular wherever it is needed. In any case, it is the responsibility of the local hierarchies, who will know their own conditions better than anyone else, to make the necessary decisions. It is for them, too, to decide how much vernacular is to be used in the liturgy. There are undoubtedly problems here, as we have already indicated, but none that cannot be solved by application and good will. If one takes the general drift of the Constitution with its repeated emphasis on the needs of the people, it can hardly be denied that it is the will of the Church that they should have a good deal of the liturgy in their own language.

Where neighbouring territories have the same language, bishops are instructed to consult together about the versions they propose to use. This is obviously very sensible, but perhaps it disguises problems as much as offering solutions. There are differences between even England and Ireland in this matter of language and a great deal will depend on whether a common style of English can be agreed upon. If we look further afield, to the United States of America and Australia, to mention no other countries, English usage is developing *away* from that of England. In the matter of 'thou' and 'thee', archaic forms which carry with them their verbal counterparts, there is a wide difference, and unless the English (and perhaps the Irish) are willing to abandon them, there is little hope of uniformity. Conversations are taking place on the subject, though of course it is too early yet to expect any decision on what is likely to be a very complex matter. What seems the wisest thing to do is to set an interval of time in which there can be experiments both at home and abroad. Various kinds of English could be tried out, the experiences of different countries compared, and perhaps after such a period of trial it would be possible to decide what versions were most apt for their purpose. The truth of the matter is that we have no living experience (or only very little) of liturgies in English. There is the noble rite of the Church of England, but there are many who belong to that church who will tell you that they have not got a vernacular. The language of the Book of Common Prayer, familiar enough to older and regular church attenders, is largely incomprehensible to those more loosely attached, and not at all popular with younger people. It is perhaps of these that we should be thinking more than we do, not because there is some mystical *cachet* attaching to 'youth' but because, whether we like it or not, they are the Church of the future. We have to take into account that in a comparatively short time English words will be impinging on their ears and forming their 'image' of the Church. Are we content to give them the impression that the Church is just an 'old-world' institution with its face determinedly turned towards the past? Should we let them think that the Church cannot speak to them in language which is recognizably theirs? Is there not a great danger of leading them to think that the Church is irrelevant to their affairs and the agonizing difficulties they are sometimes involved in? Who in short is in the greatest need of a lively and life-giving liturgy if not the younger people who are growing up in a world far more difficult than that in which comfortable clerics grew up fifty years ago? It would seem that we should think of the future rather than the past and remember that the formative influence of the liturgy is going to be exercised largely by language. We are starting out on a venture similar to that of the reformers of the sixteenth century and we should be aware of the fact that when almost all else is gone, a liturgy in the language of the people holds them to the Church as few other things can.

Translations are to be approved by the local hierarchies. From the authentic text of the *Motu proprio* of 25 January 1964 we know now that this is so. Vernacular versions are to be prepared and approved by national hierarchies 'whose actions are to be "duly approved or confirmed"' by the Holy See.[1]

The Adaptation of the Liturgy to the Culture and Traditions of Nations

One of the most far-reaching statements of the Constitution is that concerning the adaptation of the liturgy to national traditions and different cultures. It is here that the missionary outlook of the Council is best seen. It is aware of a changing world and of the need for the Church to make itself 'con-corporate' with that world. If the Church is to gain the world for Christ, then it must go to that world and not expect it to come to the Church. For four centuries the liturgy has retained a rigidity that made it impossible to adapt it to different cultures and national traditions. A highly elaborate western rite in a language that also was of the West and which, as a rite, had nothing at all to say to Asians and Africans was carried by missionary priests to the farthermost parts of the earth. The most they could do was to invent para-liturgies of one kind or another and give their converts devotional exercises which, however good, were not the Church's liturgy. Perhaps the most tragic incident was that of the Chinese rites controversy of the seventeenth century and the lowest point of appreciation of liturgy surely came with the injunction from Rome that Chinese priests might be ordained *provided they could read Latin and even if they did not understand it.*[2] It was, needless to

---

[1] Report in *The Tablet*, 14 March 1964.

[2] See the article in *Questions Liturgiques et Paroissiales* by Dom A. Robeyns, reviewing a book on the subject by P. Bontinck, *La Lutte autour de la liturgie chinoise* (Louvain, Paris, 1962). Dom Robeyns remarks that this was the triumph of 'validism' in liturgy (p. 343)

say, not just a tragedy for liturgy but for the whole Christian future of China. Now the Church has completely reversed this point of view. The statement that the Church, even in liturgy, has no wish to impose a rigid uniformity in matters which do not implicate the faith or the good of the whole community, is one of the most important ever made by the Church in modern times and its remote consequences are incalculable. The liturgy now enters upon a period of re-shaping in which countries as various as India and Africa will bring their contribution to it and eventually *their* liturgy will look very different from that of England. Chants, language, gestures, movements, everything will take on the flavour of the local culture.

There is a further principle that is even more radical. Local religious customs and what might be called rites are to be admitted to the liturgy if they can be shown to harmonize with its true and authentic spirit. One remembers Bishop van Bekkum of Indonesia speaking at the Assisi Conference of how his people expressed their religious senti-ments, of the wide range of action they used and needed and how when they came to Mass they felt there was nothing there through which they could express their joy, their adoration and their supplication. The possibility of 'bap-tizing' certain 'pagan' rites is thus opened and, with it, a magnificent opportunity for the Church in such lands. Anything bizarre or incompatible with the Christian liturgy is excluded by the proviso that there should be nothing superstitious or erroneous attaching to them and that they harmonize with the authentic spirit of the liturgy. What the Council is envisaging in this matter of adaptation seems to be primarily those parts of the Church that are still called, somewhat anachronistically, the 'foreign' missions and no doubt the need for adaptation is more acute there than in other places.

But the Constitution does not exclude the possibility of liturgical adaptation in other lands. In 38 we find the

words 'especially in the missions' (praesertim in missioni-
bus) and in one or two other places (e.g. 63, b) there are
indications that the Church does not wish to impose a rigid
uniformity even in other parts of the Church. Even with
the admission of vernacular languages into the liturgy, we
have the beginnings of a process of adaptation. The English
language, for instance, is so different from the Romance
languages of Europe that it is inevitable that we should
evolve a different kind of music and with this will come a
different style of text. If Italian, for example, can keep
much closer to the Latin and so make the adaptation of
music used for Latin texts a practical possibility, this is not
true of English. What the texts will be like that we shall
eventually use is impossible to forecast at present, but it is
conceivable that we shall devise a hymn-like form, which is
part of our national genius rather than a translation of
psalms based on their Hebrew pattern. At least this would
seem to be a need for small parish churches where a high
level of musical expertise cannot be expected. It is also
conceivable that we shall discover the need, at least gradu-
ally, to express our worship in forms different from those
of France or Italy and it would seem right and proper that
these should be allowed eventually to have a place in the
liturgy. There is little likelihood of liturgical chaos ensuing,
since the Constitution lays it down that the substantial unity
of the rite is always to be preserved and the right of approv-
ing changes rests with the Holy See.

What is of an importance almost equal to the broad
principle of adaptation is that an entirely new and radical
change is to be made in the re-shaping of the Roman rite.
Room is to be made for lawful variations and changes as
they are likely to emerge from different groups, regions and
peoples. That is to say that a principle of flexibility is to be
admitted to the Roman liturgy so as to make it an apt
instrument to incorporate the legitimate aspirations and
needs of different peoples and cultures. Although this was

the situation in fact in the early centuries when the great liturgies of East and West were forming, this is, I think, the first time that such a principle has been admitted into the Roman liturgy. It is evidence of the pastoral concern and far-sightedness of the Council in all this matter of liturgical reform. Moreover, the principle of adaptation is to be written into the very books as they are revised and room left for development: 'This should be borne in mind when drawing up the rites and devising rubrics for them' (38). Within the limits set by the typical editions (and here we shall have established 'the substantial unity of the Roman rite'), it will rest with the local conferences of bishops to suggest what adaptations are to be made in 'sacramentals, processions, liturgical language, sacred music and the arts. . . . Above all this is to apply to the sacraments' (39). The itemization and the particular emphases one finds here have their own importance. All these areas can be seen to be immediately patient of adaptation. Processions in the western fashion say nothing at all to orientals (and one wonders whether they do to us!). These will find their native expression. In music and the plastic arts there has already been a good deal of experimentation in recent years, but that in music has been hampered by the rigidity of the Roman rite and the necessity to use the Latin language. This will now be eased. Sacraments and sacramentals receive special mention, no doubt because it is here that in some ways the need for adaptation is most acute. Some of the symbolism associated with sacramental acts in both the narrow and the broad sense is either meaningless or repulsive to people of other cultures than our own. Yet these acts are intimately concerned with the great moments of their lives, and they should speak to them with the same force that their own pagan customs and rites did. It is the intention of the Council that this should be possible. The Mass is not mentioned explicitly, though we may suppose that it is included in the statements about music and lan-

guage, but if we look to the future it is possible to envisage
a liturgy that is truly Roman, with that order and sobriety
that is characteristic of it, and yet at the same time expressing the native culture and customs of the region or nation
in which it is being used. This at any rate is what we can
imagine for those parts of the world that have been western-
ized, but what is being actively discussed in the Church at
the moment is the suitability or not of some of the eastern
rites to missionary situations, far removed from European
civilization. It is generally held that there must be an
investigation of this matters, as there is enough to show that
these liturgies are much better adapted to non-European
mentalities than is the Roman.

Perhaps it is some such change as this that is dealt with
in 40. 'Even more radical adaptation of the liturgy' is
thought to be a possibility. Local conferences of bishops are
accordingly instructed to do three things: (1) They are to
institute a careful investigation into the traditions and culture of the peoples where such adaptation is thought desirable. (2) The bishops' proposals are to be submitted to the
Holy See with whom it rests to give permission to make the
changes desired. (3) To give the possibility that such changes
shall be made in the right way, the Holy See will grant a
period of time for experimentation among groups suited for
it. This is a broad and very generous arrangement that is
of immense importance. However much we should like
liturgies to grow naturally, this is hardly possible in our
time. Some experimentation is a necessity if the reforms
are not to be either merely academic exercises or on the
other hand superficial extravaganzas. Once again, one hopes
that there will be no disposition to limit these wise and
liberal regulations to missionary areas. The Church everywhere needs such permissions and it is difficult to see the
liturgy developing as the Council wishes it to if in the
western world it is to be kept in the straitjacket with which
we are only too painfully familiar.

As in other departments of reform, experts in the liturgy are to be employed (40, 3).

The whole section of the Constitution on adaptation is one of its most important parts. It sets the pattern for the future and will in the long run affect every aspect of liturgical reform. The procedures of 40 are of hardly less importance and, as we shall see, are meant to be applied, when necessary, in other matters than adaptation.

Of the Mystery of the Holy Eucharist

47. At the Last Supper, on the night when he was betrayed, our Saviour instituted the eucharistic sacrifice of his body and blood. He did this in order to perpetuate the sacrifice of the cross throughout the centuries until he should come again; and he wished to entrust to his beloved spouse, the Church, a memorial of his death and resurrection, a sacrament of love, a sign of unity, a bond of charity, a paschal banquet in which Christ is eaten, the mind is filled with grace and a pledge of future glory is given to us.

48. The Church, therefore, earnestly desires that those who have faith in Christ, when present at this mystery of faith, should not be there as strangers or silent spectators; on the contrary, through an adequate understanding of the rites and prayers they should take part in the sacred action conscious of what they are doing, with devotion and full collaboration. They should be instructed by God's word and be nourished at the table of the Lord's body; they should give thanks to God; by offering the immaculate victim not only through the hands of the priest, but also with him, they should learn to offer themselves; through Christ their Mediator, they should be drawn day by day into ever more perfect union with God and with each other, so that finally God may be all in all.

49. For this reason the sacred Council, having in mind those Masses which are celebrated with the assistance of the faithful, especially on Sundays and feasts of obligation, has made the following decisions in order that the sacrifice of the Mass, even in the ritual forms of its celebration, may become pastorally efficacious to the fullest degree.

50. The rite of the Mass is to be revised in such a way that the intrinsic nature and purpose of its several parts, as also the connection between them, may be more clearly manifested, and that devout and active participation by the people may be more easily achieved.

For this purpose the rites are to be simplified, due care being taken to preserve their substance; elements which, with the passage of time, came to be duplicated, or were added with but little advantage, are now to be discarded; other elements which have suffered injury through accidents of history are now to be restored to the vigour which they had in the days of the holy Fathers, as may seem useful or necessary.

51. The treasures of the Bible are to be opened up more lavishly, so that richer fare may be provided for the faithful at the table of God's word. In this way a more representative portion of the holy scriptures will be read to the people in the course of a prescribed number of years.

52. By means of the homily the mysteries of the faith and the guiding principles of the Christian life are expounded, during the course of the liturgical year, from the sacred text; the homily, therefore, is to be highly esteemed as part of the liturgy itself; moreover, at those Masses which are celebrated with the assistance of the people on Sundays and holidays of obligation, it should not be omitted except for a serious reason.

53. Especially on these same days there is to be restored, after the Gospel with its homily, the 'Community prayer' or 'Prayer of the Faithful'. By this prayer, in which the people are to take part, intercession will be made for Holy Church, for the civil authorities, for those oppressed by various needs, for all mankind and for the salvation of the entire world.

54. In those Masses which are celebrated with the people, a suitable place may be allotted to their mother-tongue. This is to apply in the first place to the readings and Prayer of the Faithful, but also, as local conditions may warrant, to those items of the liturgy which pertain to the people, according to the principle laid down in art. 36 of this Constitution.

Nevertheless steps must be taken to ensure that the faithful are able to say or to sing together, also in Latin, those parts of the Ordinary of the Mass which are rightfully theirs.

If an even more extended use of the mother-tongue within the Mass appears desirable in some parts of the world, the procedure laid down in art. 40 of this Constitution is to be observed.

55. That more perfect form of participation in the Mass whereby the faithful, after the priest's communion, receive the Lord's body from the same sacrifice, is strongly commended.

The dogmatic principles about communion of the faithful which were laid down by the Council of Trent are confirmed; yet communion under both species may be granted, when the bishops think fit, not only to clerics and religious, but also to the laity, in certain cases to be determined by the Apostolic See—as, for instance, to the newly ordained in their Mass of ordination, to the newly professed in their Mass of religious profession, and to the newly baptized in the Mass which follows their baptism.

56. The two parts which, in a certain sense, go to make up the Mass—namely the liturgy of the word and the eucharistic liturgy—are so closely connected with each other that they form but one single act of worship. Accordingly this sacred Synod strongly urges pastors of souls that, when instructing the faithful, they insistently teach them to take their part in the entire Mass, especially on Sundays and holidays of obligation.

57. §1. Both in the east and in the west, concelebration, whereby the unity of the priesthood is appropriately manifested, has remained in use to this day within the Church. For

this reason it has seemed good to the Council to extend permission for concelebration to the following cases:

    (i) (a) On Maundy Thursday, not only at the Mass of the Holy Chrism, but also at the evening Mass;

       (b) At Masses during Councils, Bishops' Conferences and Synods;

       (c) At the Mass for the Blessing of an Abbot.

    (ii) Also, with permission of the Ordinary, to whom it belongs to decide whether concelebration is opportune, and to regulate the way in which it is done:

       (a) At Conventual Mass, and at the principal Mass in churches when the needs of the faithful do not require that all the priests available should celebrate individually;

       (b) At Masses celebrated at any kind of priests' meetings, whether the priests be secular clergy or religious.

§2. (i) It is for the bishop, however, to regulate the discipline of concelebration in the diocese.

    (ii) But each priest shall always retain his right to celebrate Mass individually, though not at the same time in the same church as a concelebrated Mass, nor on Maundy Thursday.

58. A new rite for concelebration is to be drawn up and inserted into the Pontifical and into the Roman Missal.

II

Of the Mystery of the Holy Eucharist
(47–58)

Once again in the introductory passage to the chapter on the Mass we are confronted with one of those passages of concentrated theology so characteristic of the Constitution. Even the effort to identify its sources, revealed in tiny phrases, is a matter of some complexity.

Without repeating in so many words the earlier statements on the nature of the Christian mystery, the passage admirably re-states it in connection with the Mass. Even the title of the chapter is significant of the approach the Council made to the matter: 'Of the *Mystery* of the Holy Eucharist'. Not 'Doctrine', as appears in the heading of the relevant chapter of the Council of Trent (which it has very much in mind), but 'mystery'.[1] We have to do with the paschal mystery of Christ which he effected in his own person on the cross and which is made present, 'perpetuated', by the liturgy in his Church. 'The work of our redemption' in the historical order is made present *in mysterio* (as the Missal says) by the liturgy, but this is 'accomplished' (*exercetur*) pre-eminently by the divine sacrifice of the eucharist (2).

---

[1] The editors of the Constitution in *La Maison-Dieu*, p. 82, point out that the title of the Tridentine chapter is to be attributed to a seventeenth-century editor.

With many a reminiscence of the noble chapter from the twenty-second session of the Council of Trent,[1] the Constitution sets the institution of the eucharistic sacrifice in the context of Christ's passover: 'At the Last Supper, on the night when he was betrayed, our Saviour instituted the eucharistic sacrifice of his body and blood.' It was a *sacrifice*: 'This is my body, given (over to death) for you . . .' 'This is my blood, of the new testament, which is to be shed for you, for the taking away of sins' (Luke 22:19, 20 and Matt. 26:28). This was to be the means by which the sacrifice of the cross was to be perpetuated in the Church throughout the centuries until he (Christ) should come again (1 Cor. 11:26).[2] It was a *mystery*: this memorial sacrifice of his death and resurrection[3] was committed to his Church so that it might be perpetuated throughout the ages. It is in this way, says the Council of Trent, that mankind is in possession of a visible sacrifice which his nature demands. In that phrase of Trent, *sicut hominum natura exigit*, we have in fact the basis and justification of all liturgical worship. Just as God's approach to us is by the visible signs of a sacramental liturgy, so our approach or return to him is made, by his ordinance, through the external and 'sacramental' signs of sacrifice and liturgy. The external part of the liturgy is not just an added extra to make it more magnificent or imposing. It is an integral part

[1] Denzinger, 938 (ed. 1928).
[2] The use of the word *'perpetuaret'* seems to be 'neutral' and to raise no theological question as to the way in which the Lord's sacrifice is made present. The Council of Trent used the word *'repraesentaretur'*, 'by which he might make present the bloody sacrifice of the cross'. As Dom Odo Casel, I think, maintained, this supported his view of the 'mystery-presence' of Christ's sacrifice in the Mass. As is well known this question of if and how the saving events of Christ's redeeming work can be made present in the Mass is hotly debated. Father E. Schillebeeckx holds that since every act of the earthly Christ was an act of the divine person, the *virtue* of his acts does not pass away but perdures now in heaven and through the Mass we are united with his heavenly sacrifice. His view receives a good deal of support from the epistle to the Hebrews.
[3] Cf. the *Unde et memores* of the Canon of the Mass.

of all Christian public worship and without it you would not have a liturgy at all.

This sacramental sacrifice is entrusted to the Church which is Christ's 'beloved spouse'. If the figure of 'body' in the New Testament emphasizes the unity of the Church with Christ, that of bride indicates that it is in some way separate, with a function of initiative. Set over against her Lord, the Church needs to be redeemed, to be perfected throughout the ages (Eph. 5:26, 27), and into her hands has been entrusted the means by which this should be achieved. To the Church has been left the power of initiating the ritual act, to which Christ committed himself, by which the memorial of his death and resurrection might be recalled to men of every succeeding generation and by which the power of his redeeming work might be made present to them. Through this sacrifice men of all ages might make an encounter with Christ and so have some share in his redemption.

Objectively made present by the rite of the Mass, Christ's redeeming death and resurrection is brought into contact with the Christian especially through his partaking of the 'paschal banquet', which is described, in the words of St Augustine, as the sacrament of love, as the sign (effective) of unity and as the bond of love. By it men are united to God through Christ, drawn into the unity of his mystical body, filled with love so that they are united with one another, and make up the community of *agape* which is the Church. In words that are taken from the Corpus Christi Office,[1] the Constitution sums up the whole matter: the eucharist is the paschal banquet in which Christ is eaten, the soul is filled with grace and a pledge of future glory is given to us.

This is the vision of the eucharist that the Council gives us and it is against this background that it goes on to exhort priests and people to make of it all that they should. It is therefore the 'earnest desire' of the Church that:

[1] Antiphon, II Vespers.

(1) The faithful should not assist at it 'as strangers or silent spectators', words that are found first in the Apostolic Constitution of Pius XI (1928) and repeated in *Mediator Dei* (84), a passage it may be well to quote here: 'It is their (the people's) duty and highest privilege to take part in the eucharistic sacrifice . . . not passively or negligently or with distracted mind, but with such active devotion as to be in the closest union with the High Priest.' Some at the time wished to think that this meant no more than a purely interior offering of the Mass. Now the Constitution actually specifies what active participation means.

(2) The people are to take part in the Mass consciously, i.e. knowing what they are doing, devoutly and actively *through* an adequate understanding of the rites and prayers. The participation demanded is not just a mental one but is in the order of *action*, the rites and prayers of the liturgy (which therefore are not to be ignored) are the very means by which they enter into the mystery.

(3) The constitution then enumerates the principal actions of the Mass with which the people should be concerned: (*a*) they are to be formed by God's word; (*b*) they are to be nourished by the Lord's body; (*c*) they should join in the giving of thanks (*eucharistia*—that is what the Mass is); (*d*) they should learn to offer the spotless victim not only through the hands of the priest but by offering themselves with him so that 'through Christ their Mediator, they may be drawn day by day into an ever more perfect union with God and with each other that finally God may be all in all things'.

The combination in the above passage of the two Tables, of the word and of the eucharist,[1] is very striking. It is thus in an official document of the Church that we have restored a balance that has long been wanting and by implication the purpose of the ministry of the word is seen to be the opening of the mind and heart of the participants so that

[1] Cf. *La Maison-Dieu*, 76, p. 84. The words are Origen's.

they may fruitfully feed on Christ's Body in Holy Communion.

The emphasis on *eucharistia* too is gratifying. Perhaps even now the late medieval idea that the Mass is largely for securing benefits is not entirely dead and people need to be instructed that the Mass is itself the great, the greatest, thanksgiving man can ever make. It is through the thanksgiving, done in Christ, that we give praise and worship to God, as the very pattern of the Preface with its *Sanctus* teaches us.

In the last part of the passage we have repeated, very briefly, the teaching of *Mediator Dei* (85–110) on the meaning of the people's offering of the Mass. This is to be both interior and external. They are to offer themselves, their lives, work and anxieties in union with Christ and strive to have the mind of Jesus Christ when he too offered himself to his eternal Father for man's salvation. This they can do in a general way, but it is not sufficient. They offer with the priest, who is the indispensable minister, acting as he does as Christ's representative, but the people have external means, 'reciting prayers alternately with the priest', at times presenting the bread and wine and at others, by their alms given at Mass. The priest, it is true, makes the Victim present, but the people offer him through the priest and also with him (96). Not that they do the external rite of the priest (for that does not belong to them), but, as the Constitution makes clearer than the encyclical, they have their own part to play in the enactment of the liturgical act. Finally, as the people are to offer the Mass with Christ the Priest and his representative, they must also strive to offer themselves as victims in union with him. It is in fact by this offering in union with Christ (for the Mass *is* Christ's sacrifice) that the people's self-offering is transferred from being a merely human act to one that is of supernatural consequence. Both priest and people at the offertory do no more than place the indispensable human gesture as the prelude to the activity of Christ in making his sacrifice present and taking into it the offering of the Church, that is, the offering of both priest and people.

After this follow the principles of reform and the practical injunctions that are necessary if 'the Mass, even in the ritual forms of its celebration', is to 'become pastorally efficacious to the fullest degree' (49).

The first principle is that the rites of the Mass are to be so revised that their intrinsic nature and purpose and their inter-connection should be more clearly manifested to the end that, as always in the Constitution, 'devout and active participation may be more easily achieved'. The Mass as it is at present does not make a sufficient distinction between its various parts. The position of the priest, who has his back turned to the people even when he is reading to them, as well as when he is doing the eucharistic sacrifice, makes it almost impossible for the people to realize that the two parts of the Mass have different functions. And in fact, unless they have been liturgically instructed, they do not advert to the fact that this is so. One of the most urgently desired reforms is that the ministry of the word should be performed in a different place from that of the eucharist itself. In ancient days the bishop presided during this part of the liturgy from his throne behind the altar. It may be thought that this position should be reserved for the bishop. If that were so, then it would seem most fitting that the priest-celebrant should conduct the whole ministry of the word, leading the prayers and proclaiming the word, from an ambo or pulpit on the gospel side of the altar. If he has ordained assistants, he could then be seated in a chair behind the altar and come forward from it only to say or sing the collects. The advantage of such a procedure is that the hierarchical nature of liturgical action would be immediately obvious to the people, and on the assumption that it would be necessary for him to celebrate alone, he would be in contact with the people, leading them in prayer and speaking directly to them. Another part of the Mass that needs alteration is the offertory act, of which we will say more below. But it should be said here that its significance is almost nil for the people nowadays, especially when the priest celebrates with his back to them. This, that was once a very public act, now seems to be wholly private. The rite of the *Pax* (kiss of peace) and the fraction of the host is, it is not too much to say, completely incomprehensible to the people nowadays. Scholarship has revealed that here we have a very confused and unsatisfactory rite in urgent need of reform. One of the rites of the Mass that is almost meaningless to the people is that of the breaking of the bread (the fraction) and its mingling with the consecrated wine in the chalice (the commixtion). Of this Jungmann has said that perhaps no phase of the liturgical action of the Mass has suffered so much as this from successive rearrangements.[1] It is the unhappy conflation of three acts: first, there was the breaking of the bread for communion, recalling the gesture of Christ at the Last Supper, then the kiss of peace and finally the commingling. A simple rearrangement has been suggested in recent years[2] which would make the meaning of all this clear to the people. The *Libera nos* after the *Pater noster* would be sung or said aloud without any gestures, as on Good Friday. The prayer *Domine, Jesu Christe qui dixisti* (the prayer of the *Pax*) could be said at this point, if it is desired to keep it. Then the priest would sing the *Pax Domini* without touching the host and give the *Pax*. Only then would he break the host and put a particle of it in the chalice, without signs of the cross and while the choir (or people) sang (or said) the *Agnus Dei*. This is by no means an exact restoration of the rites as they once were, but it would make it possible for the people to appreciate its meaning. In view of the emphasis in the New Testament

---

[1] *Missarum Sollemnia*, French trans., Vol. III, p. 248 (Paris, 1954).
[2] Dom B. Capelle, 'Fraction et Commixtion', *La Maison-Dieu*, 35, p. 94.

on 'the breaking of the bread', the earliest name for the eucharist, it would seem to be strongly indicated that this rite should be made understandable to the people. What of the kiss of peace? Is it possible to restore this very evangelical gesture to the people? A hand-clasp has been suggested and it seems to be the modern equivalent of the ritual embrace.

Another comparatively small but important change to make the pattern of the consecration prayer clear is that the Preface and Canon should appear as a unity. At present it is badly broken up in various ways. The Preface seems to be a separate piece to which the Canon is only loosely attached and the very printing of the Missal gives this impression. At High Masses the celebrant usually continues with the Canon although the people are still singing the *Sanctus*. By the simple device of a rubric the celebrant could be instructed to wait until the *Sanctus* is over before beginning the Canon. Again the numerous *Amens* punctuating the prayer make it look like a series of prayers rather than one whole.

Of course all this raises the question of audibility of the Canon. In the interests of making the rite understandable, there is everything to be said for the audible recitation of the Canon, the most important part of the whole Mass, and it seems odd that the sacred words of consecration should always be hidden from the people.

A revision of the offertory act and of the *Pax* raises the question of the position of the celebrant at the altar—again, one would insist, from the viewpoint of the principles laid down here in the Constitution. If 'the nature and purpose' of the rite is to be more clearly understood and if the offertory and the *Pax* are to be even visible to the people (and how can they be understandable if they are not?), then the celebrant will have to face the people. No doubt it will be said that there are great difficulties about this and of course a *mere* change of position will not teach the people very much, but it is clear that it is a more functional thing to do to face the community *for whom* one is celebrating and who, the Constitution indicates, have a right to take a full part.

A second injunction (50, second section) carries the matter further. Always preserving their substance, the rites are to be simplified, duplications and certain additions of no great value are to be removed and other elements, which have suffered injury, are to be restored. Three things then:

(1) *Simplification.* We have already given one or two examples. Others that spring to the mind are the complication of the entrance rite of the Mass, the lack of a clear pattern in the ministry of the word and the unsatisfactory nature of the offertory act. At present we have what are to all intents and purposes, at least at low Mass, two entrance rites: the psalm *Iudica*, etc., and the introit. If we are to have an entrance chant, then it ought to appear to be such and the prayers of preparation, as they are called, were better suppressed or shortened and placed elsewhere. Nor is the *Kyrie* well placed and it confuses the pattern of entrance, prayer of assembly (collect) and lessons. Even where the lessons are concerned, the *point* of the gradual and the rest is not clear. The former is meant to be a meditation on the word just announced. Often it is not and in any case has been reduced to one or two verses. It needs to be a whole psalm again. And would it not be better for the *Alleluia* (with its verse or verses) to be more clearly made the welcoming by the people of God's word which is now to be proclaimed in the gospel? In the older Mass texts this is clearly its function. If we are to have three lessons in future, then the division of gradual, tract and *Alleluia* will be much easier. But, to sum up, entrance chant, collect, lessons with psalms, sermon and creed provide a clear pattern which is obviously organic. This is what the Constitution seems to require.

(2) *Additions.* The Last Gospel, which has already dis-

appeared on a number of occasions, could well go and the Mass should end with *Ite, missa est*. It is doubtful whether any of the private prayers of the priest have a place in the Mass. These are certainly 'additions', dating from Carolingian times when people seem to have had a strong *horror vacui*. Likewise, it cannot be said that the many signs of the cross and genuflexions that were introduced into the Canon quite late (some of them not until the Missal of Pius V) have added to the dignity of the prayer of consecration. It is highly probable that most of the signs of the cross were no more than ritual gestures pointing to the elements to be consecrated or which had been consecrated.

The offertory, from being a simple rite of presenting the offerings of the people, in which they took their part (though by the time of the Gregorian book this had become rather complicated), has become an almost purely private act of the priest, accompanied by a number of prayers which are positively misleading. They speak of the bread and wine as if they were already consecrated and all the ingenuity of commentary in the world cannot remove faulty impressions. That is why it was once called 'the Little Canon'. What seems required is that the people should be able to make their offering which might be presented by representative groups of a parish together with the bread and wine that is to be consecrated for their communion and the priest's. These might be offered together with the recital of the prayer unhappily called 'the secret' (which is in fact the one official offertory prayer of the Mass). This would make room for the one restoration that is specifically mentioned by the Constitution, the Prayer of the Faithful.[1]

(3) *Restorations.* The fact that the Council Fathers saw fit to include the Prayer of the Faithful by name is an indication of the importance they attached to it. One of the greatest lacks in our liturgy is a prayer of intercession in which the

---

[1] Articles 52 and 53 on the lessons and the homily have already been dealt with. See pp. 111–12.

assembly can voice its needs and those of the Church and the world. This was not always so. One of the most ancient forms of prayer, which may very well go back to New Testament times,[1] is an intercession, usually led by the deacon, for 'all sorts and conditions of men'. It took place at the end of the ministry of the word. It was done this way in the Roman rite in the fourth and fifth centuries and traces of these prayers can be found in the literature of the time. Perhaps because prayers of intercession were inserted into the Canon (and are still there) in the early part of the fifth century, Pope Gelasius (died 496) moved them to the first part of the Mass where the *Kyrie* now is and in doing so changed their pattern. It is highly probable that instead of the elaborate series of prayers of the sort that survive in the rite of Good Friday, he constructed a litany or litanies after the pattern of the last part of our present Litany of the Saints.[2] St Gregory shortened this litany at least for some occasions, and by the end of the tenth century it had become no more than the ninefold *Kyrie, Christe*. It was undoubtedly a great loss. In recent years this loss has been felt and, at least in low Masses, a vernacular prayer of intercession has been used widely in France, Germany and America. No doubt it is this pastoral experience, as well as a concern for an organic restoration of the liturgy, that has led to its re-insertion into the Roman rite. While fitting perfectly into the hierarchical structure of the liturgy, it is a thoroughly popular prayer in which the people easily and gladly take their part. The petition is announced by the commentator (deacon?), who invites the people 'Let us pray to the Lord' and they answer with 'Lord, have mercy'. Examples of this sort of prayer for all the Masses of Proper of Time will be found in the Bible Missal of St André, although the translation is so bad that it is unusable.

[1] Cf. 1 Tim. 2 : 1, 2.
[2] It was this part, too, that Cranmer took over, altered, and made *his* Litany of the Book of Common Prayer.

What, however, is of considerable importance is that whatever formula or formulas are drawn up, it is essential that liberty should be given to the local priest to insert petitions for the needs of the local community. It is equally important that the formula should be varied. Nothing would be more deadly than that the same words should be sung Sunday after Sunday. Ideally, the petitions should reflect, as in the St André Missal, the texts of the Mass of the day. This will mean that a book will have to be drawn up which will take its place alongside the Missal and no doubt the lectionary.

The re-insertion of the litany into the Mass is likely to affect the revision of the Canon. Many of the petitions in any litany will be duplicated in those of the Canon. Is there going to be any re-shaping of the Canon? If it were recited aloud *and* in the language of the people, it is conceivable that the petitions for the pope and bishops[1] could remain and the litany would be concerned with other matters. From another point of view, it would seem desirable that the long lists of saints should be reduced. Many are very obscure and they lengthen the Canon unduly.

These are but a few of the modifications that might be made to the liturgy of the Mass which the Council wishes to be of the greatest possible pastoral efficaciousness. They are dictated not by an itch for change but to manifest the mystery of the Mass by which the people are intended to live.

English in the Mass (54)

The statement of the Council on the use of the people's language in the Mass is very brief, almost laconic. It undoubtedly reflects in this and other respects the conflict of opinion in the Council on this subject. Nevertheless, it

[1] If this *is* an intercession of the Church for them and not a prayer that God will pacify, guard, etc., the Church *with* them. See a letter of Dom Gregory Murray in *The Tablet*, 29 February 1964.

makes three positive statements and in a fourth leaves the door open for a further extension of the vernacular in the Mass. (*a*) A suitable place is to be allotted to the vernacular. (*b*) This is explained as being especially (*praesertim*) indicated for the readings and the Prayer of the Faithful. (*c*) Where local conditions may warrant it, the use of the vernacular may be extended to 'those items of the liturgy which pertain to the people'. (*d*) Where an even greater use of the vernacular appears desirable, local hierarchies may apply to the Holy See for it, according to the procedure of 40.

Apart from those who do not wish for any English at all in the Mass, there is no difficulty about (*a*) and (*b*). But there is some uncertainty about (*c*). What, it is asked, is the meaning of the phrase, 'those parts that pertain to the people'? It is generally agreed that the texts of the Ordinary (*Kyrie, Gloria, Credo*, including the *Sanctus* and the *Agnus Dei*) are parts that belong to the people and that it is highly desirable that they should be allowed to say and sing them in their own language. The matter is not without practical difficulties of translation and the like which we have already considered and it may be agreed that some little time will elapse before suitable versions are found that can be used in public worship. But the principle is clear and it will be only one or other kind of prudential motive that will delay the translation and use of these texts. Then, if we look at the liturgy as it once was, that is, if we examine the tradition, as the Constitution says we should, we find that introits, offertory pieces and communion verses were once psalms sung by the people in alternation with the choir. If the liturgy is to be reformed along the lines of tradition, as again the Constitution says it should be, we have to envisage the day, not very far distant, when these texts will have their ancient form and the people will be given back their part in them. Is it practical to suggest that they will be able to sing these chants, varying from Sunday to Sunday, in Latin? We know it is not possible. It would be as well then to have these texts, as they now are in the Missal, in the people's language as soon as possible. After all they belong to them and one day soon they will be able and required to use them.

If it were agreed that all the first part of the Mass, that is, the ministry of the word from the beginning to the creed, was to be in English, there remains the question of the conclusion of the Mass, principally the postcommunion prayer. With this is inevitably connected the question of the collect and the offertory prayer. The first by definition is the prayer of the assembly and although it is the principal presidential text of the first part of the Mass and so properly recited by the priest, he does so in the name of the people whom he invites to join with him in the prayer and who give their assent to it at the end. What is true of this prayer is true also of the others, with the special difficulty of the offertory prayer that at present it is recited silently. Yet, it seems that the right interpretation of this complicated section of the Constitution, which was the result of compromise in the Council, is that if local conferences of bishops wish to have these prayers in the vernacular they must apply to the Holy See for permission, according to the procedure of 40. There is nothing to prevent them from doing this and every reason to suppose that their requests would be granted. Certainly, a patchwork liturgy with Latin and English alternating in successive texts would be a most undesirable thing.

There is perhaps an even more delicate matter. It is generally assumed that texts like the Preface and *a fortiori* the Canon will remain in Latin and yet there are two texts, one within the consecration prayer (the *Sanctus*) and one just outside it (the *Pater noster*), not to mention the *Agnus Dei* which comes so soon after it. Here we have what are undoubtedly 'parts that pertain to the people' not only by their very nature but by the positive declaration of the Holy See in many documents. One cannot pretend that the juxtaposition of a Latin Preface with an English *Sanctus* would be anything but an unhappy solution to a difficulty. The recitation of the Preface in English followed by the *Sanctus* in English would be tolerable even if the Canon were then said in Latin. As for the *Pater noster*, as we have seen, directives are meant to be in the language of the people. Why then should they not be allowed to pray the greatest prayer of all in their own language which is used to invite them to do so? In short, one is forced to think that the recitation of the whole Canon in the language of the people will come eventually and the Constitution leaves the way open for such a possibility. There is no limiting clause that says there are parts that must not on any account be in the vernacular and the wording of 40 seems to invite requests for such a permission: '*If an even more extended use of the mother-tongue* within the Mass appears desirable in some parts of the world, the procedure laid down in art. 40 is to be observed.' It is not to be supposed that these things will come quickly and the further liturgical education of the people, as urged by the Constitution, is a necessity before they are in a position to profit fully from such changes. But it would seem to be wise to envisage them as practical possibilities in the not too distant future.

The Council is obviously concerned that the people should not be ignorant of the traditional Latin chants and urges that steps be taken to ensure 'that the faithful are able to say or sing together, also in Latin, those parts of the Ordinary of the Mass which are rightfully theirs'. Even in this injunction about Latin, the Constitution is positive and will have no truck with those who think that the Ordinary is the business of the choir. These are the *people's* parts. What are the practical problems? A good deal has been done over fifty years or more to teach the people to sing the Ordinary in plainsong and in Latin. Vast numbers of children all over the world have been taught certain Masses, and yet congregational singing, at least in England, is very rare. It looks as if what is required is a whole new process of liturgical education and formation before we are to reap the harvest that for so long has been sown in vain. Lay-people, teachers and those in charge of choirs complain of a good deal of incomprehension on the part of the clergy about the wishes and indeed injunctions of the Church on congregational singing. What is done with great competence and devotion in schools is often enough never reflected in the worship of the parish church. If then the Council's desire is that the people should be able on occasion to sing the Ordinary in Latin, it will be in the schools that they will first have to learn to do so and then they must be given opportunities to sing what they have learnt in church. All this seems to be banal in the extreme, yet there is no chance at all of the people singing in Latin if these two simple conditions are not fulfilled.

The occasions when such singing in Latin is desired and necessary are great international gatherings, pilgrimages and so on where people of different nations gather together. Cathedrals and other great churches will no doubt establish (or continue) a tradition in the matter, and it will be there that the classical music of the Roman Church will best be heard. Most of it is in any case far beyond the scope of parish churches. Monasteries, too, are usually regarded as places where the Latin liturgy will be used, but not all of those who live in them are content that their houses should become liturgical museums. Whatever may be the solutions found for a continuation in some form of the Latin liturgy, it must be said to be a good thing in itself. It would be deplorable if through a use of vernaculars there grew up an ecclesiastical parochialism, a sort of 'Little Englandism', translated into a myriad forms and spread all over the Church. Even if the Church be judged to be over-centralized now, it has taken her centuries to shake herself free from secular pressures and nationalistic fevers and to establish a large freedom of action to carry out her purely spiritual work for mankind.

Yet, in this matter language is not decisive. The Church is held together by faith and charity as well as by loyalty and obedience to its authority. But it is precisely this underlying spiritual generosity that should enable the members of the Church to accept and learn and, when necessary, use what after all will always remain the language of the western Church.

Communion and Communion under both Kinds (55)

Repeating the teaching of the Council of Trent, of *Mediator Dei* and the Instruction of 1958 (22, c), the Constitution urges that the people receive the Lord's body from the same sacrifice, clearly meaning, as this writer sees it, from the Lord's body which has been made present at the Mass the people are attending. Although the Constitution does not quote the actual words of *Mediator Dei* (126), it seems to have them in mind and in this instance the encyclical is more explicit than the Constitution. Quoting another pope, Benedict XIV, Pius XII says that it is highly desirable to communicate at Mass but that it is preferable to receive particles consecrated at the same Mass, even if, as was to be expected, he resumes his predecessor's doctrine that it is perfectly proper to receive particles consecrated at another Mass (which surely no one has ever denied) and that even communion outside Mass for good and lawful reasons is permissible.

There can be no doubt about the Church's desire that people should communicate as often as possible and normally at Mass. Yet even after fifty years of 'frequent Communion' there is still a need to inculcate into people that it is *normal* to receive Holy Communion at every Mass they attend. Perhaps if there were a clearer theological teaching of the inter-relationship between the sacrifice and the sacrament, they would be more ready to do so.

Pius XII's recommendation that the people should communicate from hosts consecrated at the Mass they attend and its consequence, that bread should be consecrated at every Mass that is celebrated with the people present, is usually repudiated as liturgical faddism—it is unpractical; it will not work; and so on. Yet it would seem that no real thought is given to the matter and there is experience to show that it is perfectly possible in a wide variety of circumstances. If there is a problem in very big churches of not knowing how many people will communicate at any given Mass, yet at least some bread can be consecrated which at least some people may receive in Holy Communion. But the matter does raise the question whether there may not be some better way of doing things than is now customary. A recent custom whereby the people put their breads upon a paten or in a ciborium at the entrance to the nave has sought to find a solution not only to the problem of the offertory but to provide a means of establishing the number of people going to Communion. It cannot be said to be wholly successful in large parish churches. No doubt more thinking and experimentation is needed.

Communion under one kind alone was at one time looked upon as almost a mark of the One True Church. This of course was in the days when the eastern Churches, whether in union with Rome or not, were regarded with suspicion and sometimes even with hostility. In this unhappy atmosphere what was no more than a matter of discipline (itself a result of a practice that had crept in unobtrusively) was treated as almost a matter of dogma. And of course there is dogma attaching to it, as the Constitution observes. It 'confirms' the Tridentine teaching,[1] though without re-stating it, and goes on to say that nevertheless bishops may give permission for communion under both kinds not only to clerics but also to lay-people in cases to be determined by the Holy See. Thus is re-established in the practice of the Church the *principle* of communion under both kinds,

---

[1] That communion in both kinds is not of divine institution for the people nor necessary for salvation. Sess. XXI, c. I.

although its actual use looks as if it is to be strictly con-
trolled. Examples are then given of appropriate occasions
when communion may be so received: priests at their Mass
of ordination, religious in the Mass of their profession and
to the newly baptized (presumably adults) in the Mass that
follows their baptism. It is generally thought that this list
is not exhaustive and that the instances given are no more
than examples in the broadest sense. Many have hoped and
wished for communion under both kinds on the occasion
of the wedding Mass which for lay-people plays the same
part in their lives as does ordination or religious profession
in the lives of priests or religious. Maundy Thursday would
be another occasion where the practice would be very appropriate, even if we have to face the difficulty of administering communion in both kinds to a great number of people.
In a small church this would provide no difficulty and in
a large one with perhaps several priests the difficulty should
not be insuperable.

Whatever the practical difficulties of the matter, two
things may be observed. One is that this concession comes
from the increased concern for the authenticity of the sacramental sign. The sign is intended not only to secure validity
but to express the total meaning of the sacrament. At the
Last Supper Christ said, 'Take and eat' and 'Take and
drink'. He instituted the eucharist under the signs of both
bread and wine, each of which in different ways evokes his
redeeming death. Through an appreciation of this the
people, if they are allowed to communicate under both
kinds, will be able to enter more deeply into the inner
reality of the sacrament. Through the use of and contact
with the total sign of the sacrament, they will be disposed
to a more fruitful reception of Holy Communion. It goes
without saying that here too instruction will be necessary.
Secondly, with the practice, however limited, of communion
in this form the Church makes it clear not only in official
statements but *in her very liturgy* that communion under

one kind is but a disciplinary regulation and that there is no objection *in principle* to communion under both kinds. It has been accepted that it is an ecumenical gesture of some importance.

The Ministry of the Word and the Sacrifice

I have already referred to article 56 in which the Constitution insists that the liturgy of the word and the eucharistic liturgy form two parts of one single act of worship. This is important not only as giving a proper vision of what the whole rite of the Mass really is, *both* word and sacrament-sacrifice, but as establishing that the ministry of the word is an integral part of the Mass. It concludes with the practical direction, still necessary, that the people are to be taught to take their part in the *entire* Mass, from which it follows that they should be present for it from beginning to end. Attempts to achieve this have often appeared to be a lost battle. Perhaps when the people hear the Mass in their own language they will realize as never before not only what they are missing but how stupid it is to do so.

Concelebration (57)

Concelebration which might seem to be a merely clerical affair will not perhaps at first sight excite any interest in the laity. Yet this too is the fruit of the new appreciation of the importance of the sacramental sign. The Constitution speaks of it as a sign of the unity of the priesthood. It goes on to say that it has remained a practice of both the eastern and the western Church and it could be said, when considered more deeply, to be a sign of the Church itself. People have become so used to the celebration of Mass by a single priest that they have largely lost the sense of the hierarchical nature of the liturgical action. Even their vocabulary betrays this. A High Mass (or that odd pleonasm, a 'Solemn High Mass') is one 'done' by three *priests*. And it is a common misconception that every priest has an obligation to celebrate Mass every day, rather on the lines of the people having to attend Mass every Sunday. Where, then, there is a body of priests and where they can celebrate with their bishop and the assistance of deacons, subdeacons and the rest, and where the whole assembly, as envisaged by the Constitution (41), bishops, priests, ministers and people, take their proper part in the celebration, there is constructed the most striking sign of the nature of the Church. It is within this context that we should think of concelebration. Priests belong to an 'order', not in the sense of living according to a specific religious rule, but in the sense that they are by ordination (and this is what the word means) admitted into the order of priesthood of which the bishop is the head and indeed the source. So, even when the bishop is not present, priests who concelebrate are expressing the solidarity that exists amongst them by virtue of the sacrament of order that they have received. They represent and show forth the structure of the Church so far as it lies within their power to do so.

This is what lies behind the Council's decision to extend the practice of concelebration. There is no discussion of the practical difficulties that have afflicted priests for long enough when they are gathered together in numbers and wish to celebrate Mass. It is all to their credit that they have done so, since the conditions in which they have had to celebrate have often been far from worthy, much less devotional. The Council, then, has made some very generous concessions in the matter.

Mass may be concelebrated by the bishop with his priests on Maundy Thursday, not only at the Chrism Mass in the morning but at the Mass of the Lord's Supper in the evening. Councils, bishops' conferences and synods are other occasions indicated for it. An abbot at his Mass of Blessing may do likewise. With the permission of the ordinary (i.e. bishop of a diocese or a major religious superior such as an abbot for his own community), priests may concelebrate at the conventual Mass of the day when the needs of the people do not require extra Masses.

Concelebration may take place at any kind of priests' meetings, retreats, conferences, etc. This will be a great boon and will solve all the difficulties of providing for a great number of Masses in a short space of time and in one place.

It rests with the bishop to regulate the use of this permission in his diocese and priests will always retain the right to an individual celebration should they so wish.

A new rite is to be drawn up so that concelebration may be done in a fitting and proper way.

It is well known that concelebration was the normal way of offering the Mass in the early days of the Church, though very little is known as to how it was done. The practice that has grown up in the concelebrated Mass of ordination is bad, almost grotesque, a sad manifestation of verbalism: everyone has to say everything. This was certainly not the primitive practice, though we do not know exactly what was done. Hence the need, which is urgent, to draw up a rite in which the respective roles of the celebrants will be defined. At the very least it will demand an audible Canon, though one does not know whether all the celebrants will be required to recite the whole of it together. What should in any case be done is to allot places for the concelebrating priests. When they celebrate with their bishop, their proper place, as in the ancient church, is gathered round him behind the altar. With most episcopal thrones where they are this is going to be difficult. In any case they should not be used as ministers (unless there is a real necessity), much less as supernumeraries at the disposal of any busy M.C. who comes along. They are the chief and priestly participants in the rite and their status requires a place of dignity. They will take their part in the consecration, they will receive Holy Communion, they will join in the chants and responses just like anyone else, and that is all.

Of the Other Sacraments and the Sacramentals

59. The purpose of the sacraments is to sanctify men, to build up the body of Christ and finally to give worship to God; because they are signs they also instruct. They not only presuppose faith, but by words and objects they also nourish, strengthen and express it; that is why they are called 'sacraments of faith'. They have indeed the power to impart grace, but, in addition, the very act of celebrating them effectively disposes the faithful to receive this grace fruitfully, to worship God duly and to love each other mutually.

It is therefore of the highest importance that the faithful should easily understand the sacramental signs, and should frequent with great eagerness those sacraments which were instituted to nourish the Christian life.

60. Holy Mother Church has, moreover, instituted the sacramentals. These are sacred signs which bear a resemblance to the sacraments; they signify spiritual effects which are to be obtained through the Church's intercession. By their aid men are disposed to receive the chief fruits of the sacraments, and various occasions in daily life are rendered holy.

61. Thus, for well-disposed members of the faithful, the liturgy of the sacraments and sacramentals sanctifies almost

every event in their lives; they are given access to the stream
of divine grace which flows from the paschal mystery of the
passion, death and resurrection of Christ, the fount from which
all sacraments and sacramentals draw their power. There is
hardly any proper use of material things which cannot thus be
directed towards the sanctification of men and the praise of
God.

62. With the passage of time, however, there have crept
into the rites of the sacraments and sacramentals certain features
which have rendered their nature and purpose far from clear
to the people of today; hence some changes have become necessary to adapt them to the needs of our own times. For this
reason the Council decrees as follows concerning their revision.

63. Because the use of the mother tongue in the administration of the sacraments and sacramentals can often be of considerable help to the people, this use is to be extended according
to the following norms:

(a) The vernacular language may be used in administering
the sacraments and sacramentals, according to the provisions
of article 36.

(b) The competent ecclesiastical authorities for the different
regions mentioned in art. 22 (ii) of this Constitution should
prepare without delay local rituals adapted, also as regards the
language employed, to local needs. These particular rituals,
harmonized with the new edition of the Roman Ritual, are to
be approved by the Holy See, and then introduced into the
localities for which they have been prepared. In the Roman
Ritual each one of the rites is preceded by an instruction,
pastoral or rubrical in nature, or referring to the social importance of the rite. These introductions are not to be omitted
from the particular rituals or collections of rites which are to
be drawn up.

64. The catechumenate for adults is to be restored; it shall
comprise several distinct steps, and be taken into use as and
when the local ordinary may see fit. By this means the time
of the catechumenate, which is intended as a period of suitable

instruction, may be sanctified by sacred rites to be celebrated after successive intervals of time.

65.   In mission territories it is found that some of the peoples already make use of initiation rites. Elements from these, when capable of being adapted to Christian purposes, may be admitted along with those already found in Christian tradition, according to the principles laid down in arts. 37–40 of this Constitution.

66.   Both of the rites for the baptism of adults are to be revised; not only the simpler rite, but also the more solemn one which must take into account the restored catechumenate. A special Mass 'For the Conferring of Baptism' is to be inserted into the Roman Missal.

67.   The rite for the baptism of infants is also to be revised, and it should be adapted to the circumstance that those to be baptized are, in fact, infants. The roles of parents and godparents, and also their duties, should be brought out more clearly in the rite itself.

68.   The baptismal rite should contain variants, to be used at the discretion of the local ordinary, for occasions when many are to be baptized together. Also a shorter rite is to be drawn up for use chiefly by catechists in mission territories, but also by the faithful in general when there is danger of death, yet neither priest nor deacon is available.

69.   In place of the rite called 'Ordo supplendi omissa super infantem baptizatum', a new rite is to be drawn up. This should manifest more fittingly and clearly that the infant, baptized by the short rite, has already been received into the Church.
    And a new rite also is to be drawn up for converts who have already been validly baptized; it should indicate that they are now admitted to communion with the Church.

70.   Except during Eastertide baptismal water may be blessed within the rite of baptism itself by an approved shorter formula.

71. The rite of confirmation is to be revised; the intimate connection which this sacrament has with the whole process of Christian initiation is to be more clearly set forth; for this reason it is fitting for candidates to renew their baptismal promises just before they are confirmed.

Confirmation may be given within the Mass when convenient; when it is given outside the Mass, the rite that is used should be introduced by a formula to be drawn up for this purpose.

72. The rite and formula for the sacrament of penance are to be revised so that they more clearly express both the nature and effects of the sacrament.

73. 'Extreme Unction', which may also and more fittingly be called 'The Anointing of the Sick', is not a sacrament reserved for those who are at the point of death. Hence, as soon as any one of the faithful begins to be in danger of death from sickness or old age, the most fitting time for him to receive this sacrament has, beyond all doubt, arrived.

74. In addition to separate rites for anointing and for viaticum, a continuous rite is to be prepared in which the sick man is anointed after he has made his confession and before he receives viaticum.

75. The number of the anointings is to be adapted to the occasion, and the prayers which accompany the anointings are to be revised so as to correspond with the varying conditions of the sick who receive the sacrament.

76. Both the ceremonies and texts of the ordination rites are to be revised. The address given by the bishop at the beginning of each ordination or consecration may be in the mother tongue.

When a bishop is consecrated, the laying on of hands may be done by all the bishops present.

77. The marriage rite now found in the Roman Ritual is to be revised and enriched in such a way that the grace of the sacrament is more clearly signified and the duties of the spouses are impressed upon them.

'If certain peoples are wont to use other praiseworthy customs and ceremonies when celebrating the sacrament of matrimony, the sacred Synod earnestly desires that these be wholly retained.'

Moreover the competent ecclesiastical authority mentioned in art. 22 (ii) of this Constitution is free to devise its own rite suited to place and people, according to the provision of art. 63. But the rite must always conform to the law that the priest assisting at the marriage must ask for and obtain the consent of the contracting parties.

78. Matrimony is normally to be celebrated within the Mass, after the reading of the gospel and the homily, just before the Prayer of the Faithful. The Prayer for the Bride, duly amended to remind both spouses of their equal obligation to remain faithful to each other, may be said in the mother tongue.

But if matrimony is contracted apart from Mass, the epistle and gospel from the Nuptial Mass are to be read as an introduction to the ceremony, and the spouses should always be given a blessing.

79. The sacramentals are to undergo a revision which takes into account the basic principles for enabling the faithful to participate intelligently, actively and easily. The circumstances of our own days must also be considered. When rituals are revised, as laid down in art. 63, it is lawful even to add new sacramentals as the need for these becomes apparent.

Reserved blessings shall be very few; reservations shall be in favour only of bishops or ordinaries.

There are to be some sacramentals which, at least in special circumstances and at the discretion of the ordinary, may be administered by suitably qualified lay persons.

80. The rite for the Consecration of Virgins at present found in the Roman Pontifical is to be revised.

To promote uniformity, moderation and dignity in the ceremonies of religious profession and renovation of vows, a special rite for these occasions is to be drawn up. Apart from special exceptions granted by law, this rite should be adopted by those who make their profession or renovation of vows during Mass.

It is recommended that religious profession be made within the Mass.

81. The rite for the burial of the dead should express more clearly the paschal character of Christian death, and should correspond more closely to the circumstances and traditions found among the peoples in different parts of the world. This holds good also for the liturgical colours to be used.

82. The rite for the burial of infants is to be revised, and a special Mass for the occasion should be provided.

III

Of the Other Sacraments and Sacramentals
(*59–82*)

This chapter dealing with six of the sacraments, with sacramentals and one or two other matters, is very long and only the main heads can be considered here. In general, we can say that it reveals the new theological and liturgical thinking about the sacraments that has been going on in the Church for some years. The Constitution is of course a pastoral document, but it is significant that the Council felt in no way bound to repeat the statements of post-Tridentine theology about validity, divine institution and causality that form the substance of most treatises on the sacraments. It is the liturgy of the sacraments that is dealt with here and its importance is emphasized in almost every article of the chapter.

Acts of the Church and acts of Christ the Priest in his Church, the sacraments are seen as real encounters with Christ to whom man is conformed in different ways according to the varying significance of each of the sacraments. By them man is drawn into the Church and through this encounter makes contact with the redeeming Christ: 'they are given access to the stream of divine grace which flows from the paschal mystery of the passion, death and resurrection of Christ' (61). The sacraments contain and convey the power of the paschal mystery of redemption.

Three truths are stated in the opening article (59).

(1) The sacraments have a twofold purpose: to sanctify man and to give worship to God. The first is something that is taken for granted. The second is not usually noticed. The movement of God towards man in the sacraments is so marked and man's need of union with God is so great that it is this aspect of the sacramental action that is nearly always emphasized. But the sacraments themselves are witnesses of God's love, they are mysteries existing in the Church that reveal in their measure something of the greatness and goodness of God. In this sense they are acts of worship. But they are even more, since it is through them that man is drawn from his unredeemed condition in which he cannot give God worthy praise; in and through their reception he can now worship God because he is 'in Christ' through whom all human worship is made acceptable to God.

In this emphasis on the cultural nature of the sacraments (a doctrine that is found in St Thomas Aquinas)[1] thus restored to currency, we have the justification for saying that we do not merely receive sacraments, that we do not merely administer them, but that we, priests and people, *celebrate* them. For eastern Christians the sacraments are the 'holy mysteries', surrounded by an atmosphere of awe and worship. They are 'epiphanies' of God and evoke from man the deepest feelings of reverence—and this is worship. This is how we should regard the sacraments and the Council gives us back the basis for doing so.

Even in its statement about the sanctifying power of the sacraments the Council is careful to set them in an 'ecclesial' context. Part of their purpose is, through the sanctification of man, 'to build up the body of Christ'. This thoroughly Pauline phrase echoes that of Pius XII who said that the priestly Church has exactly the same aim and purpose as Christ himself, namely to build Christ into souls and to

[1] III, 62, a. 5, 63, a. 6, etc.

build souls into Christ.[1] This too is an ancient doctrine, summed up in many places by St Thomas, but reaching back to the earliest teaching of the Fathers. The sanctification offered by the sacraments is not merely an individual one; it is social by its very nature, for man is built into the Church, the body of Christ, and it is his duty to 'fill up' the Church until it reaches the measure of growth ordained by God.[2] By the sacraments a man is committed to the Church, there to live out his life as a member of the community through which salvation is to be brought to the world.

(2) The sacraments are signs that instruct. We have already said a good deal about this above and there will be no need to repeat what we have said here. But it must be emphasized that the instruction spoken of here is not merely a giving of information in the purely mental sense. The sacraments are *symbols*, concrete and graspable, and addressed to the whole personality. They speak first of all to man's senses and therefore they must be 'transparent', clear, comprehensible, making an immediate impact. Further, they are actions, which are intended to draw man into union with Christ. Granted faith, by this very process he *learns* Christ and is in every way, both through his senses and his mind as well as by the mysterious action of Christ in his soul, *formed* by the sacramental action. At the practical level, this means that the whole ritual of every sacrament with all its words and gestures must be respected and used in its celebration. The ritual is not just a decorative extra which, so long as the conditions for validity are ensured, may be neglected and undervalued. It is the total liturgical celebration that is going to teach people and form them in the ways of Christ.

(3) The sacraments are the sacraments of faith. Once again we have restored to pastoral currency a truth that has been only half-seen in recent centuries. To one used to modern theological text-books, it is sometimes a surprise

---

[1] *Mediator Dei*, 18.   [2] Eph. 2:6 and Col. 3:1.

to read so often in St Thomas' treatises on the sacraments that they are the 'sacraments of faith'. Yet he was but summing up the patristic tradition on the matter, as he so often did. A St Basil in the fourth century could write: 'Faith and baptism, these two modes of salvation, are indivisibly bound to each other. For if faith receives its perfection from baptism, baptism itself is based on it. . . . The profession of faith that leads to salvation comes first, but baptism, the seal of our commitment, comes quickly on its heels.'[1] The sacraments, even baptism, presuppose faith, but they also evoke it and strengthen it. This is in fact the aim of the sacramental signs, this is at its deepest the kind of 'instruction' that they bring to those who are properly disposed to receive them and it should be noted that the *ritual*, the prayers, texts and actions that go to make up the liturgical action, are the chief means of the evocation of faith. They dispose the soul, they open it up to Christ's action so that the recipient may profit to the fullest from the sacramental action. It is for this reason that it is so important that the signs and symbols of the sacraments should be clear and it is for this reason that it is so necessary to celebrate them in the language of the people.[2] That all this is the teaching of the Constitution cannot be doubted:

'They (the sacraments) have the power to impart grace, but, in addition, *the very act of celebrating them* effectively disposes the faithful to receive this grace fruitfully, to worship God duly and to love each other mutually.'

Article 59 concludes with a practical observation: it is for

[1] *De Spiritu Sancto*, 12, 28, quoted in this place by the editors of the translation of the Constitution in *La Maison-Dieu*, 76, p. 92.

[2] What St Basil has to say of faith and baptism might seem to be difficult to reconcile with infant baptism. But it is the teaching of the Church that infants are received into the Church on the strength of their parents' faith, for which the godparents go guarantors. Later, each child must make its own adherence or commitment to Christ. Its faith must become conscious and this is one of the main aims of Christian education.

these reasons that it is of *the highest importance* that the faithful should easily understand the sacramental signs and should use the sacraments assiduously.

No doubt to avoid a purely theological discussion (with which it is not concerned) the Constitution gives what is almost the definition of sacramentals of the Code of Canon Law (c. 1144) where they are described as sacred signs that have a certain likeness to the sacraments, with spiritual effects obtained through the Church's intercession. They dispose men to receive the fruits of the sacraments and are means by which they may sanctify their daily lives. In doing so the Constitution has however extended the definition. It attaches them more closely to the sacraments of which they are seen as the extension, from one point of view, and as a preparation from another: they evoke in their recipients the right dispositions so that they may receive the sacraments more fruitfully. Secondly, they are said to be a means by which the people may sanctify every aspect of their lives. Thus, they are a means by which the whole of life, even that part which is usually regarded as secular or 'profane', may be christianized. This is a valuable emphasis and draws the mind away from the view that they are merely external 'aids to devotion' or something of the sort. It is suggested that they are so much more than merely the wearing of scapulars and medals, though of course these things are not excluded.

In attaching the sacramentals more closely to the sacraments, the Constitution seems to have in mind an older view of them. In recent times sacramentals have usually been regarded as the external acts and practices of devotion which the Church has authorized and blessed. In fact, if you ask most modern Catholics what are sacramentals, they will usually point to some object, like a rosary, that has been blessed by the Church. The older view was that the liturgy itself, its rites and observances, was the great and the principal sacramental whose peculiar efficacy came from its

close association with the Church. This is the teaching of
Mediator Dei (29) which includes both the liturgy and
those things usually called sacramentals, and put into official
currency the term *ex opere operantis Ecclesiae*: 'In the
case of the prayers and sacred ceremonies which Christ's
immaculate Bride the Church uses to adorn the sacrifice
and sacraments, and also in the case of the sacramentals and
other rites instituted by the Church, the efficacy is *ex opere
operantis Ecclesiae*, inasmuch as the Church is holy and
acts in the closest union with her head.'[1]

Having thus established what is the nature of sacraments
and sacramentals, the Constitution goes on to say that they
are the sources of the Christian life, the means of encounter
with Christ in the paschal mystery of his passion, death and
resurrection, and lastly the means by which material things
may be used for the sanctification of man and the praise of
God. The emphasis here is not so much on the sanctification
of daily life (though that is in the background) as on the
Christian use of material things. By the sacraments and in
striking and varied ways by the sacramentals, the whole of
material creation is drawn into God's service and made the
means of giving him praise. Nothing is alien to God and all,
if properly used, can minister to his glory though it is
through man that they do so. In this sense man is the
minister of God's creation. This truth lies at the heart of
the liturgical use of things which are laid under contribution by the Church, and in the process of so being used their
essential goodness is revealed; they become reflections, even
if infinitely remote, of the God of beauty whom we worship.
All that is included in this view or philosophy of created
things is the justification of the Church's use of precious

---

[1] The term *ex opere operantis Ecclesiae* is a little difficult to translate: 'by the activity of the Church', i.e. of the Church's intercession
as Bride of Christ. This definition emphasizes that the spiritual
effects to be obtained from sacramentals are to be attributed *both* to
the intercession of Christ in his Church *and* to the personal activity
and devotion of the human individual.

materials in her worship. But, as the Constitution affirms in two or three places, the liturgy must have a noble simplicity and we must not confuse pomp and over-elaborate ceremonial with dignity. As many of the Council Fathers have pleaded, the Church needs to strip herself of much that is merely imposing and some that is pretentious in a world that is looking for austerity and genuineness even in worship, perhaps especially in worship.

In the articles that follow, one thing strikes one forcibly. There is the by now usual insistence of the need to clarify, improve and, where necessary, adapt the rites, but there is also evident a determination to relate the sacraments to the eucharist. This of course is a return to an older tradition manifested by the sacramentaries in which all the sacramental rites were contained. It gives a much more organic view of the sacraments which are seen as leading up to the eucharist (baptism, confirmation, ordination) and as applying its effects (marriage). The eucharist appears as the source of the whole of the Christian life as well as the climax to which in one way or another all the other sacraments lead.

In article 62, then, we are told that the rites have suffered in the course of time from the addition of features which have obscured their purpose (it is interesting to be told that addition is not necessarily a good thing in liturgy) and hence that there are to be changes and adaptations to make them more fit 'for the needs of our own times'. Some of these changes are indicated in subsequent articles and the possibility of adaptations is suggested.

The first change, which could also be said to be an adaptation, is in the matter of language:

'The vernacular language may be used in the administering of the sacraments and sacramentals.'

This laconic statement conceals the background of lively

debate of which it was the result. It first included words to the effect that the 'form' of the sacraments was normally to remain in Latin. This gave great dissatisfaction to a large number of the Council Fathers and they sent back the proposition which then appeared in the form given above. Some missionary bishops said bluntly that if the form were to remain in Latin, it would make it look like a magic formula to their people. So the language is to be that of the people throughout the rite. The excessive concern for 'validism' was thus rejected by the Council.

What is equally important is that *all* the sacramentals may be administered in the people's language. This in effect means everything in the Ritual. The funeral rites, for instance, that come after the Requiem Mass are to be found in the Ritual and it is to be hoped that permission will be given as soon as possible for the use of the vernacular here. Priests who are engaged in pastoral work are aware of the difficulties caused by the retention of Latin in this place and to them it seems simply cruel that when their people are in their greatest anguish the Church should seem to be indifferent to it. Moreover, present at almost all funeral services are a number of our separated brethren and others with no church allegiance at all. Even the use of a commentator (which does make some difference) is not sufficient to get one over all the difficulties, and non-Catholics are frankly puzzled by the Church's apparent insistence on the use of Latin here.

In 63, b we have a good example of the sort of pattern that will emerge in the near future. Local conferences of bishops are instructed to draw up rituals in the local language and adapted to local needs and these rituals are to be harmonized with the Roman Ritual, which is to be revised. Thus we have the happy possibility of a combination of the local with the Roman.

The Constitution points out that in the Roman Ritual each of the rites is prefaced with an instruction either pastoral or rubrical in nature. The pastoral instructions of the Ritual have been much praised and this book, in some ways unsatisfactory, is in fact the most pastoral liturgical book we have. One of the best examples of these instructions is that which precedes the rite of the Visitation of the Sick, so rarely read and even more rarely acted upon. It shows a deep compassion for the sick and a delicate and detailed concern for their well-being. These introductions, no doubt revised in the light of modern conditions, are to be included in local rituals.

The compilation of such rituals offers an opportunity to examine anew the ancient rituals of England, usually called *Manualia*. They were the handbooks of the pastoral clergy for many centuries and the Sarum *Manuale* was published as late as the beginning of the seventeenth century, thus indicating that the missionary priests and martyrs used it. It is possible that an examination of these books would yield a number of customs that could well form the basis of new local rituals. The Sarum books generally are redolent of an optimistic spirit that was characteristic of old England. They delighted in processions, a custom that is now more characteristic of Anglican worship than of ours.

In 1962 the Congregation of Rites, in response to requests from bishops both in Europe and in the mission territories, drew up and issued a revised form of the longer rite for the baptism of adults and thus provided the framework of a liturgical catechumenate. The rite in the Ritual is the conflation into one service of the various observances that were once spread over a period of time. These have now been rearranged, though the differences between the new rites and those in the Ritual are not great and may be used wherever bishops set up a catechumenate. According to article 64, this catechumenate for adults is to be restored and its use made possible for the whole Church. The reason given is important:

'By this means the time of the catechumenate which is intended as a period of suitable instruction may be sanctified by sacred rites to be celebrated after successive intervals of time.'

No doubt this new arrangement envisages people who are unbaptized. In these circumstances there will be no difficulty about the procedure. In France such catechumenates have been in operation for some years. In England and America, those who come to the Church, although often without any church allegiance, have been baptized. But there would seem to be no reason why an adaptation of the catechumenate to our circumstances should not be made and this would be fully in the spirit of the Constitution. Many priests for some long time have felt that our way of dealing with catechumens is unsatisfactory. It is unduly intellectual, consisting of not much more than a series of talks. Conversion is an initiation into the life of the Church and cannot be a purely intellectual process. The Constitution speaks of instruction and rites in the same sentence and throughout constantly emphasizes the teaching power of the liturgy. How very much more effective our instruction would be if it were part of a liturgical process in which teaching went hand in hand with an ever deeper initiation into the Church's life. This at any rate is an opportunity the Constitution opens up to us.

The most important point in article 65 is that the Council agrees to what might be called the 'baptism' or christianization of certain pagan rites, when and if they can be shorn of superstitious or other undesirable features. This is a direct application of the principles laid down under 37–40 and shows the determination of the Council to carry its prescriptions to their logical conclusion. It is important because now for the first time there is a practical possibility of the integration of local usages and customs in the liturgy. A bridge will be built between what has formed part of the very life of certain peoples and the Christian life into which they are being inserted by baptism.

Baptism

Baptism is given the large proportion of five articles (66–70), that very fact emphasizing its importance. Recent liturgical teaching and practice have been insisting on this for some time and the reforms projected here will enhance its importance in the minds of the people.

The two rites in the Ritual, the traditional one for adults and its rearrangement in connection with the catechumenate are both to be revised. Everyone is aware that the adult baptismal rite is in a state of decay. It is filled with all sorts of observances which it is very difficult to make intelligible to modern people, and there are constant repetitions that are intolerable. Even the revised rite, which was not much more than a reprinting of what is in the Ritual, has some unhappy features which are revealed by the very fact that the Holy See has left certain rites to the discretion of local hierarchies. The revision of these rites is a work of some magnitude. A much greater simplicity is indicated and there is the rite of Hippolytus to point the way to a new and more organic baptismal liturgy which will speak to the people.

The rite for infants is equally unsatisfactory. As is well known, it was not a rite for infants at all. It just happened to be shorter than the one for adults and was put into the Ritual of the seventeenth century and prescribed for infants. They, although unconscious, are constantly addressed, prayers repeat each other and envisage an adult coming to the church, and there are at least four exorcisms. The impact of all this on the modern mother is that her child is a limb of Satan. One supposes that the rite of spittle will be abolished and that if that of the salt is to be retained its significance will be made plain by the formula accompanying it. The white garment wobbles unhappily between the robe that was once put on the baptismal candidate and the chrisom cloth that at a later date was put on his head. The parents of the child nowhere appear in the picture and god-parentage has too often become a social formality. This is to be remedied and the roles of them both are to be made explicit in the revised rite.

Variations to provide for a large number of baptisms are to be inserted and especially for missionary territories a shorter rite is to be devised for use by lay-people in danger of death. Even here it is suggested that this simple rite should consist of something more than the mere pouring of the water and the saying of the 'form'. No doubt in cases of extreme urgency the shortest rite will be permissible.

Great numbers of priests are unhappy about the order for supplying what was omitted from the rite when it was done in cases of urgency.[1] It does seem to be not much more than a piece of ceremonial whose purpose and meaning are obscure. One wonders whether it is at all meaningful to retain exorcisms in such a rite? In any case the attitude of the Constitution is positive: the new rite is to emphasize that by baptism the child is received into the community of the Church. In these circumstances, why could there not be a simple rite expressing this and taking place after the gospel of a Sunday Mass?

Reception of Converts

The new rite for converts who have been baptized will be of special interest to countries like England and the United States of America where there are always a number of Christians of other communions joining the Church. The rite as it is at the moment is a daunting little affair, con-sisting essentially in nothing more than a sixteenth-century profession of faith. The new rite is to indicate that such converts are being admitted to communion with the

---

[1] One is grateful to the Council Fathers for not saying 'supplying the *ceremonies*'; the Constitution puts simply '*omissa*'.

Church. This means that the very rite will have a more communal character which will express by text and action what is the meaning of the event taking place. It would best be done in the presence of the local community, and if the profession of faith could be done *with* that community, as we have suggested above, the practical difficulties would disappear and the nature of the act be clearly established. A further step would be to harmonize the whole matter with the restored catechumenate (such converts would form a special category) and to have such receptions taking place at the same time of the liturgical year as that for adult baptism, namely Easter.[1]

Henceforth the baptismal water is to be kept in the font only for Eastertide and a rite of blessing is to be provided for use at each baptism. This is a splendid change. There will hardly be any priest who has not opened his font with dismay a few months after Easter. If the accretions of the present baptismal rite are removed there will be room for a prayer which could become a principal feature of the new rite. No doubt it would not be over long, but surely long enough to recall the events of the history of salvation and especially the baptism of the Lord. The same alteration opens up the possibility of having flowing water in the font and thus the symbolism of water would almost literally come alive: it would be a 'spring of water leaping up to give eternal life' (John 4:14).[2]

Confirmation

The Constitution has four things to say about confirmation. It is to be revised so that its relationship with the process of Christian initiation is made clearer. The baptismal promises may be renewed on this occasion and the sacrament may be

---

[1] There would always be legitimate exceptions to such regulations and the liberty of the spirit would always be carefully safeguarded.

[2] Various ways could be thought of which it is unnecessary to go into here. In the great baptistery of the fine abbey church of St John's, Collegeville, U.S.A., there is flowing water.

celebrated within the Mass (no doubt at the end of the ministry of the word which would provide a place for the proper sacramental catechesis), and when it is given outside Mass a further formula is to be drawn up for use beforehand.

Confirmation as usually administered in England and America (after first Holy Communion) has broken away from the order of the sacraments of initiation, which was baptism, confirmation and Holy Communion. Now an opportunity is given of restoring that order, though the administrative problems will not perhaps be easy. At any rate, the union of the sacrament with the Mass (and the Pontifical to this day assumes that the candidates are going to communion) is a good thing and will do something to relate the two sacraments to one another. Further, the rite itself is to be revised in this direction. This could be done by the addition of scripture texts (among others Acts 8:14–17), and by catechesis, for this sacrament already provides a classical pattern in this respect. The bishop speaks to the candidates about the meaning of the sacrament, leads them into it, opens their hearts to a fruitful reception and then administers it. The catechesis might well end with the renewal of the baptismal promises and if a formula similar to that used at the Easter Vigil were drawn up, it would link confirmation with the paschal mystery and with baptism. Something will have to be done about the vestigial kiss of peace (the tap on the cheek), and in view of the difficulty of the bishop giving it to each candidate it looks as if it will have to go. It cannot be said to be exactly a live symbol.

Penance

The rite and formula of the sacrament of penance are to be revised, though the article (72) is very laconic. What can be done? One suspects that this will be a matter for prolonged discussion. The formula in the Ritual is unnecessarily heavy-handed and legalistic. Why should penitents be absolved from excommunications they have never incurred? The *'deinde'* was once a rubric which the Congregation of Rites in the nineteenth century refused to suppress and the principal gesture, and one of great importance, the imposition of hands (now just a raising of the right hand), cannot be seen. What has been tried in many countries is to have a service of the Bible devotion type (35, 4) made up of Bible readings, prayers, even a general examination of conscience, all taking place while some of the penitents are actually in the confessionals. This is possible in big churches with a good supply of priests, but not elsewhere. What seems required is that, while the privacy of the confessional should be strictly preserved, ways should be found to show that penance is an act of the Church and that sin and repentance are both relevant to the common life of the Church.

The Anointing of the Sick

Of Extreme Unction (73), which may now 'fittingly' be called 'The Anointing of the Sick', we are told in carefully chosen words that it is not reserved for the moment of death but for those *who are beginning to be in danger of death* from sickness or old age. This is entirely in line with recent theological writing[1] and marks a decisive point of return to the older view of the sacrament, which indeed had never been wholly lost sight of. In this case, casuistry has been rather in advance of theology. It is interesting that old age is mentioned, again something not entirely new but indicating now officially that this is an occasion when the sacrament may properly be given. No doubt when all this has been reflected upon, it will be found that the number of occasions when the sacrament may be given will be much greater than in the recent past. It will be *seen* by the people to be the sacrament of healing and it will be possible to relate it in a more telling fashion to the healing work of Christ upon earth.

[1] See C. Davis, *The Study of Theology*, ch. XIX (London, 1962)

Secondly, viaticum is to be restored to its proper place as the sacrament of the dying and as the climax of the whole Christian life. Some years ago, the Germans received permission for the insertion of a continuous rite into their ritual in which the proper order of confession, anointing, viaticum was maintained. This is now to become the rule. Another small regulation is of considerable interest. It is envisaged that this sacrament will be given in a variety of circumstances and to meet various needs the prayers are to be revised so as to fit them. Some will receive this sacrament who are near death or who are suffering from incurable diseases. It would be grotesque to be praying that 'they may return to their former duties'. The old need comfort and reassurance. These and other conditions of life will be taken into account in the compilation of the prayers. Further, the number of anointings is to be adapted to the occasion. In an earlier age the anointings were applied to those places where the pain was greatest. No doubt this would not be appropriate always with our modern medical knowledge, but evidently the intention is to underline the healing properties of the sacrament. These new anointings will, it is to be presumed, have different 'forms' also, emphasizing this. At present all of them speak only of the taking away of sin. Although one does not want to see an unduly lengthy rite, it is to be hoped that room will be found for a number of scripture texts which could be read *ad libitum* by the priest for the comfort of the sick person.

Holy Orders

The revision of the Pontifical had already started before the opening of the Council. Perhaps that is why so little is said of it here (76). The rites and texts of ordination are to be revised and one must say that there is a great need of simplification. Once again one would point to the noble but simple rites of the *Apostolic Constitution* of Hippolytus (about A.D. 215) which express very adequately the meaning of episcopal, priestly and diaconal orders. No doubt the 'tradition of the instruments' will remain, but in a simpler form, and perhaps it will be no longer necessary for the priest to try and touch them with his hands bound. One change signalized by the Constitution is that in the consecration of a bishop all the bishops present shall lay their hands on him. This is in fact a return to the rite of Hippolytus and expresses liturgically the collegiate nature of the episcopate. The new bishop is 'ordered' or ranked with or taken up into the episcopate of the Church. Finally, the addresses given before each rite of ordination or consecration may be in the vernacular. But, as the Constitution says, these too will need revision. They are very ancient texts, that for the priesthood perhaps going back to the fifth century, but like many others they have been interpolated and there are one or two rather odd passages that do not suit modern times. The people are asked to give their assent to the raising of these men to the various orders; in view of the fact that the matter is all settled and the people have no say in it, this would have to be changed. Likewise, they would be not a little shocked to hear subdeacons being exhorted to be *no longer* idle, neglectful, given to drunkenness and various sorts of levity! [1] It is these and a dozen other anomalies that have been hidden from the people for centuries by the Latin language.

The rites of the Pontifical for the consecration and blessing of churches have already been (provisionally) revised, but it is generally felt that the rite for pontifical Mass is in equal need of revision. At present such a Mass requires a veritable army of assistants and servers all of whom have to be highly competent. If the bishop's rite were much simpler, it would be possible for him to celebrate the Sunday *sung* Mass in parish churches, and in view of the inclusion of confirmation in the Mass this will become a real need.

---

[1] These observations are made by the writer in *La Maison-Dieu*. 77, p. 152.

If there were such a simplification, then it would be possible for the parish clergy to con-celebrate with him and thus the true pattern of worship would be established before the very eyes of the people. No doubt the simplification will reach the episcopal vestments which must be very uncomfortable and are in some ways grotesque. Why should a bishop be required to wear horse-riding garments in church and when he has never ridden a horse in his life?

Marriage

The rite for marriage in the Roman Ritual is jejune in the extreme and it is not generally known that the reason for this is that that ritual assumed the existence and use of local rites and did not wish to supersede them. This was noted by the Council of Trent whose statement is repeated in the second paragraph of article 77: 'If certain peoples . . .' and the Council expressed its view that such local customs and rites should be 'wholly retained'. First, then, if a country has its own rite, as we in England have, it may keep it. Our rite is, with one or two verbal differences, that of Sarum which we have kept all through the centuries and is a precious link with the past. It conforms to the one requirement of the Constitution that the priest must ask for and obtain the consent of the contracting parties. It will then always be kept. But, again in accordance with the Constitution, there is no reason why it should not be improved. In the Belgian, German and Irish rituals there is a litany of intercession for the bride and bridegroom which has proved to be very acceptable to the people. With the insertion of the rite of marriage into the Mass (78) this litany could be said immediately after the marriage and as part of the Prayer of the Faithful.

The two most important changes are that the marriage rite is to take place within the Mass and that the prayer over the bride is to be changed into a prayer for both bride and bridegroom to remind them of their equal obligation to remain faithful to each other. This prayer may be said in the vernacular. The insertion of the rite into the Mass emphasizes that marriage is comparable *in the life of the laity* to ordination and religious profession. The couple are being consecrated to God and are dedicating their human love to him. Further, since the Church herself is the Bride of Christ, the human couple are showing forth the holy and mystical union that exists between Christ and his Church. They are in fact becoming two in one flesh through their participation in the bridal mystery of the Church. For long enough people have been asking for a revision of the wedding prayer and the inclusion in it of the husband.[1] If this prayer which dates from the sixth century, if not before, was advanced in its view of the dignity of women, much, very much, has happened since then to make it unsuitable. The surgical operation on it that will be necessary will be a delicate one, but no doubt its substance will be preserved.

The intention of the Council in inserting the rite of marriage is evidently that it should be preceded by the proper catechesis and it may well be that other Masses (for baptism and confirmation) will be modelled on this one. And even when there is no wedding Mass the epistle and gospel are to be read before the exchange of consent. The bride and bridegroom are always to be given a blessing, presumably the one in the ritual.

Sacramentals

Little enough in detail is said about them and a General Council could hardly be asked to penetrate into the jungle of rites and blessings and prayers that make up so large a part of the Ritual. Simply, they are to be revised so that the people may 'participate intelligently, actively and easily'.

[1] This suggestion was made by Donald Attwater some years ago in *Liturgy*, 'The Rites of Christian Marriage', Vol. XXIX, No. 4. October 1960.

The circumstances of our day are to be taken into account when they are being revised and new sacramentals may be instituted. An example of the last category would be a rite for the renewal of baptismal vows at the time of adolescence. It would recall baptism and confirmation, and, *ex opere operantis Ecclesiae,* renew the grace of these sacraments and stimulate the participants to a fuller commitment of themselves to Christ and to his Church.

Reserved blessings which are now numerous are to be reduced in number and reserved only to bishops and ordinaries. This will mean a drastic simplification, which is called for, but it has very little interest for the laity. Various religious orders have had the right to impart blessings of one sort or another and the parish clergy have had to get permission to do so from them. It looks as if this situation is now to be brought to an end.

In some circumstances the bishop may allow lay-people to administer certain sacramentals in special circumstances. An obvious example is the early stages of the restored catechumenate where the presence of the priest is not indispensable.

Religious Profession

The rite for the Consecration of Virgins is ancient, very beautiful and of great significance, but it too has suffered from accretion, so it is to be revised.

A uniform rite for religious profession and the renewal of vows is to be drawn up and normally these two observances should take place within the Mass.

The many modern congregations have a great variety of observances in this respect and it is now thought that the time has come to put a little order into the matter. This reform will no doubt be in the direction of deepening the significance of such acts and so leading to a more profound theology of the religious life.

Christian Death

The liturgy associated with Christian death has in recent centuries been considerably affected by notions that are not strictly Christian at all. Black velvet hangings 'decorated' with skulls and cross-bones, not perhaps usual in Anglo-Saxon countries, are symbols of a very partial view of this event in the life of every man. The late Middle Ages with its obsession with the Last Judgment as exclusively a time of terror and punishment had already added its quota with texts like the *Dies irae* (not originally intended for use at the Requiem Mass at all) and the *Libera me*. In earlier times, Christian death was seen as a sharing in the passover of Christ, as part of the process whereby the Christian is conformed to Christ in his death, that he may rise again with him in his resurrection. The very passage of the body from the home to the grave was seen as a triumph of which the most striking evidence in our present liturgy is the *In paradisum*, now somewhat reduced in its use. This is in fact a conflation of texts which formerly were antiphons to the psalms sung during the procession of the body to the grave. One of these psalms was the paschal psalm, *In exitu*, which clearly expressed the paschal character of Christian death. It is no doubt texts like this that will be re-inserted into the rite and given a new prominence. The texts of the Mass on the whole express the idea of Christian death very well and the *Subvenite* with which the body is welcomed into church is redolent of an authentic Christian hope and tenderness. One would like to see this latter, or another similar to it, replacing the *Libera me*.

The question of the colour of the vestments to be used for funerals has been raised at one time or another in recent years. Dark red or even green has been suggested. The Constitution suggests the possibility of change in certain circumstances, but it is almost certain that it is thinking of missionary territories in which different conventions obtain. White in some places is the colour of mourning and may in the future be used. That there will be a change in the west is improbable, but at least the kind of vestment that looks as if it came out of an undertaker's wardrobe could be avoided.

Infant Burial

Every priest who has had to preside at the burial of infants has felt the inadequacy of the rite, and when to this was added the obligation to say it all in Latin, he felt that his pastoral work was being positively and unnecessarily hampered. It is all very well to assume, as the rite does, that the babies have gone to heaven, as they have. Parents happen to love their children and experience a deeper grief on these occasions than perhaps at any other time. If then the Church is concerned to usher the babies into heaven, she should show an equal concern for the grief of the parents.

Often in the past the Mass of the Angels has been used for these occasions. Yet it is not entirely desirable. Babies are not destined to be angels and never will be. A new Mass formula is to be compiled.

Of the Divine Office

83. Christ Jesus, high priest of the new and eternal covenant, taking human nature, introduced into this earthly exile
that hymn which is sung throughout all ages in the halls of
heaven. He joins the entire community of mankind to himself,
associating it with his own singing of this canticle of divine
praise.

For he continues his priestly work through the agency of his
Church which is ceaselessly engaged in praising the Lord and
interceding for the salvation of the whole world. She does this,
not only by celebrating the eucharist, but also in other ways,
especially by praying the divine office.

84. By tradition going back to early Christian times, the
divine office is devised so that the whole course of the day and
night is made holy by the praises of God. Therefore when this
wonderful song of praise is duly performed by priests and
others who are deputed for this purpose by the Church's
ordinance, or when the faithful pray together with the priest
in the approved form, then it is truly the voice of the Bride
addressed to her Bridegroom; it is the very prayer which Christ
himself, together with his body, offers to the Father.

85. Hence all who render this service are not only fulfilling
a duty of the Church, but also are sharing in the greatest

honour of Christ's spouse, for by duly offering these praises to God they are standing before God's throne in the name of their Mother the Church.

86. Priests who are engaged in the pastoral ministry will offer the praises of the hours with greater fervour the more vividly they realize that they must heed St Paul's exhortation: 'Pray without ceasing' (1 Thess. 5:17). For the work in which they labour will effect nothing and bring forth no fruit except by the power of the Lord who said 'Without me you can do nothing' (John 15:5). This is why the apostles decided to institute deacons, for they said: 'We will devote ourselves to prayer and to the ministry of the word' (Acts 6:4).

87. In order that the divine office may be better and more perfectly prayed in existing circumstances, whether by priests or by other members of the Church, the sacred Council, carrying further the restoration already so happily begun by the Apostolic See, has seen fit to decree as follows concerning the office of the Roman rite.

88. Because the purpose of the office is to sanctify the day, the traditional sequence of the hours is to be restored so that they may be genuinely related again to the time of the day when they are prayed, as far as this may be possible. To effect all this, it will be necessary to take into account the modern conditions in which daily life has to be lived, especially by those who are called to labour in apostolic works.

89. Therefore when the office is revised, these principles are to be observed:
(a) By the venerable tradition of the universal Church, Lauds as morning prayers and Vespers as evening prayers are the two hinges on which the daily office turns; hence they are to be considered as the chief hours and are to be celebrated as such.
(b) Compline is to be drawn up so that it will be a suitable prayer for the end of the day.

(c) The hour known as Matins, although it should retain the character of nocturnal praise when celebrated in choir, shall be adapted so that it may be recited at any hour of the day; it is to be made up of fewer psalms and longer readings.

(d) The hour of Prime is to be suppressed.

(e) In choir the hours of Terce, Sext and None are to be observed. But outside choir it will be lawful to select any one of these three, according to the time of the day.

90.   The divine office, because it is the public prayer of the Church, is a source of piety and nourishment for personal prayer. And therefore priests and all others who take part in the divine office are earnestly exhorted in the Lord to attune their minds to their voices when praying it. The better to achieve this, let them take steps to improve their understanding of the liturgy and of the Bible, especially of the psalms.

Those who undertake the revision of the divine office are to adapt its ancient and venerable treasures so that all those to whom they are handed on may more extensively and easily draw profit from them.

91.   So that it may really be possible in practice to observe the course of the hours proposed in article 89, the psalms are no longer to be distributed throughout one week, but through some longer period of time.

The work of revising the psalter, already happily begun, is to be finished as soon as possible, and is to take into account the style of Christian Latin, the liturgical use of psalms also when they are to be sung, and the entire tradition of the Latin Church.

92.   As regards the readings, the following points are to be observed:

(a) readings from sacred scripture should be arranged so that the riches of God's word may be easily accessible in more abundant measure;

(b) readings excerpted from the works of the fathers, doctors and other ecclesiastical writers should form a better selection;

(c) the accounts of martyrdom or lives of the saints are to accord with the facts of history.

93. To whatever extent may seem desirable, the hymns are to be restored to their original form, being purged of whatever smacks of mythology or ill accords with Christian piety. Also, as occasion may arise, let other selections from the treasury of hymns be incorporated into the divine office.

94. That the day may be truly sanctified, and that the hours themselves may be recited with spiritual advantage, it is best that each of them be prayed at a time which most closely corresponds with its true canonical time.

95. Communities obliged to choral office are bound to celebrate the office in choir every day in addition to their conventual Mass. In particular:

(a) Orders of Canons Regular, monks and nuns and of other regulars bound by law or constitutions to choral office must celebrate the entire office.

(b) Cathedral or collegiate chapters are bound to recite those parts of the office imposed on them by general or particular law.

(c) All members of the above communities who are in major orders or who are solemnly professed, except for the lay-brothers, are bound to recite privately whichever canonical hours they do not sing in choir.

96. Clerics not bound to office in choir, if they are in major orders, are bound to pray the entire office every day, either in common or privately, as laid down in article 89.

97. The occasions on which parts of the office may be replaced by liturgical services are to be defined by the rubrics.

In particular cases, and for adequate reasons, ordinaries can dispense their subjects wholly or in part from the obligation of reciting the divine office, or they may commute the obligation.

98. Religious who, according to their constitutions, are to recite parts of the divine office, are thereby joining in the public prayer of the Church.

The same may be said of those who, in virtue of their constitutions, recite any short office provided this be drawn up after the pattern of the divine office and has been duly approved.

99. Since the divine office is the voice of the Church, that is, of the whole mystical body publicly praising God, those clerics who are not obliged to office in choir, especially priests who live together, or assemble for any purpose, are urged to pray at least some part of the divine office in common.

All who pray the divine office, whether in choir or in common, should fulfil the task entrusted to them as perfectly as possible; this refers not only to the internal devotion of their minds but also to their external deportment.

It is strongly recommended, also, that the office, both in choir and in common, should be sung when possible.

100. Parish priests should see to it that the chief hours, especially Vespers, are celebrated in common in the church on Sundays and the more solemn feasts. And the laity, too, are encouraged to pray the divine office, either with the priests, or among themselves, or even individually.

101. §1. According to the ancient tradition of the Latin rite, clerics must use the Latin language in the divine office. But in individual cases the ordinary has power to grant the use of the vernacular to those clerics for whom Latin constitutes a grave obstacle to their praying the office as it should be prayed. The vernacular version, however, must be one that is drawn up according to the provisions of article 36.

§2. The competent superior has power to concede the use of the vernacular for the divine office, even in choir, to religious, including men who are not clerics. The version, however, must be one that is approved.

§3. Any cleric bound to divine office fulfils his obligation if he prays the office in the vernacular together with a gathering of the faithful or with those detailed in §2 above, provided that the text used is one that is approved.

IV

Of the Divine Office
(83–101)

The Church holds a high doctrine of the divine office, yet its practice must be said to be low. In few churches, even cathedral churches, is the office sung or recited and in hardly any parish church is any part of the office ever heard. It is one sector of the liturgy of which the laity know hardly anything at all and which in recent times has given the clergy a great deal of anxiety. Weighed down as they are in most countries with a heavy load of pastoral work, they have found it increasingly difficult to find a proper place in their lives for the official prayer of the Church. In addition, the reform of the office which has been in process since the time of Pius X has proved to be a very complex matter.

Let us then look first at the doctrine and secondly at what the Constitution proposes.

The first paragraph of chapter IV follows very closely the passage in *Mediator Dei* on the same subject (150–152). It will be useful to set it out in full here:

'The "divine office" is the prayer of the mystical body of Jesus Christ, offered to God in the name of all Christians and for their benefit, since it is recited by priests,

187

by other ministers of the Church, and by religious, who are officially appointed by the Church to that function. . . .

'The Word of God, when he assumed a human nature, introduced into this land of exile the hymn that in heaven is sung throughout all ages. He united the whole community of mankind with himself, and associates it with him in singing this divine canticle of praise . . .'[1]

To this the Constitution adds two things that are worthy of note. First, it describes the prayer of the Church as the voice of the Bride who addresses her Bridegroom. This takes up an ancient teaching of the Church which has formed the theme of papal documents on the divine office for a very long time.[2] It is for this reason that the French commentators can say that the divine office is at once the voice of the Bride and the prayer of the total Christ made to the Father.[3]

'Hence all who render this service are not only fulfilling a duty of the Church, but are also sharing in the greatest honour of Christ's spouse, for by duly offering these praises to God they are standing before God's throne in the name of their Mother the Church' (85).

Secondly, for the first time the 'christifideles' without distinction are reckoned among those who offer this prayer of the Church whenever they take part in it with the priest.[4]

There are three reasons why the praying of the divine office has run into difficulties for priests engaged in pas-

[1] The passage continues with a quotation from St Augustine about Christ praying as our priest in the psalms and praying with us as man (*Enarr. in psalmos,* 85, 1).
[2] E.g. the bull *Divinam psalmodiam* of 1631 attached to former editions of the Roman Breviary.
[3] *La Maison-Dieu,* 77, p. 162.
[4] The question whether they do so when they pray it by themselves without the presence of the priest is not explicitly answered, though one could argue for it from art. 98 (and perhaps art. 100) which might very well include secular institutes whose members are lay-people.

toral work: (i) what is essentially public prayer has had to be prayed in private; (ii) the continued use of Latin (which in fact has made it almost impossible to sing the office in parish churches and so taken away even that opportunity of public prayer from the priest); (iii) the increased burden of pastoral work which is given in article 88 as the principal reason for revision.

The Constitution insists on the importance of the office for the personal spiritual life of the priest and is obviously concerned to make of it a usable instrument of prayer for him, but perhaps it does not pay sufficient attention to the need to pray it in public. It *recommends* (99) that where possible priests not bound to choral recitation should pray the office in common or at least some part of it. But the only chance the parish clergy have to do this is with their people and one would like to think that this is being taken into account in the revision of the hours. It is difficult for modern people to pray a number of psalms without intermission and they have a great desire to express their needs in petition. If a renewed form of *Preces* were added to Vespers this would give the office a popular element that is much desired.

The Constitution's insistence, however, on Lauds and Vespers as the morning and evening prayer of the Church is important and valuable. These were in fact the principal hours of prayer for what are now called the secular clergy and they are intended to be prayed in the morning and in the evening respectively. This is emphasized in article 94 where the purpose of the office to sanctify the day is insisted on and priests are exhorted to say the various hours of the office at the time to which they correspond. Thus the undesirable practice (never sanctioned) of 'blocking' the office is here repudiated.

Throughout the chapter the distinction between the pastoral clergy and the monastic is kept well to the fore and the differing nature of the two vocations is expressed in the different obligations of the two groups. With the arrangements laid down by the Constitution the pastoral clergy now have an office that is manageable in bulk: Matins, Lauds, one Little Hour, Vespers and Complin. It is another matter whether these offices in their actual form are apt for their purpose. The Constitution then lays down the principles of reform.

As with the other parts of the liturgy, the Constitution exhorts priests to cultivate an understanding of scripture, especially the psalms, and of the liturgy. This is the first condition for a prayerful use of the office.

(1) The psalter is to be distributed over a longer period of time. In the Ambrosian Breviary this is a fortnight. In the Book of Common Prayer it is a month. The purpose of such a rearrangement is that the use of the hours as laid down in article 89 will be practically possible. But experience shows that it is difficult for us nowadays to pray a considerable number of psalms at one time, and if we keep in mind the possibility of the people joining with the clergy at least on occasion in the office, it is all the more necessary that there should not be too many at once. Thus, even in English, four psalms at Vespers (as in the Benedictine office) would seem to be sufficient. Again, certain psalms, like the long historical psalms of Saturday, are less apt for prayer. They could more easily be used as lessons.

(2) The lectionary of the Roman Breviary is its least satisfactory part. It was arbitrarily shortened in the early Middle Ages for reasons that had nothing to do with the liturgy and has remained the pitiful thing it is ever since. This is to be put right (92, a), and this will probably give more trouble than any other single item of reform. A new lectionary will have to fit in with that of the Missal and certain decisions of principle will have to be made. Are we to take it that the *whole* Bible, every word of it, is going to appear in the office? Is it necessary that genealogies and lists of kings should form part of the lectionary? One may even

ask whether certain parts of Exodus and Leviticus which are no more than lists of things are suitable reading in the office? In other words, the *purpose* of the lectionary will have to be established first, and if we may judge by the Constitution (90), since the office is for the nourishment of the spiritual life, such parts of the Bible will be excluded. The whole Bible is God's word, but it does not follow that every single part of it is equally appropriate to the office, which has a different purpose from study. Finally, one would like to plead for some scripture lessons to be restored to Lauds and Vespers, and if the latter is to become part of parish worship again, it will be necessary to do so.

(3) The patristic readings have suffered the same fate as the scriptural ones and now on Sundays are reduced to mere snippets. They have been selected from a very narrow range of the Fathers and many of them (allegorical jugglings with numbers) say absolutely nothing to us today. They are just an exacerbation of the spirit. But if the patristic lectionary is to be of any real value to the modern priest the readings will have to be much more extensive than they have been since the early Middle Ages and their very bulk will pose new problems. From the material point of view they could be accommodated in a separate book. But would it be wise to impose the reading of them as of obligation? And at least an ordinary reading of them would be right and sufficient. For lessons at any rate it seems odd that we should have to move the lips *as if* we were in choir. No doubt this is a matter that will be left for the schema on the discipline of the clergy to deal with.

Other ecclesiastical writers are mentioned and no doubt there is a case for their inclusion. But those already in the office are not always appropriate to liturgical prayer and almost everyone finds encyclical letters a difficulty. It might well be that each country could have some of its own writers (e.g. Newman for England) which as *spiritual reading* would be helpful.

(4) The historical lessons of the office have been under reform ever since the sixteenth century. They are still in need of a drastic revision, first from the point of view of historical criticism and then from that of the style in which they have been written. They are singularly uninformative and rarely if ever indicate the importance of the saint in the history and life of the Church. Apart from really important saints' feasts, often an historical note and a commemoration is all that is required. If certain legends that are regarded as more ancient (though they are always of several centuries later than the existence of the martyr) are to be retained, it is to be hoped that they will be re-written. Some of the jingles in which they abound are irksome in the extreme.

The whole question of what saints are to be included in the calendar of the Roman Church is another complex problem and perhaps the whole question of the saints in the economy of salvation will come in for re-examination.

(5) Hymns are another sore point. They are to return substantially to what they were before Urban VIII and his unhappy servants 'classicized' them. But someone will have to take a hard look at all of them. Some of them are undistinguished whether just as poetry or as religious poetry and are not much help for prayer. They could probably be reduced in number. There does not seem to be any good reason why every office every day should have hymns.

Article 97 incorporates a regulation that so far has appeared only in the *Ordo Instauratus* of Holy Week, namely that when the clergy are engaged in another liturgical service in church, the office corresponding to this time may be omitted. Henceforth this is to be written into the rubrics.

It is good to see that in article 99 the Council insists on the importance of the public recitation and singing of the divine office. It is equally gratifying to find that the parish clergy may say or sing the divine office with their people in their own language. This, it can be said without doubt, is the condition of the restoration of offices like Vespers and those of Holy Week to parish worship. Further, the laity are encouraged to pray the divine office themselves even in the absence of the priest (100). It is in fact no longer to be regarded as a clerical preserve.

In article 90 the Constitution affirms that the office is for the priest a source of piety and nourishment for his personal prayer. In article 101, §1, it says that bishops may grant to individual priests permission to say the office in their own language if Latin is a grave obstacle to their praying it *as it should be prayed* (in the words of the old prayer before the Office, *digne, attente et devote*). The grounds for such permissions would seem, by the terms of the Constitution itself, to go far beyond a mere material difficulty with Latin. Priests are exhorted to make their office *above all things* prayer. The mere saying of words, even with a broad intention of union with Christ, does not constitute real prayer and there are great numbers who have an adequate knowledge of Latin for reading purposes but who find it difficult if not impossible to pray at length in Latin. For these reasons it is held[1] that the regulation of the Constitution should be interpreted *cum magnanimitate*.[2]

Apart from the interpretation of the Constitution, great numbers of priests feel that both their pastoral life and their spiritual life would be enriched by the practice of saying the office in their own language. They would, as they say, have a much more ready use of scripture from which their sermons would benefit and they themselves would respond much more easily and naturally to God's word as they read it.

[1] Cf. C. Howell, S.J., *Clergy Review*, March 1964.
[2] The phrase is that of Mgr Wagner and Fr Jungmann quoted at the end of Fr Howell's article.

Of the Liturgical Year

102.   Holy Mother Church considers it her duty to celebrate the saving work of her divine Spouse by devoutly recalling it to mind on certain days throughout the course of the year. Every week, on the day which she has called 'The Lord's Day', she keeps the memory of her Lord's resurrection; once in the year, by the most solemn festival of the Pasch, she celebrates his resurrection together with his blessed passion.

As each year passes by, she unfolds the whole mystery of Christ, from the incarnation and birth until the ascension, the day of Pentecost and the expectation of blessed hope and of the coming of the Lord.

Reflecting thus upon the mysteries of redemption, the Church opens to the faithful the riches of her Lord's powers and merits, so that these are in some way made present for all time, and the faithful are enabled to lay hold upon them and become filled with saving grace.

103.   In celebrating this annual cycle of Christ's mysteries, Holy Church honours with especial love the Blessed Mary, Mother of God, who is inseparably involved in the saving work of her Son. In her the Church holds up and admires the most perfect fruit of the redemption, and joyfully contemplates, as in a faultless image, that which she herself desires and hopes wholly to be.

104. The Church has also included in the annual cycle days devoted to the memory of her martyrs and her other saints. Raised up to perfection by the manifold grace of God, and already in possession of eternal salvation, they sing God's perfect praise in heaven and offer prayers for us. By celebrating the passage of these saints from earth to heaven the Church proclaims the paschal mystery achieved in those who have suffered and been glorified with Christ; she proposes them to the faithful as examples drawing all to the Father through Christ, and through their merits she pleads for God's favours.

105. Finally, at various times of the year and according to traditional methods of training, the Church completes the formation of the faithful by means of pious practices for soul and body, by instruction, prayer and works of penance and of mercy.

Accordingly the sacred Council has seen fit to decree as follows:

106. By a tradition handed down from the apostles and going back to the very day of Christ's resurrection, the Church celebrates the paschal mystery every eighth day; with good reason this, then, bears the name of 'the Lord's Day' or 'Sunday'. For on this day Christ's faithful should come together into one place so that, by hearing the word of God and taking part in the eucharist, they may call to mind the passion, resurrection and glorification of the Lord Jesus, and may thank God who 'has begotten them again, through the resurrection of Jesus Christ from the dead, unto a living hope' (1 Pet. 1:3). Hence the Lord's Day is the original feast day to be proposed to the piety of the faithful, and they should be taught to observe it as a day of joy and of freedom from work. Other celebrations, unless they be truly of great importance, must not have precedence over the Sunday which is the foundation and kernel of the whole liturgical year.

107. The liturgical year is to be revised so that the traditional customs and training methods of the sacred seasons shall be preserved, or else restored to suit the conditions of modern

times; their specific character is to be retained, so that they
duly nourish the piety of the faithful who celebrate the mysteries of Christian redemption, especially the paschal mystery.
If certain adaptations are considered necessary on account of
local conditions, they are to be made in accordance with the
provisions of articles 39 and 40.

108.   The minds of the faithful must be directed primarily
towards the feasts of the Lord whereby the mysteries of salvation are celebrated in the course of the year. Therefore the
proper of the time must be given the preference which is its due
over the feasts of the saints, so that the entire cycle of the
mysteries of salvation may be suitably recalled.

109.   The season of Lent has a twofold character; primarily
by recalling or preparing for baptism and penance, it disposes
the faithful who persevere in hearing the word of God and in
prayer, to celebrate the paschal mystery. This twofold character
is to be brought into greater prominence both in the liturgy
and by instruction. Hence:

(a) More use is to be made of the baptismal features proper
to the lenten liturgy; some of them, which used to flourish in
bygone days, are to be restored as may seem good.

(b) The same is to apply to the penitential elements. As
regards instruction it is important to impress on the minds of
the faithful not only the social consequences of sin but also that
essence of the virtue of penance which leads to the detestation
of sin as an offence against God; the role of the Church in
penitential practices is not to be passed over, and the people
must be exhorted to pray for sinners.

110.   During Lent penance should not be only internal and
individual, but also external and social. The practice of penance
should be fostered in ways that are possible in our own times
and in different regions, and according to the circumstances
of the faithful; it should be warmly encouraged by the authorities mentioned in art. 22.

Let the sacred paschal fast be observed everywhere on Good
Friday and, where possible, let it be prolonged throughout

Holy Saturday, so that the joys of Easter Sunday may be attained with uplifted and clear minds.

111. The saints have been traditionally honoured in the Church and their authentic relics and images are held in veneration. For the feasts of the saints proclaim the wonderful works of Christ in his servants, and display to the faithful fitting examples for their imitation.

Lest the feasts of the saints should take precedence over the feasts which commemorate the very mysteries of salvation, many of them should be left to be celebrated by some particular church or nation or religious order; only those should be extended to the universal Church which commemorate saints who are truly of universal importance.

V

Of the Liturgical Year

(*102–111*)

In the opening paragraphs of this chapter, three points of
some importance are made:

(1) The liturgical year is the celebration of the paschal
mystery of which the centre is the feast of the Passover when
the Church recalls and makes present the passion, death
and resurrection of her Lord. This is the emphasis of the
liturgical movement since the war and its place here at the
head of the chapter bears witness that that point of view
has entered formally into the thought and life of the Church.
In *Mediator Dei* there is no mention in the section on the
liturgical year of the paschal mystery and the treatment of
the year is diffuse, reflecting the outlook of a former age.
Further, this same article (102) is careful to put things in
their right order, first the mention of the weekly paschal
feast, the Lord's Day, and secondly its annual celebration
at Easter. This is in fact how they emerged in the history
of the Church's worship. First there was the celebration of
the Lord's Day of which the heart was the *anamnesis* of the
eucharist in which the Church recalled (and made present)
the redeeming mystery of the passion, death and resurrection of Christ. Then, it would seem, in the second century
came the more solemn annual celebration of the Lord's

Passover which ran from Friday (which we call Good Friday) to the end of the paschal liturgy early on Sunday morning. This has always lain at the heart of the Church's life and liturgy and from it in one way or another the whole of the liturgical year has evolved.

(2) It is of this that the Constitution goes on to speak in the next paragraph and even the order of things is significant. The Church unfolds the *whole mystery of Christ* from the incarnation until the ascension and the day of Pentecost. Finally comes the mention of the last part of the liturgical year which is seen as overlapping on Advent. The Constitution does not endorse the view that Advent is the beginning of the liturgical year and by linking it with the last Sundays after Pentecost suggests that its eschatological content is more important than its incarnational one. The liturgical year, then, is the celebration of the different stages of the paschal mystery. Of these, after Easter, Christmas was the first to emerge in the middle of the fourth century, when it appeared at the head of a list of martyrs. By the end of the century it had already become a 'mystery' feast of which forty years later St Leo was the magnificent interpreter. For him Christmas was part of the Christian mystery because it marked the beginnings of our redemption. We note too that the Constitution speaks of the *day* of Pentecost as the end of the paschal celebration proper, excluding it would seem the octave and emphasizing the sacred 'fifty days' which is the oldest part of the liturgical year.

(3) In more recent times the liturgical year has usually been regarded as a series of historical commemorations of sacred events that happened long ago. They are recalled so that we may meditate on them and, through so doing, receive grace. In this view there is no more than a moral connection between Christians now and the events of the redemption in the past. This led to putting saints' feasts almost on the

level of the feasts of the Lord[1] and to the tedious 'considerations' which appeared by the thousand, and gave rise to
those *fervorini* of the pulpit whose exuberance was equalled
only by their vacuity. The Constitution moves in another
world and although discreetly avoiding theological opinions,
states that the mysteries of redemption are *in some way*
(*quodammodo*) made present to the faithful so that they are
able to lay hold of them and so be filled with grace.[2] The
keeping of the feasts is always associated with the celebration of the eucharist which makes present the whole redeeming mystery of Christ, and thus it is *through* the Mass
ultimately that the people are able to lay hold of the
different stages of the mystery and make them the sources
of grace.

The order of consideration in this chapter is the mystery
of Christ, the position of Our Lady in the liturgy, and finally
the place of the saints. These three articles are the introduction to the whole matter on the liturgical year. It is for
this reason that we have a brief passage on Our Lady whose
unique place in the Church's life and devotion is thus
indicated. She, it is said, is inseparably linked with the
saving work of her Son, she is the most perfect fruit of it and
she is the spotless image of its effects and the model or
exemplar of the holiness each Christian hopes to achieve. In
the history of the Church, the liturgical feasts of Our Lady
have been a factor in theological development. If the prayer
of the Canon in which we venerate the ever blessed Virgin
Mary, Mother of God, was most probably inserted into it
after the Council of Ephesus, yet devotion to her was no new

[1] Guéranger's reactions to a suggestion for the curtailment of
saints' feasts was very violent. The Catholic faith was being
attacked!

[2] This marks an advance on *Mediator Dei* which, although teaching with some force that 'the liturgical year is no cold and lifeless
representation of past events, no mere historical record', fights shy
of 'mystery' language, for which it showed a dislike. But it goes on
to affirm that the *mysteries* of Christ (note the plural) are still now
constantly present and active and the sources of grace (176).

thing. It was the *people* who in the basilica broke out in protestations against Nestorius who would call her no more than Mother of Christ. From then on devotion and theology went hand in hand and in all the early feasts, the Annunciation, the Assumption, with which we must put Christmas and its epilogue, Candlemas, it is difficult to separate the Mother from the Son. In fact the new Code of Rubrics has done much to re-establish the connection between Mary and the saving work of her Son. Candlemas is now once again a Feast of the Lord and the incarnational content of the Annunciation reminds us that it too was a feast of the Lord. With new theological insights came the Immaculate Conception which has always been appropriately placed in Advent, and the Assumption, the crown of the Marian feasts, which is shown to be the final fruit of the redeeming activity of Jesus, her Son. This is the organic perspective given by the liturgy and it is one that contemporary theological reflection is doing more and more to support.

In this brief paragraph there is indeed a wealth of theology of the most authentic kind, but it would take us far from our purpose to comment upon it. We note simply that the phrase 'spotless image' is one that leads us to see the full effect of the redemption in Mary who personally becomes the Bride of Christ and so the model and exemplar of the whole Church and of every member of it.

These are the fundamental reasons for Mary's place in the liturgical year and for the Church's constant recourse to her.

The Constitution reveals a similar sense of tradition in its article on the saints. The martyrs are put first. Then, with the other saints, they are spoken of as being perfected by God's manifold grace, but—and it is here that the ancient view of sanctity and especially martyrdom is expressed—the Church is seen as celebrating their *passage* from earth to heaven and by consequence their sharing in the paschal mystery of Christ which is achieved in those who have suffered and been glorified with him. In the early Church the martyr was regarded as the *typical* saint, not because there were no other holy people, but because he shared most deeply in the paschal mystery of Christ. His giving of his life out of the deepest love ('Greater love than this no man has . . .' for Christ) meant that he shared in the death of his Saviour as no one else did, and that through the resurrection he was raised up to be in glory with him. It was this *transitus*, this passing over in Christ, that conformed him to his Lord, and very early it was seen as fitting that this paschal death should be celebrated in connection with the Mass in which the passion, death and resurrection of Christ is made present. Other saints, whose feasts began to be kept in the fifth century, mostly bishops, were conceived of as being made like to Christ in their *lives* and by their apostolic activity as witnesses (*confessores*, the Latin word for *martyres*) to Christ and his truth. The ancient liturgical texts for confessors show that the Church was conscious of this likeness between martyr-saints and those who were not. Because of their likeness to Christ the Church honours them in festivals and because of their closeness to Christ she seeks their intercession.

The intention of article 105 is to show that the Church regards the liturgical year as a means of spiritual formation for the people, by prayer, instruction, fasting and works of mercy. This, at the level of living, is the *point* of the liturgical year. It is not just a series of ceremonial observances but, at its deepest, the way by which the people may live out the life of the mystical body. This is the teaching of *Mediator Dei* (163) which seems to be reflected here:

'In reminding the faithful of these mysteries of Jesus Christ the sacred liturgy seeks to make them share in them in such a way that the divine head of the mystical body lives by his perfect holiness in each of his members.'

At the practical level if the people *are* to live the life of the mystical body, it will be through their participation in the liturgical year. Pius XI, who said to Dom Capelle that the liturgy is the *Church's* teaching, observed in his encyclical *Quas primas*, instituting the feast of Christ the King, that the celebration annually of the feasts of the Church was a more powerful means of teaching the people the Christian faith than the writings of theologians. This means of course that it is the *authentic* liturgical year that is presented to the people and not just some adventitious devotions which, however good, are never as good as the liturgy which 'by its very nature far surpasses any of them' (13). Yet this article does make room for devotional services and practices which are mentioned and recommended in *Mediator Dei* (39 and 185–196), though Pius XII concludes that there should be 'not many devotions but much devotion'.[1] At the same time, there seems to be a reference here (among others in the Constitution) to the Bible devotions which are recommended under article 35, 4. It is these that best correspond with the directives of both *Mediator Dei* and the Constitution that these devotions are to lead to the liturgy and, to some extent at least, are to be modelled on it.

The Christian Sunday (106)

The article on the Christian Sunday is remarkable for the prominent place given to it in the chapter, for its length and above all for its doctrine. By its position, after the general introduction and before any discussion of reform, it appears as in a sense the chief celebration of Christ's paschal mystery. The paschal feast kept at Eastertide is indeed the centre of the Church's year and Sunday is set forth as the weekly celebration of that same mystery. At one blow the Trinitarian character of Sunday, which dates from the early tenth century, is done away with and one hopes that

---

[1] This phrase is actually the paragraph heading of the English translation of the encyclical (197).

with it will go the Preface of the Trinity and the 'revisions' of one or two Sunday hymns of the Breviary which were perpetrated in the seventeenth century. Explicitly, Sunday is spoken of as the *'primordialis dies festus'*, the feast from which all other feasts of the Lord came, including Easter. It should then be proposed to the people as such, to be kept by them as a day of joy and gladness.

As for the doctrine, the Constitution rapidly summarizes what has been the theme of many books and articles in recent years.[1] Already in New Testament times the first day of the week (1 Cor. 16:1) had become the Lord's Day (Apoc. 1:10—*kyriakē hēmēra*) and had superseded the sabbath. It was the day of the Lord's triumph, of his resurrection, although, as the Constitution says, it was the day of a total celebration of the paschal mystery. The early Christians, instructed by the facts of Christ's appearances to them on the first day of the week, met together and kept vigil from Saturday night to Sunday morning[2] and celebrated the events of redemption, passion, death and resurrection. In this way the old Sabbath was superseded and the first day of the week, which, the gospels tell us, was the day of the Lord's resurrection, became the chief festival, for some time the only festival of the early Church. But the *idea* of the sabbath was not obliterated. It was spiritualized. In the Old Testament the Lord in the creating of the world ceased from his labours on the seventh day and for the Jews the Sabbath was a day of repose. For the Christians, it was taken out of the temporal order and called the eighth day to signify that with the completion of the Lord's redeeming work the people of God had now entered the new age. This day was the symbol of the eternal rest and joy of heaven in which all those who followed Christ and looked eagerly for his

---

[1] See *Dimanche et Vie Pascale*, by Dom J. Hild (Turnhout-Paris, 1949) and *Public Worship* by J. A. Jungmann, pp. 231-4 (London and Collegeville, 1957).

[2] It is not clear that they met *every* week-end in New Testament times, though this had become the custom in the second century.

return would share. Sunday, which the Constitution is careful to call the *Lord's* Day, is thus the summary of salvation: Christ's community meet together to hear God's word, to take part in the eucharist which recalls and makes present his passion, death, resurrection and ascension and turns men's minds to the second coming of Christ, to the glory and joy that awaits us all. It is therefore 'a day of joy and freedom from work'.[1] The pastoral importance of this teaching is considerable and, if properly presented, will help people to see that attendance at Mass is not just a legal obligation but an opportunity to enter into the depths of the Christian life. And it is because of the unique dignity of the Christian Sunday that other celebrations are not to take its place unless they are of truly great importance. The Constitution does not say simply 'feasts' but 'celebrations', which is a wider term. It implies that various occasions, not always liturgical ones, which have sometimes by 'privilege' been able to take with them certain Masses, should no longer be observed on Sunday. Even what is unhappily called the 'external solemnity' of feasts would seem now to be contra-indicated for Sunday.

Revision of the Liturgical Year

After thus laying the theological foundations, the Constitution, as is its habit, goes on to give the general rules for the revision of the liturgical year (107, 108).

The heart of the injunctions, to be found in article 107, is that the paschal mystery, meaning the celebration of it from Maundy Thursday evening to Easter Day, is the centre of the liturgical year and it must always appear to be so. Next to this come the (other) mysteries of redemption. The liturgical year is to be revised so that the celebration of the mysteries may 'duly nourish the piety of the faithful'.

[1] For a brief account of Sunday as the eighth day see *La Vie Spirituelle*, special number, *Le huitième jour* (Cerf, April 1947), pp. 495–501.

Secondly, the celebration of that part of the year called the
Proper of Time is to be given preference over the feasts of
saints 'so that the entire cycle of the mysteries may be suitably recalled' (108). Much has been done since 1955 to
achieve the simplification of the liturgical year and if any
single act gave back to it its correct perspective it was the
reform of the liturgy of Holy Week, first celebrated in its
new form in 1956. The reduction in rank of the saints'
feasts which began then and was continued with the new
Code of Rubrics of 1960 has given a prominence to the
Proper of Time it has not had for hundreds of years. We
have only to recall the liturgical year before 1955 with its
many commemorations and its interweaving octaves, to
realize what great progress has been made. Yet still the
Council is not satisfied and it may be admitted that there is
room for improvement. If the Sundays are to remain sacro-
sanct (and they have been the chief casualties in the course
of ages), then only a feast of the Lord should have precedence here. It would be a good thing to raise the Sundays
after Easter to the first class, like those of Lent, for paschal-
tide is the oldest and most important part of the liturgical
year. In fact, if the ranks or classes of feasts are to reflect
reality, it would seem that only feasts of the Lord should
be of the first class. This would solve a number of problems
and would by itself make the pattern of the liturgical year
clearer to the people. If Advent is to remain an important
season, feasts during this time should be restricted and
Mass formulas for all or most of its days are required.
Perhaps something should be done, by the choice of texts,
to emphasize its eschatological content. The season after
Christmas (which except in Latin, and possibly in Italian,
has a title in the new Code of Rubrics that is untranslatable)
is still in a very confused condition. Is it to be a season in
which the great themes of Christmas are to be reflected in
the texts or are we to continue to have a somewhat uneven
series of historical commemorations of the infancy gospel

and one or two things connected with it?[1] Likewise, the Epiphany season needs revision. The Sundays after Epiphany should have a distinctive character, new lessons and preferably a different name.

In the matter of keeping feasts, perhaps it is necessary to recall that the expression means festival, festivity, and there is something unreal about feasts that bring with them nothing more than an obligation to go to Mass. A *'holiday of obligation'* is almost a contradiction in terms, and although we live in a wicked world which we cannot be expected to give way to, the multiplication of feasts which can only be kept by a bunch of ecclesiastics hardly seems to express what the Church has always meant by a feast, that is a festival. Article 107 admits the principle of adaptation, and even in our western world there would seem to be a case for re-examining the whole question. The two greatest feasts, Easter and Christmas, do coincide with secular holidays, but the rest? Whatever is done, the Constitution is of the view that all these matters are not just the concern of clerical rubricians. On what is done will depend whether the people can make the liturgical year a source of piety or not.

The principles of revision are carried forward into the next two articles on Lent (109, 110) which could be very far-reaching. Lent has too often been regarded as a prolonged meditation on the passion of our Lord, with special emphasis on his physical sufferings. In fact, it is a time of spiritual discipline and renewal and in the liturgy there is little enough mention of the passion at all. As the Constitution points out, it has a twofold character: baptismal and penitential. It is a preparation for the celebration of the paschal mystery that comes at its end[2] when it is renewed

[1] If the feast of the Holy Name is to be retained, it must have a new formula which is more meaningful. Apart from a use of 'name' which is out of date by the standards of modern scriptural scholarship, it has one of the worst liturgical formulas in the Missal and the Breviary.

[2] Originally, the last three days were counted as *outside* Lent. The Church was and is celebrating precisely the paschal mystery.

within us, among other things by the renewal we make of
our baptismal promises. This element of Lent is now to be
given a new prominence in the revision that is to be made
of it. One way of doing this would be to see that the restored
rites of the catechumenate are integrated into it and that
there should be a baptism during the Easter Vigil. If this is
not possible, then catechumens (baptized) who have been
prepared during the earlier part of the year could take part
in an adaptation of the catechumenate and make their
solemn profession with the people at the Vigil. So far as the
texts of the Lenten liturgy are concerned, what is most
required is that the great scriptural passages concerning
baptism that used to be read on the third, fourth and fifth
Sundays (with which would come their corresponding
epistles) should be restored to their former places.[1]

The intention of the Constitution in restoring the penitential element of Lent is evidently to bring back to people's
minds the social nature of sin and the 'ecclesial' nature of
penitence. When we sin we injure the whole body of
Christ, and when we repent we are re-entering the fellowship of the faithful. This was how the ancient penitential
discipline thought of it. Even if it is not a matter of grave
sin, the Constitution still insists that people should be
taught about the role of the Church in all this matter of
penitence. Lent is indeed the great season when the Church
by prayer, preaching, the reading of God's word and exhortation, exercises the mission of reconciliation and forgiveness that was committed to her by her Lord. Of this the
sacrament of penance is a specific if the most potent example. What the Constitution envisages is that the whole
biblical and liturgical teaching on penitence should be
given to the people and that through it they should live more
earnestly during Lent and come to the sacrament of penance

[1] These are the incidents of the Samaritan woman (John 4:42),
of the Man born blind (John 9:1–38) and the raising of Lazarus
(John 11:1–44). These are now read on various days in different
weeks of Lent.

at its end ready to profit from it to the fullest. The Easter confession would then be seen as part of the renewal of the Christian life which is the whole aim of Lent.

What can be discerned in the background of the Constitution's teaching here is among other things the use of Bible services (35, 4) which are explicitly recommended for Lent. It is from them that the people will be able to learn what the scriptures have to say about repentance, about the following of Christ in his suffering and generous self-giving. It is in services such as these that there could be urgent prayer for sinners (among whom all would count themselves) and also for catechumens. This could of course be made part of the normal Lenten liturgy by the insertion of prayers for catechumens and sinners in the Prayer of the Faithful, and it is to be hoped that it will.

About the way in which 'penances', in the conventional use of the term, should be presented to the people, the Constitution is flexible and, where fasting is concerned, reserved. The Council realized that in the present state of the world, with people suffering various kinds of deprivation, the question of physical expressions of penitence and self-denial is a very delicate one. Therefore while enjoining that the practice of penance should be fostered in various ways, it encourages the use of the principle of adaptation, pointing explicitly to local episcopal authorities who should see to this matter.

Only once is fasting mentioned and that is when the Constitution recalls it in terms that are a reflection of the earliest view of it. It urges that the sacred paschal fast be observed everywhere (and so it is considered to be *possible* everywhere) and urges its prolongation until the celebration of the Easter Vigil. What the Constitution has in mind here is the absolute fast that was the custom, at least among the most devout, in the second century. It lasted from the day we now call Good Friday until the Vigil, the days, in the words of Tertullian, *ubi ablatus est sponsus*, when the

Church's Bridegroom was taken away from her. Here too the ancient notion that the fast was part of the joyful waiting for the coming of the Lord is brought back into currency.

The total view of Lent given in the Constitution is a noble one, ancient without in any way being archaeological. It is not in any way a return to old customs for their own sake, but witnesses to a determination to draw on the depths of spiritual doctrine that our liturgy still contains.

The Saints (111)

The most striking phrase in the brief article on the saints is that showing they proclaim the wonderful works of Christ in his servants. To know the saints is in some sense to know Christ who is their model and inspiration. Therefore they are to be honoured, as the Church from the second century has honoured them. But their feasts should not take precedence over the mysteries of salvation (this is the third time this has been repeated), and in an endeavour to keep down the number of saints' feasts the Constitution urges the ancient custom of *local* celebrations. In all the early centuries of the Church, and indeed until quite late, saints' feasts were celebrated only in those localities with which they (the saints) had a physical bond. This is no longer entirely possible or desirable, so the Constitution admits the celebration of other saints' feasts in the Calendar of the Roman Church only when they can be shown to commemorate saints of truly universal importance.

For over a thousand years saints' feasts have been invading the Proper of Time. Pius V by his reform in the sixteenth century did much to reduce them, but by the end of the nineteenth century they almost dominated the scene. Even in our own time, the number of saints' feasts inserted into the calendar has been very great. Granted that it is very difficult to establish who are saints of truly universal importance (and no one has yet suggested any workable criteria), the principle is important and if honestly observed would eliminate the unhappy condition of recent times. It becomes all the more important to make the most of local calendars, though here too there are possibilities of abuse. Probably the solution to the whole problem is to be rigid about the classification of feasts. It is this that was the chief weakness of the Pian reform and one which was not sufficiently corrected by that of Pius X. If saints' feasts are kept down in rank, they will never come in conflict with any of the greater feasts of the Lord or with the Sunday. This, it would seem, is what the Constitution wants.

Of Sacred Music

112. The musical tradition of the universal Church is a treasure of inestimable value, greater even than that of any other art. The main reason for this pre-eminence is that, as sacred song united to the words, it forms a necessary or integral part of the solemn liturgy.

Holy scripture, indeed, has bestowed praise upon sacred song, and the same may be said of the Fathers of the Church and of the Roman pontiffs who in recent times, led by St Pius X, have explained more precisely the ministerial function supplied by sacred music in the service of the Lord.

Therefore sacred music is to be considered the more holy in proportion as it is more closely connected with the liturgical action, whether it adds delight to prayer, fosters unity of minds, or confers greater solemnity upon the sacred rites. For the Church approves of all forms of true art having the needed qualities, and admits them into divine worship.

Accordingly the sacred Council, keeping to the norms and precepts of ecclesiastical tradition and discipline, and having regard to the purpose of sacred music—which is the glory of God and the sanctification of the faithful—decrees as follows:

113. Liturgical worship is given a more noble form when the divine offices are celebrated solemnly in song, with the

assistance of sacred ministers and the active participation of the people.

As regards the language to be used, the provisions of art. 36 are to be observed; for the Mass, art. 54; for the sacraments, art. 63; for the divine office, art. 101.

114.   The treasury of sacred music is to be preserved and fostered with great care. Choirs must be diligently promoted, especially in Cathedrals; bishops and other pastors of souls must be at pains to ensure that, whenever the sacred liturgy is to be solemnized with song, the whole body of the faithful may be able to contribute that active participation which is rightly theirs, as laid down in articles 28 and 30.

115.   Great importance is to be attached to the teaching and practice of music in seminaries, in the novitiates and houses of study of religious of both sexes, and also in other Catholic schools and institutions. To impart this instruction, teachers are to be carefully trained and put in charge of the teaching of sacred music.

It is desirable also to found higher institutes of sacred music whenever this can be done.

Composers and singers, especially boys, must be given also a genuine liturgical training.

116.   The Church acknowledges Gregorian chant as specially suited to the Roman liturgy; therefore, other things being equal, it should be given pride of place in liturgical functions.

But other kinds of sacred music, especially polyphony, are by no means excluded from liturgical celebrations, so long as they accord with the spirit of the liturgical action, as laid down in art. 30.

117.   The typical editions of the liturgical songbooks are to be completed; and a more critical edition is to be prepared of those books already published since the restoration of sacred music by St Pius X.

It is desirable also that an edition be brought out containing simpler chants, for use in small churches.

118. Religious singing by the people is to be skilfully fostered, so that in popular devotions, as also during liturgical services, the voices of the faithful may ring out according to the norms and requirements of the rubrics.

119. In certain parts of the world, especially in the mission lands, there are nations which have their own musical traditions, and these play a great part in their religious and social life. For this reason due importance is to be attached to their music, and a suitable place is to be given to it, not only in forming their attitude towards religion, but also in adapting worship to their native genius, as indicated in articles 39 and 40.

Therefore when missionaries are being given training in music, every effort should be made to see that they become competent in promoting the traditional music of these peoples, both in schools and in the liturgy, as far as may be practicable.

120. In the Latin Church the pipe organ is to be held in high esteem, for it is the traditional musical instrument which adds a wonderful splendour to the Church's ceremonies and powerfully lifts up man's mind to God and to higher things.

But other instruments also may be admitted for use in divine worship, with the knowledge and consent of the competent territorial authorities as laid down in articles 22 (ii), 37 and 40. This may be done, however, only on condition that the instruments are suitable, or can be made suitable, for use in divine worship, accord with the dignity of the sacred building, and truly contribute to the edification of the faithful.

121. Composers, filled with the Christian spirit, should feel that their vocation is to cultivate sacred music and increase its store of treasures.

Let them produce compositions which have the qualities proper to genuine sacred music. And they must not confine themselves to composing works which can be sung only by large choirs, but should provide also for the needs of small

choirs and for the active participation of the entire assembly
of the faithful.

The word-texts intended to be sung must always be in conformity with Catholic doctrine; indeed they should be drawn
chiefly from holy scripture and from liturgical sources.

VI

Of Sacred Music

(*112–121*)

Speaking of the introduction (112) to this chapter Père Gelineau[1] remarks that 'it is the most condensed, the newest and the most considerable part because it applies to music the spirit and doctrine of the whole Constitution'.

We may note (1) that music has an importance all its own in the realm of art as used by the liturgy because it is an integral part of it. No other form of art comes so close to the liturgy and enters in the same way into its substance. It is by the voice of the celebrant, using song, that the consecration prayer is begun and formerly was wholly sung, so that the eucharist could be said to have been effected by the use of music. It is true that this applies only to sung liturgies and the Constitution inserts in this place the word 'solemn', meaning sung. But if we look at an earlier age than our own, if we turn for a moment to the eastern liturgies, there we see that the liturgy was and is always sung, and where, as in some rites there is a simpler form nowadays, at least the words of consecration are always sung aloud. No doubt in the circumstances of our time it would be utopian to look for Masses that were always sung, but we are heavily conditioned by our recent past. We

---

[1] *La Maison-Dieu,* 77, p. 193.

always think nowadays *first* of a low Mass, which we think is the norm. In the history of worship, whether pagan or Christian, our way of thinking is precisely abnormal and therefore it is possible to hold that music is integral to worship and playing a role that is given to no other art-form. That this goes a little beyond what the Constitution says cannot be denied and it will have taken modern conditions into account. But it does serve to show the importance of music in worship, which the Constitution is so concerned to promote.

(2) The second thing we may note is that music is said to have a ministerial role in worship. It has a function of serving not merely the liturgy to enhance its solemnity but of serving the people who are engaged in it, and the Constitution goes on to specify how it fulfills this role. It adds delight to prayers, fosters unity of minds and confers greater solemnity on the sacred rites. In a word, it is *a mode of prayer* and it is in this that its dignity and importance lies. It is this too that the modern Christian least appreciates. He has become so accustomed to occupying himself with private devotions during public worship that he finds singing a 'distraction'. Even those who see that singing is right and take their part in it, often have a vaguely puritanical feeling that when they are singing they are not really praying and that they would be doing very much better to be quietly contemplating the sacred mystery of the Mass. It is all part of the hidden Manichaeism of modern 'spirituality'. Only that that is purely mental is valid in prayer. The body has no place and you cannot really worship God by action, gesture and voice. Well, if music has a ministerial function in the liturgy, it must be allowed to operate and people must be persuaded that by singing they are praying.

The same introduction refers to holy scripture, the Fathers of the Church and the teachings of the popes in the matter. Holy scripture is indeed full of sacred song, of which the psalms (which were, almost all, meant to be *sung*) form one book, but some of the Fathers were uneasy about music in worship. We all remember St Augustine's doubts. But they might have had the same doubts now if they thought they were being asked to accept certain musical manifestations of our day into the liturgy. They too were faced with a pagan and often lascivious music and this they rightly felt was incompatible with the sacredness of worship.

In fact, it is the pronouncements of the popes in more recent times that have given the most important encouragement to music in worship and spoken most penetratingly of its significance. Père Gelineau, noting with pleasure the mention of Pius X in the Constitution, says of his *Motu proprio* (1903) that no other document has surpassed it or attained the same degree of liturgical and pastoral depth.[1] This was followed by the Apostolic Constitution of Pius XI, *Divini cultus* (1928), by *Mediator Dei* (203-205) which resumes and reinforces the two previous documents, and finally by *Musicae sacrae disciplina*, entirely devoted to sacred music in all its forms.[2] All these documents are found to be underlying this chapter of the Constitution, which takes their teaching a stage further.

From all its teaching it is clear that the Constitution has a truly pastoral attitude to music in the liturgy and sees it as the means by which the liturgical assembly may give glory to God and achieve sanctification. We may go further and say that it sees music as part of the liturgical sign which it enhances, gives it another voice and makes clear to the people that they are in fact one in mind, heart and voice in offering worship to God. This is why it can be said to apply the spirit and doctrine of the whole Constitution to sacred music.

The most striking example of this fidelity to the spirit of

[1] Op. cit., p. 198.
[2] Translations of the *Motu proprio* and the *Divini cultus* in 'The Popes and the Liturgy' (Society of St Gregory Publications, 1945) and of *Musicae Sacrae* in *Sacred Music* (published by Challoner Publications for the Society of St Gregory, 1957).

the Constitution is to be found in its concern for the people.
Bishops and pastors are to see that when the liturgy is sung,
'*the whole body of the faithful* may be able to contribute
that active participation which is rightly theirs, as laid down
in articles 28 and 30' (114). Every kind of religious singing
by the people is to be fostered and skill brought to bear
on it (118), and even where composers are encouraged to
dedicate their gifts to making music for the liturgy, they are
not to confine themselves to works that can only be sung by
large choirs, they are to keep in mind the needs of small
parishes and the active participation of the entire assembly
(121). There can be no more formal or clearer teaching than
this and, with all respect, one can but draw the attention of
musicians to it. Already for some years, since the popular
liturgical movement has got under weigh, tensions have
been felt between the legitimate rights of the congregation
and those of composers and choirs. But however difficult the
solutions at the practical level, the Constitution clearly indicates the sort of *liturgical* thinking that must go to the
composition of music for worship. For about a thousand
years, choirs and composers have had it all their own way.
The elaborate plainsong of the post-Gregorian centuries, the
emergence of polyphony and the riot of ornate music that
characterized the period of the Baroque have all too suc-
cessfully taken away from the people the parts of the Mass
that rightfully belong to them. With the decline of a sense
of what was due to liturgical worship, there came those
'Masses' of the great Baroque and romantic composers which
consisted precisely of highly elaborate and very beautiful
settings for the *people's* texts of the Mass, the *Gloria,
Sanctus*, etc. Then came their miserable followers who
filled the air and choir cupboards with the second-rate stuff
that is still, alas, regarded by many as 'Church Music'. On
the other hand, it is well known that the plainsong of the
Proper was so difficult that it was (and is) either sung to a
psalm tone or not at all. The whole organic relationship of

celebrant, choir and people has been broken up and we have arrived at a stage of liturgical and artistic confusion. Composers and choirs may well feel worried. One is tempted to say that it is about time they did, though that would be unjust. They have usually been doing no more than working within a framework laid down by someone else and the clergy have rarely given the instruction that was required or even the attention the matter deserved.

Anyway, for the future there has to be some new thinking. Happily, a number of composers both here and abroad have already seen the problem and have made some attempts to solve it.[1] Choirs will need to learn their function, which is to lead the people and to sing certain things they cannot; and composers will have the enormously difficult task of writing music for the liturgy which will give to the people's voices their proper place.

In addition, there will have to be a process of education of the people. One of the most daunting features of our age is the enormous gap that exists between what may be called popular culture and that of the artist. Any new expression of art in any medium either leaves people cold or is actively resisted by them. How this particular problem is to be tackled, it is difficult to say. That it must be tackled is certain. But further, the people will have to be educated liturgically. Frankly, they will have to be weaned from what seems an excessive affection for low Masses and 'said' services. Probably, if they could be shown that sung Masses do not mean pompous performances of (to them) boring and irrelevant music, if they could be led back to the simpler and more appropriate forms of music, they would soon begin to realize that by singing, their offering of the Mass is enhanced and they are giving themselves more generously to God in their worship. But whether it is the composer, the choir or the people, it is always the liturgy and liturgical

---

[1] In England the name of Mr Arthur Oldham and in France that of Père Gelineau readily come to mind.

formation that provides the ultimate solution to these problems (cf. article 115).

As for plainsong, the Constitution repeats what has been said by the popes. The Gregorian chant is specially suited to the Roman liturgy (in Latin). Other things then being equal, it is to have pride of place. It has in fact this pride of place in the more solemn, 'ministerial' parts of the Mass: the celebrant may only use plainsong when he sings the liturgical texts that belong to him, in particular the consecration prayer. What will be the situation when the celebrant is able to sing in his own language remains to be seen. A process of adaptation would seem to be indicated and if syllabic chants can be artistically adapted to modern languages, this would be the right thing to do. The plainsong recitative is of unique beauty and wholly apt for the solemn proclamation of prayers and scriptural texts in the liturgy. There is room for unprejudiced experiment here.

One notes (117) that, in the re-editing of the liturgical chant books, simpler chants suitable for small churches are to be devised. This more than anything could keep alive in parish churches the treasure of plainsong which, among other kinds of music (114), is to be preserved and fostered. Everyone knows that even in the *Kyriale* there are only two or three settings of the people's parts which they can really sing. Simplified *Kyries*, etc., are an absolute necessity if plainsong is to be kept alive *for the people*. But there are other places too where a simplification is necessary. Even the *Venite, adoremus* of Good Friday is too difficult for most congregations, and yet this is pre-eminently their chant. Likewise, the threefold *Alleluia*, so grand and magnificent, of the Vigil Mass is completely beyond the people and most celebrants too. *All* the chants that concern the people, but especially those where they are required to reply to the celebrant, are in need of simplification.[1] The

[1] Cf. art. 31. Of little use will it be to write into the liturgical books the people's responses if they cannot sing them.

same must be said of the repertoire of the Gradual and indeed of the Vesperal. Hymns, psalm tones, responsories, all have suffered from a process of musical complication in the course of centuries and if they are once again to become popular chants they will need to be revised. What is the use of having an impeccable treasury of plainsong if it cannot be sung *at all* (as it cannot) in small parish churches and most big ones too.[1] Introits, offertories and communion chants were originally responsorial in form: the schola or cantor sang the verses (perhaps to a more elaborate chant) and the people replied with a simple refrain. The same is true of the gradual. It is not the complete preserve of the choir; the people have their part in it and if it is once again to be shared with the people, then even the gradual will have to be simplified.

It may be that it is the use of Latin that has inhibited people from singing and composers from writing. Experience shows that people will easily enough learn chants in their own language, even if they are more difficult than plainsong ones, and composers will not be encouraged to write music for the people unless they know they are really going to sing it. Untll now this has been impossible in the language of the people, at least for the Mass, which is the only service attended by the vast majority of Catholics. Article 119 speaks of the use of the traditional music of different nations and peoples and recommends that it should be used in the liturgy. True, the context is missionary, but with the extension of the vernacular to the Mass and other parts of the liturgy in all the countries of the Church, musical traditions are going to become very important. In England we have a long and very fine tradition of choral music of many styles and different periods. English composers are still writing music for Anglican worship, even if much of it is not of the first class. But they have a long

---

[1] Even monasteries, one notes, rarely sing *all* the plainsong given in the book for a Mass.

experience of setting English words to music, and in the promotion of traditional music 'in schools and in the liturgy' (119) it would be well to consult that tradition. Composers will need encouragement from the highest authority if they are to work in this tradition to give to our worship the music it demands. It is conceivable that with the promotion of a genuine English school of sacred music, the people would acquire a certain enthusiasm for it and would be more willing to give their time and energy to learning it. Thus would be solved the problem of getting choirs together, a problem that has increased enormously in more recent years. If there is any part of the Constitution that offers opportunities for a change of our liturgical habits it is this.

Of Sacred Arts and Furnishings

122.   Very rightly the fine arts are considered to rank among the noblest activities of man's genius, and this applies especially to religious art and to its highest achievement, which is sacred art. These arts, by their very nature, are oriented towards the infinite beauty of God which they attempt in some way to portray by the work of human hands; they achieve their purpose of redounding to God's praise and glory in proportion as they are directed the more exclusively to the single aim of raising men's minds devoutly towards the Divine Majesty.

Holy Mother Church has always been the patron of the fine arts and has ever sought their valued help, with the special aim that all things set apart for use in divine worship should be truly worthy, becoming and beautiful, signs and symbols of the supernatural world. The Church has, indeed, trained artists and craftsmen to make such things. Moreover she has, with good reasons, reserved to herself the right to pass judgment upon the works of artists, deciding which of them are in accordance with faith, piety, and cherished traditional laws, and thereby fitted for sacred use.

The Church has been particularly careful to see that church furnishing should worthily and beautifully serve the dignity of worship, and has admitted changes in materials, style or ornamentation prompted by the progress of the technical arts with the passage of time.

Wherefore the Council fathers have decided to issue the following decrees on these matters:

123. The Church has not adopted any particular style of art as her very own; she has admitted styles from every period according to the natural dispositions and circumstances of her peoples, and the needs of the various rites. Thus, in the course of the centuries, she has amassed a treasury of art which must be very carefully preserved. The art of our own days, coming from every race and region, is also to be given free scope provided that it adorns the sacred buildings and holy rites with due reverence and honour; thereby it is enabled to contribute its own voice to that wonderful chorus of praise in honour of the Catholic faith sung by great men in times gone by.

124. Ordinaries, by the encouragement and favour they show to art which is truly sacred, should strive after noble beauty rather than sumptuous display. This principle is to apply also to sacred vestments and ornaments which ought not to be unduly expensive.

Bishops should carefully and insistently remove from churches and other holy places the works, produced by some artists, which do not accord with faith, morals and Christian piety, and which offend true religious sense either by depraved forms or by lack of artistic worth, mediocrity and pretence.

And when churches are to be built, ordinaries must see to it that the design of these churches is such as to facilitate the celebration of the liturgy and the active participation of the faithful.

125. The practice of placing statues and pictures in churches so that they may be venerated by the faithful is to be maintained; but their number should be moderate and their relative positions should exemplify right order. For otherwise they might provoke astonishment among the people, and foster devotions of doubtful orthodoxy.

126. When passing judgment on works of art local ordinaries must listen to the opinions of the Diocesan Commission

of Sacred Art and—in those instances which call for it—also to
those of others who are specially expert, and of the commissions
referred to in articles 44, 45 and 46.

Ordinaries must be very careful to see that sacred furnishings and works of value are not dispersed or allowed to fall
into other hands; for they were intended to add to the splendour of God's house.

127.   Bishops should have a special concern for artists, so as
to imbue them with the spirit of sacred art and of the sacred
liturgy. This they may do in person, or through suitable priests
who are gifted with a knowledge and love of art.

It is also very desirable that schools or academies of sacred
art should be founded in those parts of the world where they
would be useful, so that artists and craftsmen may be trained.

All artists who, prompted by their talents, desire to promote
God's glory in the Church, should ever bear in mind that they
are engaged in a kind of holy imitation of God the Creator,
and are concerned with works destined to be used in Catholic
worship, to edify the faithful, and to foster their piety and
their religious formation.

128.   Besides the revision of the liturgical books ordered in
article 25, there is to be an early revision of the ecclesiastical
laws and statutes which govern the provision of material things
involved in public worship. These laws refer especially to the
worthy and well-planned building of churches, the shape and
construction of altars, the nobility, position and safety of the
eucharistic tabernacle, the dignity and fitness of the baptistery,
the suitable placing of sacred images, embellishments and vestments. Any laws which seem less suited to the reformed liturgy
are to be brought into harmony with it, or else abrogated; and
any which are helpful are to be retained if already in force, or
introduced where they are lacking.

According to the principle of article 22 of this Constitution,
the local bishops' conferences are empowered to adapt such
things to the needs and customs of their different regions; this
applies especially to the materials and styles of church furnishings and of sacred vestments.

129. During their philosophical and theological studies, clerics are to be taught about the history and development of sacred art, and about the basic principles governing the production of its works. In consequence they will be able to appreciate and preserve the Church's ancient monuments, and be in a position to aid, by good advice, artists who are engaged in producing works of art.

130. It is fitting that the use of pontificals be reserved to those ecclesiastical persons who have episcopal rank or some particular jurisdiction.

VII

Of Sacred Arts

(*122–130*)

As the Constitution comes to consider those things connected with the liturgy but which also belong to the realm
of art, its statements must necessarily be less precise. This
is seen particularly in what it has to say in this chapter. At
first sight much of it would seem to be no more than repetitions of what has been said often enough before in documents emanating from the Holy See, and the impression
that one gained from press reports during the first session
was that here were not much more than innocuous and so
ineffective commonplaces. This is not borne out by a closer
examination of the text. But even if the Council had said
nothing very precise on sacred art, it does not seem to be
generally appreciated that this would be a good thing.
Artistic creation cannot be dictated by law nor organized
by rubric except in a negative way. The Church can and
does say what is fitting for her worship and reserves the
right to pronounce upon the *liturgical* fitness of individual
objects. The great virtue of this chapter is that it is positive,
seeking for what is best in this area and giving encouragement to artists. Restrictive clauses are very rare.

To unfold the philosophy implicit in the introduction to
the chapter would take us very far. We merely note one or

two points. Things made by human hands are the fruit of
the contemplation of the artist who seeks to discern the
hidden 'form' of objects so that he may express them and
so enhance their worth in the sight of men. In this he is
trying to work along with God who made them and to reveal
the beauty that is inherent in them. It is through this sort of
activity, a combination of mind, heart and hand, that the
artist reveals that beauty which then is seen as a reflection
of the infinite beauty of God (122 and compare 127). In this
sense, all artistic activity is basically religious, and if the
artist is working to provide objects for worship and if he
has some measure of success in his work (and success is not
always to be had for the asking), the things he makes will
give glory to God and help those who use them to do
likewise.

But in working for the liturgy, he accepts a restriction.
Whatever the artefacts are, whether statues or pictures to
help the contemplation of others, or chalices and vestments
which are essentially *for use*, he must be aware that he is
serving something greater than himself. He is serving God
in his own way, yes, but he is also the servant of the community whose function it is to worship God by using the
means he supplies. This does not mean that he must scale
down his vision to the L.C.M. of the sentimental and wit-
less, but it does mean that he himself must realize that *as a
man* he is a member of that community, that in some way
he must make himself one of them, learning by whatever
ways are open to him (and that means above all by worshipping with them) what are their fundamental spiritual
and emotional needs. Once given a sense of the dignity of
matter and the purpose for which it is to be formed (use in
worship), it is this sense of community more than anything
else that will enable the artist to give to the people he serves
things that are apt in themselves and will lead to contemplation. In the brief passage of *Mediator Dei* (207) where this
matter is referred to, it is significant that Pius XII empha-

sized the communal aspect of liturgical art: the artist should take into account the needs of the Christian community.

Just as music, so the plastic arts, though more remotely, become part of the sign of the liturgy (122) and it is this power to enhance the purely liturgical signs that makes art in worship so important. If the objects used in worship are debased, sentimental, meretricious, they are conveying to the people who are confronted with them wrong notions of God and of the worship they are engaged upon. If the altar appears to be no more than a shelf on a wall for the support of flowers, it will hardly teach them that it is the place of sacrifice and the table of communion. If weak and effeminate statues are constantly before their gaze, how can they not think of our Lord or the saints as weak and effeminate characters? Mercifully, the statues of this sort (which, daunting thought, are reproduced by the million throughout the Church) are literally so insignificant that after a time the people do not *see* them at all. They are just there, so many articles of 'church furniture'. But if the harm is minimized by familiarity, the justification for the use of statues (125) is also taken away. But, in conclusion, it is the relationship to the sign with which they become incarnated that gives to liturgical objects their importance and value.

In our own time it has been realized that it is not the most elaborate or 'imposing' objects that offer the best vehicle for worship. The signs of the liturgy should be stripped and simple, eloquent through the economical use of the best materials. The liturgical sign will become transparent when married to objects conceived and carried out in this spirit. There has been a great cry in the Church, voiced time and again in the Council by bishops, that the Church should appear to the world as 'poor'. This word, that constantly recurs, usually in foreign languages, should probably be translated 'austere'. The Church should appear to the world as wholly concentrated on essentials, as concerned with Christ's poor, with those whom the psalms and

Jesus called the 'poor ones', those who are in most need of God's help both for their souls and their bodies. The Church in her liturgical expression, whether in worship or in the things she uses or the buildings she builds, should appear as stripped down, 'austere', eschewing the pompous, the complicated and all that is merely sumptuous (124). If it be thought that we are being asked to return to puritan meeting houses, that would be a mistake. There is a case, and a strong one, for the removal from our churches of a great number of objects which no longer perform any useful function and, to judge from the neglect they are subject to, are no longer wanted. Some churches are a veritable forest of shrines, statues and banners obscuring the main purpose of the church, which is to provide the people of God with a place where they may meet to take their part in offering Christ's sacrifice. Everything should be subordinated to this and nothing should be allowed to distract attention from it. This would seem to be the sense of article 125 where a due hierarchy of objects in church is insisted upon. But if there is to be a proper austerity, this can be redeemed by the quality of the materials used in the building of churches and of those things that are placed in them. A noble and ample vestment made of natural fabrics when seen against a stone background gives an impression that is at once simple and splendid. This is the sort of austerity the Church is thinking of and asking for.

It will be as well to move from this subject to one of the most helpful articles in the chapter. New churches are to be built in such a way as to make the active participation of the people possible and easy (124). Ordinaries are to see to this. If this principle is really acted upon, then it will forward the revolution in church design that has been in progress in Europe for some twenty years and will produce the sort of churches we so badly need. The article actually mentions two principles: the celebration of the liturgy and the active participation of the people, but they really come to the same thing. The liturgy, in the mind of the Constitution, is the people's as well as the priest's; they are concerned with it as much as he. Liturgical worship is essentially worship *with* the people and all other kinds of celebration are abnormal. Therefore churches must be constructed so that the people can play their part. For this three things are required: (1) There must be room for the proper performance of the Roman liturgy whose typical service is *not* the low Mass. (2) The altar must be so placed that the people can not only see it but be near it. (3) This dictates the shape of any church which must be the place of assembly of the worshipping people. Whether square, circular or elliptical or whatever other shape may be devised, it must allow the people to gather near the altar and there take their part in the liturgy. This means that the church is essentially what has been called the 'eucharistic room' in which takes place the celebration of the liturgy by the priest with his people. All else in this part of the church must be severely subordinated to this overriding purpose. Shrines, 'side-altars' (unhappy name) and the rest are best out of the main body of the church so that nothing distracts from the place of sacrifice. Yet the Church is not only the place of public worship and prayer; it is also the place of private prayer. Chapels *are* needed, shrines where people go for their devotions should be provided, but out of the main ground-plan. These principles are largely agreed upon nowadays and several hierarchies in different parts of the world have issued 'directories' setting out the basic liturgical requirements of church design.

It perhaps needs to be said that such liturgical requirements in no way dictate style. The Constitution states that the Church is in no way committed to any historical style and commends 'the art of our own days'. This is to be given free scope, provided that it adorns the sacred buildings and holy rites with due reverence and honour (123). Every church poses problems of its own and their solution is the concern of the priest and his architect. No blueprint can be given for the 'liturgical church'. Such an animal does not exist. All churches are 'liturgical', though some make the performance of the liturgy insuperably difficult. No, the architect remains free, *but* just as the musician and the artist, so he must be imbued with the spirit of the liturgy and he especially has an obligation to obtain the necessary information.

In fact, the obligation to see that those who work for the church should be imbued with the right spirit is laid upon bishops who are told to have a special concern for artists (among whom we must put architects) and to encourage them in their work. This they may do either themselves or through priests appointed by them (127). The status of the Christian artist needs to be secured in the Church and one reads with appreciation that they should be consulted by diocesan commissions for sacred art (126). But respect for the artist's role and the limitations of clerical rights in this matter need to be further defined. In matters of art, almost all priests are 'laymen'. Normally they do not practise the arts and cannot be in a position to pass judgment on certain aspects of the objects that are brought before their notice. It is here that they need to have the humility to recognize the role of the artist and to listen to what he has to say. They may, for purely non-aesthetic reasons, feel bound to reject a given object, but they should make clear what are the grounds for rejection. The Constitution gives no countenance to the kind of thinking that expresses itself in meaningless clichés, 'modern', 'contemporary'—as if when one had said that one had said anything at all! There is good modern art and bad modern art and one needs to have some ability to distinguish the one from the other.

One of the plagues of the Church today is the proliferation of mass-produced statues and other objects of worship which are taken for granted by both clergy and laity. There is nothing in the Constitution that approves of them and article 124 could very well be regarded as disapproving of them: bishops are instructed to *remove* from churches objects that offend the religious sense either by reason of their depraved forms or *by lack of artistic worth* or *on account of their mediocrity and pretentiousness.* Under these successive hammer blows fall almost all the contents of most of our churches (including a number of altars made of faked 'marble'). But it cannot be expected that our bishops will go round our churches in an iconoclastic fury sweeping away all this pretentious and fundamentally irreligious farrago. However great the temptation, it is one that must be resisted. *As things are,* it would of course be a grave pastoral error; people in varying degrees need these things. The only way to get rid of them is to encourage good artists, to use them, to commission them and to pay them. Many Catholic artists of great skill live by what commissions they receive from Christians of churches other than our own. Of course there are risks, of course there will be disappointments, but it is naïve to suppose that artists always achieve success when no one else, including ourselves, does so in any department of life. But one thing is certain: the debased objects that disfigure our churches will only be expelled when, by steady pressure, they are replaced by statues and the like that are the fruits of man's contemplation and manual skill. It is this sort of artistic product alone that is worthy of the liturgy and of the Church's encouragement.

The Council, rightly despairing of dealing with the matter of art and architecture in a single chapter of the Constitution, promises that a further code of laws will be drawn up in which rules are to be laid down that will do much to improve the situation. In particular it is interesting to note that the designing of churches, a matter of major importance, is to be taken in hand. The shape of altars, the place of the tabernacle, the position of the baptistery, the siting of statues and the quality of vestments will all be considered. This indicates that the rubrics and other laws governing these matters are largely obsolete, reflecting as they do the Baroque world of the *Caeremoniale Episcoporum* which for too long has canonized the epoch of display which article 124 repudiates. No doubt in the world into which we have moved, where everything is so various and different cultures are ready to add their contribution to the liturgy (128), the rules will be flexible and concerned with general *liturgical* principles. In this way the greatest possible liberty will be given to designing churches that will be 'sacraments' of God's presence among men and to the making of things that will reflect his beauty.

A Declaration of the Second Vatican Council on Revision of the Calendar

The Second Ecumenical Sacred Council of the Vatican, recognizing the importance of the wishes expressed by many concerning a fixed Easter and an unchanging calendar, having carefully considered the effects which could result from the introduction of a new calendar, declares as follows:

1. The sacred Council would not object if the feast of Easter were assigned to a particular Sunday of the Gregorian Calendar, provided that others whom it may concern, especially the brethren who are not in communion with the Holy See, are agreed on this matter.

2. The sacred Council likewise declares that it does not oppose efforts designed to introduce a perpetual calendar into civil society.

But, among the various systems which are being suggested to stabilize a perpetual calendar and to introduce it into civil life, only some will be unopposed by the Church. These are the systems which retain and safeguard a seven-day week with Sunday, and which do not insert any extra days considered as belonging to no week, so that the succession of weeks may be left intact as far as possible. If serious reasons appear to dictate otherwise, the Holy See will judge of them.

APPENDIX

A Declaration of the Second Vatican Council on Revision of the Calendar

In this declaration the Council expresses its willingness to consider the practical possibility of a fixed date for Easter. It is a statement of principle that has great value. It could form the basis of any discussions the Church wished to enter into with those whose business it would be to deal with the matter. But the Council shows a concern for the sentiments of others and especially for those of the brethren not in communion with the Holy See. This refers principally to the Eastern Orthodox for whom the dating of Easter has always been a matter of special concern. If the Holy See itself actively promoted the cause of a fixed Easter, it might very well seem to be emphasizing a difference between the two churches. It has no desire to do this.

All this might seem to be only remotely connected with the liturgy, yet a fixed Easter would solve many matters connected with the liturgical year. It would be easier to organize the period between Christmas and Lent. Candlemas could be arranged always to fall outside the three Sundays before Lent. The Sundays after Epiphany would always have a fixed number and certain feasts could be arranged so that at least they never occurred in Passiontide. All this would help the Church to do what the Constitution

237

desires, to make the pattern of the liturgical year so clear that it can be a source of Christian life for the people.

The second subject of the declaration is much more complex. This has to do with a perpetual calendar. Various systems have been suggested at one time or another. In this declaration and in accordance with what has been said in the Constitution, the Council wishes to make clear that the Church holds to the sacredness of Sunday, and unless there were very serious reasons to the contrary, would reject any system that infringed upon it. Finally, it leaves the matter to the judgment of the Holy See.

READING LIST

PAPAL DOCUMENTS

The Mystical Body of Jesus Christ (Mystici Corporis), encyclical, 1943 (Eng. trans., C.T.S.).

Christian Worship (Mediator Dei), encyclical, 1947 (Eng. trans., C.T.S.).

An Instruction on Sacred Music and Liturgy, 1958. English translation by Fr Clifford Howell, S.J. (London and St Louis, 1959).

The Rubrics of the Roman Missal and Breviary. The General Decree, *Novum Rubricarum* of S.C.R., 26 July 1960. Latin text and English translation by J. B. O'Connell (London, 1960).

PAPAL DOCUMENTS CONCERNING
   SACRED MUSIC

Pius X, *Motu proprio (Tra le sollecitudini)*, 1903 (Eng. trans., 1947); Pius XI, Apostolic Constitution, *Divini Cultus*, 1928 (Eng. trans., 1947); *Musicae sacrae disciplina*, 1955. English translation, *Sacred Music*, 1957. These three documents have been published by the Society of St Gregory, England.

The Constitution on the Sacred Liturgy. English translation by Rev. Clifford Howell, S.J., Whitegate Publications, Cirencester, Glos., 1963. Latin text, French translation, *La Maison-Dieu*, 76 (Editions du Cerf, Paris, 1964). Commentary, *La Maison-Dieu*, 77.

ON THE CHRISTIAN MYSTERY

I. H. Dalmais, O.P., *Introduction to the Liturgy*, especially chapter IV (London and Baltimore, 1961).

I. H. Dalmais, O.P., 'The Christian Mystery and the Mystery of Salvation', in *True Worship*, ed. L. C. Sheppard (London, 1963, and Baltimore, 1964), pp. 1–13.

C. Davis, 'The Christian Mystery and the Trinity' in *The Study of Theology* (London, 1962), chapter 9. Published in U.S.A. under the title *Theology for Today* (New York, 1963).

On the paschal mystery in the liturgy of Holy Week, *The Paschal Mystery* by Louis Bouyer. The English translation (Chicago, 1950, and London, 1951) is now out of date in some respects as it was written before the restoration of the Holy Week liturgy. A subsequent edition in French has brought it up to date.

Dom Odo Casel's view on 'mystery presence' will be found in *The Mystery of Christian Worship* (Westminster, Md., 1961, and London, 1962).

THE HISTORY OF SALVATION

A brief account for sixth formers but useful for everyone is *God Speaks to Us*, by Hubert Richards (London, 1963), the first in the series *'Where We Stand'* issued by Darton, Longman and Todd. *Till Christ be Formed* (London, 1964), by Derek Lance is a teacher's guide book in the same series.

THE HISTORY OF THE LITURGY

See for a compendious treatment J. D. Crichton, 'An Historical Sketch of the Roman Liturgy' in *True Worship*, ed. L. C. Sheppard, op. cit.

For the Mass, first of all, J. A. Jungmann's *The Mass of the Roman Rite*, two volumes (New York, 1951 and 1955) (one volume edition issued in England, London, 1957).

A shorter treatment, *History of the Mass* by F. Amiot, Faith
and Fact series, 109 (this series is published in U.S.A. as
Twentieth Century Encyclopedia of Catholicism (New
York); the volume numbers are the same for both series).
For eastern rites, *The Eastern Liturgies* by I. H. Dalmais,
111, and for the liturgical year, *The Christian Calendar*
by Noële Denis-Boulet, 112.

For a general treatment of the Mass, *The Liturgy of the
Mass*, by Pius Parsch, third edition, translated by H. E.
Winstone (London and St Louis, Mo., 1957).

THE SACRAMENTS

What is a Sacrament? Faith and Fact (20th Century Encyclopedia of Catholicism), 49. Other books in the same series,
What is a Priest? by J. Lécuyer, 53; *Christian Marriage*
by J. Fabrègues, 54 and *The Last Rites* (unhappily
named) by J. C. Didier, 55.

C. Davis, *The Making of a Christian* (London and New
York, 1964).

THE DIVINE OFFICE

The Breviary Explained, by Pius Parsch (London and St.
Louis, Mo.).

The Divine Office, by P. Salmon, O.S.B. (The Liturgical
Press, Collegeville, U.S.A.).

The Psalms are Christian Prayer, by T. Worden (London
and New York, 1962).

THE LITURGICAL YEAR

The Church's Year of Grace, by Pius Parsch, five vols. (The
Liturgical Press, Collegeville).

SACRED MUSIC

The only book known to me that is really fundamental is
that of J. Gelineau, *Chant et musique dans le culte chré-*

tien (Paris, 1962), of which I understand a translation by Father Clifford Howell, S.J., is to appear shortly as *Music in Christian Worship* (Liturgical Press, Collegeville).

SACRED ART

On architecture, *Liturgy and Architecture*, by P. Hammond (London, 1960, New York, 1961).

Towards a Church Architecture, ed. P. Hammond (London, 1962).

General Index

Africa, 122, 123
Anointing of the Sick, 110, 157, 166n., 174–5
Apologetics, 26
Architecture, 53, 84, 231; church design, 232–3, 234–5
Art, 22, 61, 84, 125, 224–38; the artist, 229; church furnishings, 226; statues and pictures, 225, 229–30, 234
Asia, 122
Austria, 118

Baptism, 10, 38, 42, 57n., 66, 67, 77, 78, 91–2, 110, 130, 156, 163, 170ff., 207
Belgium, 53, 81, 95, 177
Benedict XIV, 148
Benoit, P., 44n.
Bible, Bible services, *see* Scripture
Bishops, 65, 70, 73, 75, 76, 78, 85, 119–20, 176; and regulation of liturgy, 16, 19–22 *passim*, 77, 80, 81, 98, 130, 149, 167, 234; leaders of the flock, 21, 22, 76, 101, 126
Bontinck, P., 122n.
Breviary, 99, 108, 110
Buckley, J. C., 84n.

Capelle, Dom B., 138n.
Casel, Dom Odo, 23, 133n.
Catechumenate for adults, 155–6, 168–9, 208
China, 122
Christ, 9, 10–11, 50, 56, 64, 67; as priest, 11, 33, 34, 37, 42, 45, 47–9 *passim*, 66, 67, 94, 160, 182; mystery of Christ, 24–5, 36, 49, 70, 112, 199; second coming, 49, 51, 52
Church, nature, 1, 5, 11–12, 26, 39–40, 42, 67, 78, 230–1; new pastoral situation, 4–5; as revealed by Council, 5; whole Church involved in reform, 7–8, 98; missionary function, 7, 55, 56, 122;

Christ's presence, 10–11, 40, 42, 45, 46, 47; mystical body of Christ, 11, 33, 49, 50, 68, 203; and liturgy, 17, 21, 92 (*see also* Liturgy); mystery of the Church, 26–7, 37, 39, 41, 86; and covenant, 32; manifests Christ, 40, 41, 47; a holy nation, 63–5 *passim*
Church of England, 86, 110, 121, 168, 222
Clergy, 77, 79, 112, 113, 227; and liturgy, 13, 14f., 17, 43, 70, 72–3, 81, 113; and divine office, 182ff., 187ff.; priest at Mass, 67, 68, 151–3
Commentator on liturgy, 104
Communion of the sick, 110
Confirmation, 77, 78, 157, 172
Congar, Y. M-J., 28–9, 29n., 40n.
Constitution on the sacred liturgy, 3, 24; its aims and importance, 3, 4, 7, 8, 61; change necessary, 8; a pastoral document, 160; *References to the articles of the Constitution*
(1) 1, 61
(2) 1–2, 26, 27, 33, 39, 40n., 41, 101
(3) 2, 61
(4) 2, 8
(5) 9, 25, 27, 30, 33, 34n., 39, 42n.
(6) 10, 37
(7) 10–11, 33, 35, 37, 42, 44, 46–8 *passim*, 90–1, 92, 101
(8) 11, 49ff.
(9) 11–12, 54
(10) 12, 49, 57
(11) 12, 62
(12) 12–13, 58
(13) 13, 63, 82, 203
(14) 13–14, 63, 68, 70
(15) 14
(16) 14, 70
(17) 14, 72
(18) 14–15, 73
(19) 15